BECOMING ANNA

ANNA J. MICHENER

Becoming Anna

THE AUTOBIOGRAPHY
OF A SIXTEEN-YEAR-OLD

THE UNIVERSITY OF CHICAGO PRESS
CHICAGO AND LONDON

The University of Chicago Press, Chicago 60637
The University of Chicago Press, Ltd., London
© 1998 by The University of Chicago
All rights reserved. Published 1998
Printed in the United States of America
07 06 05 04 03 02 01 00 99 98 1 2 3 4 5

ISBN 0-226-52401-9 (cloth)
ISBN 0-226-52403-5 (paper)

Library of Congress Cataloging-in-Publication Data

Michener, Anna J., 1977–
    Becoming Anna : the autobiography of a
sixteen-year-old / Anna J. Michener.
        p.   cm.
    ISBN 0-226-52401-9 (cloth : alk. paper)
    1. Michener, Anna J., 1977–   . 2. Abused
children—United States—Biography.
    3. Psychologically abused children—United
States—Biography. I. Title.
    HV6626.52.M54   1998
    362.76'092—dc21
    [b]   98-11049
                                                    CIP

♾ The paper used in this publication meets the
minimum requirements of the American National
Standard for Information Sciences—Permanence of
Paper for Printed Library Materials, ANSI Z39.48-
1992.

For my Uncle Bob

The names of all institutions
and all persons except the members
of Ms. Michener's new immediate
family have been changed.

My grandmother says I destroyed my mother before I was even born. A little flame of hate burns behind her ordinarily cold gray eyes when she says that. When she says, "You were so big, you tore her apart."

My mother gives a slightly different version of the story of my birth, but I still don't know what went wrong. Why was I a caesarean? Why did my mother need surgery afterwards? Whatever the reason was, it happened again when my brother was born two and a half years later. How come no one blames him too?

"It was all the surgery that caused her pancreas to go into shock."

In other words, when the paramedics came one night to take my mother away in a diabetic coma, it was my fault.

I was only four the first time it happened. I watched in stunned silence from my doorway as strange men in uniforms wheeled my mother away on a stretcher. There was a needle jabbed in her hand, and a little trickle of blood ran from it. The whites of her eyes flicked back and forth like metronomes gone mad beneath her half-closed lids. A little cloud appeared suddenly on the mask over the bottom of her face. I heard a desperate *khuhh* sound, and it vanished slowly. She didn't see me, didn't see anything, couldn't tell me what was going on, that it would be O.K.

My mother came back eventually. But it happened again. It happened many times during my childhood. Each time my grandmother sat me down to say to me, "It looks like your mother is not going to live this time. Don't you wish you had been less stressful to her?"

My grandmother did not move next door to us until I was six. My grandmother made a deal with my mother: whenever my mother was in the hospital or otherwise ill, or whenever my mother just didn't want to deal with one or both of her children, she could send us to my grandmother. But my grandmother was to have complete control of us, and my mother was not to interfere.

From one night to up to a month at a time, my brother and I were shipped next door. During our stay, we were not allowed to go near our own house, to set foot in our own yard. We had no contact with our parents, not even with my mother when she was in the hospital.

A thunderstorm raged outside the huge front window of my grandmother's house while I slept on the couch one night. I dreamed that my mother had died in her bed. The tree out front shook violently, and I thought God was angry with me because I was killing my mother. I wanted to scream but my grandmother would not allow me to make a sound. She said if we cared for our mother we would have no need to cry. I bit the blankets.

My grandmother had a Ph.D. in child psychology. She had worked for about thirty years at a center for children with "emotional disturbances" and "behavior disorders." This meant that if she believed I was crazy, she was not going to be disputed.

I would call it nothing less than an obsession, my grandmother's drive to find every last "problem" of mine, no matter how slight or even nonexistent, and "bring it to light." When I was seven I dreamed of being a ballerina and I flitted around on my toes a good deal of the time. My grandmother said the children at the center who were schizophrenic walked on their toes.

She would have me sit across from her for hours at a time and listen to her "diagnosis." I had no conscience. I had no self-discipline. I cared for no one but myself. Apparently I was sociopathic. I was a pathological liar. I was a viciously manipulative pervert who could never love. (And thus "did not deserve to be loved," was the obvious conclusion.)

My grandmother claimed to love me, however. She used to say that if she did not love me she would not have bothered to try to "save" me. She would not have pointed out everything I did wrong and explained how everything I did well could have been done better. She would not have carried a stopwatch around her neck to remind me just how long it was taking me to get dressed in the morning. She would not have had the bus rerouted to drop me off at her house instead of my own every day after school so that I would have to go straight to her to be hovered over as I did my homework. She would not have called my teachers and school counselors constantly to see what trouble I was causing and to explain what a trained psychologist did with a "child like Tiffy." She would not have had me bend over the sofa or hold out my hand so that she could inflict numerous welts across the bare flesh of my arms and legs with a thin metal knitting needle that had a heart welded on top.

Perhaps if she had not "loved" me so much I would have felt a little love for her. I was not even impressed by the times she made cookies with my brother and me, took us to the park to sail boats, or allowed us to play with her toys for an afternoon. We could only "earn" these things from her by doing whatever she said we had to do for them. Nothing came for free, in the true spirit of grandmotherly love. While my brother was easily controlled with bribes, I resented them more than the thin metal rod my grandmother kept at the top of the stairs.

I was always the "willful" one. When my grandmother could no longer make me cry out when she whipped me, she whipped my little brother in my place. She knew I would rather die than see him hurt.

Although I could never be bullied into anything, my

grandmother could manipulate me with the large crocodile tears that spilled out of her eyes sometimes when she spoke of "loving me so and hating to see me on the road of a person with bad character," or whined about my "poor, weak mother" and my "callous treatment of her."

She put it into my head that if I loved my mother I would have, from the age of six, kept the house clean and made dinner every night, done all the chores, and taken care of my brother, as well as maintaining perfect grades at school. I should have sacrificed everything for my mother, thought of her above all else. I should never have asked her for anything. I should never have even touched her. My grandmother called being touched by children "unnecessary stress."

I felt completely responsible for my mother's physical health and emotional state. No one else even tried to help her. My grandmother sure didn't do the things for my mother that she always said I should be doing. In fact, my grandmother did the complete opposite of reducing stress for my mother. Around my grandmother, or even just when thinking about her, my mother got the look on her face of a prisoner who longs to climb a fence of barbed wire but never dares.

Soon after my mother was first diagnosed as a diabetic, my father moved from their bedroom into the basement. During the last ten years of my parents' marriage, I saw them touch each other only once. My mother was always telling me that my father had said he wouldn't sleep with a "worthless cripple." My father never commented on the situation.

Throughout my entire childhood, I cannot recall my father ever touching me except to spank me or hit me on the head. He never took any interest in me, never asked how I was doing, never did anything with me unless my mother had told him to come along, never gave me anything that my mother hadn't picked out, never said he loved me. He spent most of his time at the convenience store where he worked overtime, and spent the remaining hours in front of the television, or cutting out pornographic pictures and pasting them into notebooks.

I hated it when my mother left me and my brother alone with our father, that stranger I knew nothing more about than the horrific things my mother told me. I hated it even more when my mother told my father to "settle" something between her and one or both of us children. Furious at being pried away from the television, he would stomp up the stairs to the room my brother and I shared, gnashing his teeth and popping his eyes, and "settle" things by shouting and cursing and mocking and ordering and hitting.

My brother and I shared a room until we were nine and seven years old. Then a wall was built across the end of the garage that was attached to the house, leaving a small, cold room that smelled like gasoline. When my father went to "settle" me there, my mother could pretend better than ever that she didn't hear my crying and screaming. In the garage I was set apart from the rest of the family, from the rest of the world.

What most horrified me about that room was that it didn't have a window to the outside. They put a window in the wall that faced the garage. It wasn't much of a view—the lawn mower—and anyone could look in on me. For five years I lived in that room. For five years my mother promised me curtains but never got me any.

My brother resented the fact that the room that was built for me took up all the space where we used to keep our toys—resented it with a fury. By that time I don't think there was any reason we couldn't find to hate each other.

In the beginning it had not been that way. We used to talk, to tell jokes and make tents and act out stories. He adored my imagination, and I was glad to have someone to play with. We fought like normal siblings do, in the beginning. But our mother and our grandmother poisoned him against me. They told him not to play with me, not to look at me because I was a bad influence, because he

didn't want to be like me. He learned from the way everyone else in the family treated me that I was a disgusting
specimen, that I had caused all the family problems. He
caught on pretty quickly that he could do anything he
wanted and say I had told him to do it. Then I would be
punished instead of him.

Naturally I hated him for doing that. I hated him for
receiving the larger share of what little attention there was
to receive. I hated him for shifting all the burden of the
family onto me because he was younger, because he was
not as smart, because he had a learning disability (so of
course the rest of the family did not expect as much from
him). I hated him for turning to the enemy, for kissing up to
them to get what he needed, instead of standing with me.

The only person I ever loved throughout my entire
childhood was my mother. Soon after she became diabetic
she acquired neuropathy as well, a disease that caused great
pain and poor circulation to her hands and feet. In the
morning before she went to work she put on thick men's
socks and tennis shoes that were two sizes too large. In
the evening when I watched her peel them off, the tops
of her shoes would be deeply imprinted on her swollen
feet.

There were times that were much worse than others, as
far as my mother's physical health was concerned. There
were times when she was in remission and she could do
all the things that healthy twenty- and thirty-something
people can do. But these times were rare, and her emotional
health and mental stability were always on a steep down-
ward slide from my earliest memories of her.

My mother kept the other knitting needle from the little
set with the hearts welded on top. Unlike my grandmother,
who executed her whippings in the same cold, methodical
way she buttered her toast in the morning, my mother
would lose her temper and be screeching at the top of her
lungs as she grabbed an arm or whatever she could and let
the blows fall in a haphazard fury.

Once she ran outside while my brother and I were playing with some neighborhood children in the sand pile. She
thought she saw me throwing sand. In the frenzy of activity
the sand flew everywhere, stinging in my cuts, gagging my
screams. The little neighbor children ran shrieking in fear
at the top of their lungs to their mother, who never
whipped them.

When she decided I was too old for the knitting needle,
my mother would attack my face, slapping me over and
over until I was blubbering for mercy. My mother may have
been in too much pain to take me places and do things
with me, but she was never in too much pain to fly into a
violent rage.

I was twelve when she attacked me in the shower. It
would seem that I would have been old enough to defend
myself from a handicapped woman. But she was always
twice my size, even now, and she was my mother. Everyone
knows you can't hit your mother, even in self-defense. I
never did, just cowered against the wall, shivering and naked while she beat me. I couldn't have been more powerless.

My mother was the most emotionally crippling of anyone in my childhood. She took the things I said to her in
confidence and threw them back in my face later, mocking
me, sneering at me. She would be hugging me and telling
me she loved me one minute and screaming that I was a
vile little brat who would never amount to anything the
next.

I defended myself as best I could when she attacked me,
as I defended myself from all of them. I could not hit, I
could not swear, but I could argue that I was right, that I
was a good person. I could scream that she was wrong and
I hated her for it. I could stand with a defiant "I don't care
what you do" look on my face. And under the very worst
barrages, I could scream that I hoped she died a slow, painful death and I would be better off then.

Each year, as I grew older and more articulate, she grew

ten times more abusive. We would shriek for hour after hour after hour until I was faint from lack of air and the room spun and my chest hurt and I shook and cried and vomited with emotion. Always I fared the worst in these endless battles. She was an adult, and I was a child who only wanted my momma to hold me and make the pain stop.

Unlike anyone else in my family, my mother broke her torrent of abuse now and then to tell me she loved me, or to hug me, or to give me just what I wanted for my birthday or Christmas. I told myself and anyone else who would listen that this was the way my mother would always be if it weren't for her pain medication or something like that.

Why I refused to see through those token gestures she used to ease her conscience and prove herself a good mother, I don't know. Why, when the truth about everyone else in my family was never less than obvious to me, did I love my mother and believe in spite of everything that she loved me?

Perhaps it was because she was so pitiful. She used to cry so mournfully in front of me. She told me all her troubles. So many troubles, and no one to tell but me. She needed me.

But I needed her too. If I hadn't been under the delusion that my mother loved me, then I would have been faced with the cold, hard fact that no one in this world loved me.

And what child can live with that?

Even denying that, I had enough troubles. Constantly watched, judged, picked at, accused, and punished, I cannot remember a time in my life when I felt good about myself. The one lesson drilled mercilessly into my head from every angle for the first fifteen years of my life was that I was not "good enough" and never would be.

At school and other organized activities, my vulnerability, the fact that I thought everyone else was better than me and knew what they were doing when I did not, might as well have been printed on my forehead. It showed in my frightened eyes, my hunched shoulders, my trembling hands. The other children teased me, not because there was much to tease me about, but because it was easy to do. My defenses were already broken down by my family. I knew nothing else to do but take everything personally and cry.

During my entire elementary school career I had not one friend. I can count the number of social events I was allowed to go to during that time on one hand. My family did not encourage any social life for me.

Nor did they have one themselves. Sure, they knew people, talked to them at work and such. My father ran for city council twice and did rather well. People who knew my grandmother and my parents casually, liked them. All three were intelligent, well educated, and knew how to hold interesting conversations. They could be friendly when they wanted to be, smiling and sweet-talking. They even praised me in front of their acquaintances (it would have made them look bad to share all of the things "wrong" with their own flesh and blood). But no one was close to them. No one came to the house who wasn't an aunt, uncle, cousin, or grandparent. Ever.

The only fun I had during my childhood, besides my few private moments in which I read, drew, wrote stories, play-acted, or daydreamed, was when I was allowed out within a few designated neighborhood blocks. Although I could not go into anyone's house, I could play with whomever came out to me. All the children in my radius were younger than me. I didn't care; that made me the leader. I might have been anyway; they all loved the games I thought of.

But my grandmother and my mother cared. They didn't like me to play with younger children. When I was eleven they forbade it. Did I want those children's parents thinking I was some kind of pervert? A pedophile?

So just at the time when I most needed strength, the

year I began junior high, I lost the one thing that had kept me strong. I had nothing left in my life but school and sitting around my or my grandmother's house. (At that point I was old enough to look out for myself when my mother was in the hospital, but my mother sent me to my grandmother's house now and then because she "didn't want to look at my face.") No one to play with. No one to talk to. No exercise and contact with nature and fresh air. No way to release the stress of constant emotional and mental manipulation and torture.

School made me about as miserable as being at home did. Although I was to discover later that my teachers actually had no problem with me, my family was constantly telling me that my teachers were very unhappy with me and that I was about to fail everything. This threw me into a frenzy of studying, doing extra work for extra credit, and even handwriting practice (some of the kids at school already called me "the typewriter" because my printing was so meticulous). Everything had to be perfect. I worked and worried myself to exhaustion and sickness. Then I missed school and fell behind and worried more than ever.

My first experience with a psychologist came when I wrote a short story for extra credit in English class. It was about a girl who didn't fit in anywhere, whose family hated her and kept her in the garage, where a little mouse she caught was the only thing she had to talk to, and where she sat and wondered about killing herself.

The teacher told my parents to get me professional help because I *thought up* such a thing. I went to a family counselor all by myself a few times, stared at the dollhouse in the middle of her office, and nodded in answer to whatever she was talking about at the time.

She didn't seem to care anything about my family or what they did to me except that they kept me in the garage, away from the rest of them. When she expressed her negative view of this to my parents, they moved me upstairs. However, they were so furious at the idea that they were the least bit responsible for my unhappiness, that there was anything that they should do differently, that I was never sent to that counselor again.

I was given my mother's room, and she took the one in the garage. My father had an absolute fit and threw all the furniture around and shouted about how he had built that room just for me and I was a goddamned ungrateful snot-nosed brat not to be damn glad of it. My grandmother told me angrily that if my poor, ill mother fell down the stairs or grew so weak climbing up two flights to go to the bathroom at night that she died, I would really be happy then, wouldn't I? My mother bought an intercom system so that she could still be in touch with my brother at night. He was eleven at the time, and I had been nine when I was moved down to that room by myself.

All of this was no better than living in the garage, so I wasn't too impressed by my first encounter with the mental health community. Little did I know that was just the beginning.

By the age of thirteen I was completely exhausted from merely existing in the cold, limited world my family had created for me. Although I escaped this world by sleeping as much as possible, I had constant rings under my eyes like bruises. The chronic, stress-induced stomach pain and nausea I had suffered ever since I could remember was considerably worse by the time I became a teenager, as were the headaches, dizziness, and fatigue. I was weak and sickly, always suffering from a cold or sinus infection or bronchitis. My skin was puffy and yellow, my hair dried out.

I thought I was one of the ugliest and most despicable creatures alive, inside and out. When I wanted someone to pay attention to me, or care about me, I made up lies.

It was funny how no one had believed or cared about the truth. When I had gone to my teachers, or the counselors, and told them about the abuse I endured . . .

But the things I made up, people cared about!

I told the children around me, and the teachers, that I had had an older brother who was killed in a car accident. They offered me their sympathy. I wrote a story about it that impressed the English teacher, and she asked if she could enter it in the school journal.

One day some other students had been calling me names, and I sat in the back of the classroom crying silently and shaking hard. I have always started trembling like a leaf at the slightest stress, but on that particular day some other girls noticed and one shrieked that I was having a seizure.

I was sent to the nurse's office. She spoke kindly to me and sent me home. Home, away from those children who tormented me, away from those teachers I thought hated me, away from the shame that I was less than a perfect student . . .

So I started faking seizures. I missed days, weeks of school in the next four months. But best of all, when I was at school, the teachers and the nurse began asking with concern how I felt that day. The other kids took an interest in me. Some that I had been with in every grade since kindergarten finally asked me what my name was and told me they were sorry I was so sick.

My parents took me to a lot of doctors. I had an EEG and an MRI and some other tests, which I found much more interesting than my endless daily routine of school and sitting at home being screamed at. At last it was recommended that I spend a few days in the hospital.

Those were the best two days of my life. Compared with anything else I had ever known, the hospital was heaven. My roommate, who was in for insulin regulation (she was diabetic like my mother) chatted endlessly to me as no other person my age had ever done before. She gave me tours of the hospital and knew where to get crackers and peanut butter any time we wanted.

The nurses all around smiled at me, looked kindly upon me, and touched me softly. They took care of me. The only time I felt a little twinge of unhappiness was when I looked at the fold-out chair beside my hospital bed. Each bed on the children's ward had one of those chairs beside it so that a parent could sleep near their suffering child. It didn't bother me so much to look at my chair and know that no one related to me cared to be near me for any reason (they never even visited, as my roommate's parents constantly did). It bothered me to look at it and remember I had family back home.

All the children on the ward who could walk or be wheeled to the classroom went to school every weekday for a few hours. Some were bald and swollen. Some were burned and disfigured. Some would never walk again. Some were dying. I knew that they all suffered. But they all had emotional support, from their loving families, from the people at the hospital, from each other.

I would have traded places with any one of them.

After three days a man in a white coat came into my room with my parents. He was pop-eyed anyway, and even more so from disgust as he glared at me over his glasses. He said curtly, "You're going home. You don't belong in *this* kind of hospital, missy."

And what excuse did I have to offer when my great crime was discovered? When it was known that I had faked seizures, maliciously pulled the wool over the eyes of my trusting family, my teachers, and the medical establishment? That I had been mocking people with "real" problems, stealing a hospital bed from someone who might have needed it, playing hooky from school, and robbing my family of a small fortune in medical bills?

I just wanted attention.

Oh yes, that phrase was forever sneered at me with utmost venom: *You nasty little worm, you just want* attention, *don't you?* Or spat out through curled lips to anyone who might have otherwise cared: *Don't go near her, she just wants* attention.

My parents and grandmother were in a frenzy when I

returned home. They had been right about me! Hah! There was something dreadfully wrong with me! I was crazy, just as they had always said!

My mother told me that the people at the hospital had found a "chemical imbalance" in my head that was apparently "triggered" by the onslaught of adolescence. I was going to have to see a psychologist who worked at the psychiatric part of the hospital. Also, my mother told me that I was going to be "monitored" at school and that I was not going to be allowed to go unsupervised for a moment anymore. There was no telling what I might do these days.

They had been such beautiful, unstressful times, those times in the past when everyone in the house had been at work or somewhere and I was alone, blissfully alone for a few hours. But now, while my younger brother was still allowed to play outside and stay home alone, my mother and father arranged their schedules to "baby-sit" me twenty-four hours a day.

Although my grandmother refused to be officially figured into the schedule, my mother would often call her after she and I had been in an especially nasty screaming match (and we had at least one a day). She would whine piteously that she had had such a hard day and "taking care" of her sick brat of a daughter was more than she could bear.

After one of these calls, I simply sat and refused to go over to my grandmother's house and endure hours of her lecturing. My mother, who had claimed in tears a minute ago to be "too weak" to deal with me, leapt upon me in a fury, snatching my arm and twisting it behind my back until I was bent over in pain. She growled like an animal to my grandmother, "There, take her arm like that, it's the only thing the little beast will listen to."

My brother took full advantage of the fact that I wasn't to be trusted. He thought it would be cool to have a dead-bolt on the door to his room, so he whimpered to my mother that he was afraid I was going to kill him in his sleep. It was a ridiculous lie, if for no other reason than the fact that he had four inches and forty pounds on me. But it got him a deadbolt.

As for my door across the hallway, of course it had no lock. I was not even allowed to close it anymore. Eventually my parents took it off its hinges so that I could be watched better. Even when I went to the bathroom or took a shower, I was to leave the bathroom door cracked.

It was a living hell, worse than the way prisoners are treated, and instead of wardens, it was my own flesh and blood treating me this way. I slept with a knife under my pillow that I had found in my father's basement, where I did the family's laundry every week. Before the knife, I had kept a large, heavy monkey wrench with me for years. I dreamed of killing my family, and the precious freedom I would have if only it were not discovered that I had killed them.

My brother saw one day that I had my father's knife. He waited until one o'clock in the morning, however, to tattle. I was sitting up with a flashlight, writing in my diary. When I heard the sudden footsteps charging up the stairs, I barely had time to slip it between my bed and the wall before the covers were suddenly ripped off me and my head knocked against the wall.

My father hit me three more times in the face, swinging his hand back and forth like a pendulum. Then he and my mother tore up my room looking for the knife until it was found.

Three days later I sat as usual in front of my bedroom window at my easel-desk with my guinea pig. Opie was my best friend in the world. I had made one human friend when I started junior high. For a time I had actually been allowed to visit her, and she could even come into my house now and then. She had ingeniously arranged this for me by telling my parents ever so innocently that her parents thought it was "kinda weird" not to let me out or let anyone come over. The last thing anyone in my family wanted was to be looked upon by anyone on the outside as "kinda weird." But after I had faked the seizures, they had an excuse for what they did to me—I was crazy. As afraid as I was that my friend's parents believed this, I had nowhere else to go when I escaped.

My mother seemed to be particularly affected by her medication that day. I could hear her raving to herself downstairs as I sat with Opie and stared listlessly out my window, as I often did in those particularly harsh years. At last I went down to see if I could be any help to her. As usual, she was sitting on her metal stool by the stove. There the stove fan sucked up some of her cigarette smoke. The butts were piled up in her ashtray on the stovetop next to her Walkman. She spent at least a few hours of every day, sometimes all day, at that stove, just smoking and listening to the same songs playing over and over.

She started screaming the minute she saw me, this time about the plants and how no one ever watered them. Her face was drawn and pale, her swollen hands trembling violently.

So I started watering the plants.

I spilled water on the table under a hanging plant I couldn't quite reach. She leaped off her stool shrieking about how clumsy I was and things like that. If she had stayed, I might have started screaming about how I had come to help her and this was the thanks I got, and so forth, and the day would have gone on like any other day of my life.

But she didn't stay. After all those months of constantly watching me, she just stormed out of the house and sped away in her car the way she used to do before it was decided I had to be baby-sat. Her last words to me before she left were that she was going to get my father to "fix me."

I slipped out the back door then, crawled under the window of my grandmother's house, and ran all the way to my friend's house. I spilled my guts to her parents. Sobbing and hysterical, I begged them not to send me back home because I just didn't see how I could stand another day of the way they treated me. My friend's mother listened silently until I was finished. Then she told me that when she was about my age her older half-sisters had broken her nose and cheekbone and jaw.

For a minute I thought she was telling me that this was abuse, and that what I endured, yelling and a few little scratches and bruises, was not abuse. I was suddenly ashamed of myself. But then my friend's mother told me that what my parents did was abuse too, and that she knew how I felt. Unfortunately she did not know what to do about it. She told me that it was illegal for a minor to run away from home, and that if I stayed there, she and her husband could be accused of aiding and abetting a runaway.

So, having been gone only a few precious hours, I called my mother. I was still crying miserably when I told her where I was and that I did not want to come home. I told her that my friend's parents had offered to let me spend the night and let things cool down a little. My mother answered in a cold, detached voice that it was my "decision to feel that way but there is no choice about where you live and your father will come get you right away."

Being walked home by my father in silence and darkness, I had never felt more utterly defeated. If my only friend's parents, one of them a victim of abuse herself, couldn't help me, then I could think of nothing short of suicide to save me from years of endless, steadily worsening misery.

When I entered my house I found my grandmother and my mother at the breakfast table, where my father soon joined them. McDonald's wrappers littered the kitchen. At the time that was my favorite food, and they had bought my brother and themselves some just to spite me. At least my stomach was too upset to allow me to eat anyway.

My grandmother was speaking in her pleasant public voice into the telephone.

"Ah, here she is now . . . yes . . . she's been such a burden for her poor mother lately . . . Oh, yes (a little chuckle) . . . Then you will take her on Monday morning? Good. See you then."

The phone clicked, and there was a long, close, smoke-filled silence.

At last a hateful grin spread across my mother's face as she glared at me over her cigarette. "That was Dr. Burns on the phone. Now you will see what happens to ungrateful, disobedient children. Now you will see."

Dr. Burns was the psychologist who worked at the psychiatric part of the hospital.

T W O

It was May 6, 1991, a Monday after-
noon, when I sat for the last time in Dr. Burns's office.
My family had called him the Friday night before, but
the psychiatric unit of the Magna Carta Medical Center
did not take new admissions on weekends except in emer-
gencies.

Since I had been walked home from my friend's house,
I had not been allowed out of my family's sight for a single
second. They even kept me home from school that Monday. On Friday, Saturday, and Sunday nights, my grandmother came into my room and slept on a cot set against
my bed.

I hardly ate or slept the whole time under those conditions, under their constant hateful glares and nasty words,
and with the knowledge that, for better or for worse, everything I knew was about to change.

My mother told me that before Dr. Burns was called,
my father and grandmother had called the police to have
them take me to jail. She claimed that she had talked them
out of it because she thought I was not responsible for my
"behavior" and that perhaps I could be "helped" in an institution.

When I did not look terribly grateful, my mother
switched from her martyr tone to anger and told me I was
damn lucky that she didn't send me to jail to be fondled
and raped and beaten by *other girls*.

My grandmother drove my mother to Magna Carta separately so that my mother "would not have to bear the bur-

den of sitting in the same car with *that child.*" I sat hunched up by myself in the back of my father's car.

Although my brother had been running around for the past three days chanting, "Loony bin, loony bin, you're going to the loony bin!" I never believed for a second that my family could get away with such a thing. Dr. Burns never seemed to understand me or sympathize with me, but surely he would not allow such an injustice to occur.

My parents and my grandmother went into Dr. Burns's office first, while I sat in the waiting room on a ratty black vinyl couch. My feet dangled over the floor. The stained and worn carpet had game boards and letters and numbers printed all over it in what used to be bright colors. There was a little plastic playhouse across from me, and an assortment of scratched plastic toys and naked dolls were strewn across the floor. Except for the hum of a fan somewhere, the room was dead silent.

For two of the longest hours I have ever known, I had nothing to do but stare at a dirty, naked pink doll that lay face down on the floor. I had always been insulted to be taken to such a childish place as Dr. Burns's waiting room, but it was all I could do not to snatch up that doll and squeeze it tight.

At last Dr. Burns's office door swung open, and my family began to shuffle into the waiting room. My father, a short man with gray-white hair, glasses, and a gut that wobbled over his belt, went right by me to a chair as if I were a stranger. He sat still and calm, his colorless eyes holding the same lack of emotion they had always held for as long as I can remember. As I stood up, my grandmother took my place on the vinyl couch. Her jowls quivered as she pinched her mouth tight. Her little, piercing eyes glared up at me. She would not touch my mother, but sat defensively beside her. My mother, a large, tall, rather pretty woman, was wailing and carrying on, pressing her languid hand against her throat and then her cheek: "Ohhhh, my baaaby! Why must she go? Why? Can't we give her one more chance? Isn't there another way? I don't want to lose my baaaaby, ohhhhh . . ."

I stood in the middle of the room, shifting uncomfortably as Dr. Burns patted my mother on the shoulder, held out a box of Kleenex for her, and said in the tone one uses for a wounded child, "There now, try to calm yourself. It's for the best."

Lord help me. He had just swallowed every bit of whatever my family had spent the past two hours telling him about me.

His tiny office was hot and stuffy, even though the window was open for air. He was wearing a brown tie and slacks. I sat in my usual place across from him while he watched me over his glasses.

During all of our sessions I had always been immensely uncomfortable. I would look around and chew my nails and try to explain that yes, I was unhappy—"depressed," as he called it—but wouldn't anyone be who was being treated by their own flesh and blood the way I was?

That day's session was short because my family had already used up more than the allotted time. He said to me, "I hear you have been having some problems at home lately."

I did not know how to answer. I knew that what he meant was, "I hear you've *been* a problem at home lately."

The pleading inside my head was so loud I was sure he could hear it. If not, it surely showed in my eyes: *You are the only person who can help me. You cannot let them do this terrible thing to me, and you cannot let them take me home. Surely you know what else there is to do with me. I don't, I'm only a child. You're an adult, you're a psychologist, help me, help me . . .*

He laced his fingers over his knee, crossed one ankle over the opposite thigh, and tried a different approach.

"Would you like a little vacation, Tiffany?"

My eyes nearly popped out of my head. *A vacation? Oh,*

yes, that's just what I need! Oh, just a little while away from those horrible people, from that horrible school, just a little rest and I could get strong again, I could feel good again, I could go on again . . .

Dr. Burns leaned forward and said, "I think you would like it at the hospital."

My face fell.

He continued in a rush. "There are lots of kids your own age, and someone who cares is always there for you to talk to. Wouldn't you like that, Tiffany?"

I did not know whether to trust Dr. Burns's description or not. I had no concept of what mental hospitals were like, only that it was a terrible mark of shame to have been to one. All I could think of was my parents and my grandmother in the next room, and my brother at home. I thought of what it would be like if I went back with them. If Satan had come to me at that moment and asked me if I would like to go to hell with him, I would have said yes.

So I said, "Yes" to Dr. Burns.

Dr. Burns smiled wanly. "I'm glad to see you won't be a problem. I'll take you upstairs."

I sure didn't like the way he said *that.*

He stood quickly and ushered me out into the waiting room, where my wailing mother tried to grab me and hug me. I pulled away in horrified disgust, even though I didn't figure Dr. Burns would approve of a child rejecting her own sobbing mother. He led me silently down a hall I had never seen before and to an elevator that took us to the third floor of the building.

When the elevator door opened again, the first thing I saw was a bare wall across from me. On the right was a large blue metal door. The sight of it, the strange feeling that it gave me, made the little hairs on the back of my neck stand up.

To my left was a long hall that stretched an equal distance in both directions from where I was standing. In the middle of this hall was a counter not unlike the drive-through counter at a bank. Dr. Burns led me silently to this counter and spoke a few words to a woman behind it.

Then he left me.

The woman came out and led me down the left side of the hall to the very end. I never got a good look at her. I guess I didn't really care at that point. I was on the verge of collapse from the terror I was holding inside me with my arms.

At the end of the hall was a door with a rectangular, wire-embedded window in it. The woman unlocked this door and ushered me in, saying, "This is your room."

Then she was gone.

I stood silently. My heart thumped against my throat and I was trembling all over.

The room contained a cheap desk and chair set, a locked wardrobe, and a metal bedframe with the flimsiest mattress I had ever seen. The walls were thick and bare except for a picture called *At Harbor's Edge*, which was bolted to the wall and covered in Plexiglas, and a small rectangular window right under the ceiling in back. The curtains were a revolting mix of Halloween colors, and the thin excuse for a carpet was just brown.

I continued to stand numbly just inside this uninviting room until I was so shaky and light-headed that I couldn't stand anymore. Then I went timidly to the metal bed and sat down.

I realized that I was shaking not only from emotion, but from the temperature as well. It was spring outside, and warm, but in that room it was freezing cold. I certainly hadn't expected that, and as I sat there in shorts and a short-sleeved shirt, goosebumps spread across my bare flesh, and my teeth rattled.

After a long debate with myself as to whether I should, I stood on the bed to study the window above me. All that could be seen out of it was a building to the left, a building to the right, the roof of a building below, and a little piece of unreachable blue sky sandwiched in between. I discovered that I could not open the window because it had not been built to open. I almost cried, because it had been the only way I could think of to obtain a little warmth. Also, I saw that the window was made of thick Plexiglas instead of glass. What kind of a person did they think I was to put me in a room with a "window" that could not be opened or broken?

As I sank back down on the bed, I wished more than anything else in the world that I had brought something, anything, familiar and comforting with me. I had been left in that place with nothing but the clothes I was wearing.

I didn't even have a watch, but I knew it had been at least an hour. Wasn't anything more going to happen? I could take anything but nothing! Had I been forgotten?

I got up and peered cautiously out the door, which I had never bothered to close. Maybe I was not supposed to close the door here, as I was not supposed to close the door at home.

All there was was that hall. No one, no sign of anyone, not even a sound. I went back to the bed and sat with my arms wrapped tightly around my knees. I was baffled. Except for my three-hour escape, I had been watched continuously for I wasn't sure how long, because I was supposedly crazy. If this was a place for crazy people, why was no one watching me?

Then it occurred to me that perhaps a place like this had more sophisticated techniques for monitoring "crazy" people than just sitting around them all the time. Maybe this room was bugged, or had a hidden camera. Maybe they had even secretly hooked me up to a machine that could read my mind, like that kid in *Flight of the Navigator!*

I eyed my surroundings with feverish terror, my heart beating even more rapidly. Somehow the idea of being monitored by hidden machines was more humiliating and horrible than having a person sit and stare at me (not that that was a joy either).

It was at least another hour before I heard voices in the hall, the first I had heard since the woman had said, "This is your room." I froze, trying to distinguish what the voices were saying. I wanted to look out into the hall and see who they belonged to, but I was afraid to leave the room where I had been put, or even poke my head out again. Soon the voices were gone, and I sat even more frightened that I had either been forgotten or was being monitored in a way that would never allow human contact again.

It was about half an hour before I heard the voices again. And this time they seemed just a little nearer.

I was straining my ears when all of a sudden a girl appeared in my open doorway. She was just an average-looking girl in a T-shirt and jeans with medium-length brown hair. She stopped and looked a little startled at the sight of me.

I had been perched on the edge of the bed, locked in the same tense position, for over an hour, shaking in spasms of cold and terror. My eyes must have been as round and frightened as a wild rabbit's.

And the girl said, "Hi, I'm Sandy. Are you new here?"

Sandy was a bit on the chubby side and rather plain, but pleasant-looking. I was so desperately relieved to see another human being that I couldn't think of a response.

"You look real scared," she noted. "Is this your first place? Don't worry though. This place sucks but you'll get used to it." She paused, cocked her head to study me, and continued knowingly, "You're kinda small, and pretty. I used to have long hair like yours."

I still couldn't say anything. My throat was dry and my mind numb with shock. I just kept staring at her as if I'd never seen a person before.

It didn't seem to bother her that she was having a one-sided conversation because she just went right along, "Don't be scared, some staff's you gotta watch out for but most are real nice and they'll take you outside and stuff . . . Oh! Just remember . . . "

Sandy stepped closer to me, into the room, and lowered her voice to tell me a secret,

"*Never* tell them you wanna kill yourself because you'd get in deep shit then, let me tell you . . ."

"Sandy!"

I jumped as a male voice shouted down the hall, and then I heard footsteps coming toward us.

"Why are you in another patient's room and what was that word I just heard you say? You know the rules! Go to Time Out! *Now!*"

Sandy muttered and went away. A few seconds later the man was in my doorway. He barked at me just as angrily as he had at Sandy, "My name is Biff. I am a staff member. Follow me."

I followed him, silently, nervously, trembling. He had a big pot belly that hung over his belt and black hair and steel-blue eyes that held no emotion. He led me down the hall to a room labeled "Dining Room."

Inside there was a cafeteria-like bar and four small tables. I was given a tray and motioned to sit at one of those tables, all empty at the time. Biff sat across from me and glared at me.

Of course I could not eat a bite. I simply sat stunned in my chair, unable to even cry. After a terribly uncomfortable silence, I ventured to whisper, "I don't like it here." It was the first thing I had said since I had come to the ward, hours and hours ago. My throat was raw and my voice sounded strange in the empty, quiet room. I stared up at Biff, waiting for an explanation or an acknowledgment of some mistake.

And do you know what he said? He looked me straight in the eye and told me, "Well, you should have been good and you wouldn't be here."

There was nothing I could say to that. I just stared at this person who had met me all of five minutes ago and could say such a thing. At last he told me to put my tray away and said something about how "stubborn little kids don't get away with refusing to eat around here." Then Biff called to a woman down the hall to get me some "stuff."

The woman led me to a very large closet in the hall and handed me two sheets and a thin pillow with a pillowcase. She asked if I had anything with me. I said no, and she handed me a small jar of lotion, Kleenex, a toothbrush and toothpaste, a comb, and two hospital gowns, explaining that I could put one on backwards to cover my rear.

I was rather horrified at the prospect of sleeping in hospital gowns, and I asked why I couldn't sleep in my clothes. The woman gave me a disgusted look and said that it was against the rules for *patients* to sleep in their clothes.

She said it was also against the rules for *patients* to walk around barefoot, and she handed me some fuzzy blue socks. I was told to come back in the morning and get a towel and washcloth and soap for a shower. Then I went back to the room that had been assigned to me.

I hadn't liked the way that woman said *"patients."*

Sandy walked by my door and said, "Good night, new girl," and that made me feel a little better. She seemed quite nice.

I got ready for bed in a tiny room with a toilet and sink situated between my room and the room next to mine. I folded my clothes so that no one could see my underwear and put them on the chair. I made up the metal bed, turned out the lights, and crawled between the sheets.

I lay freezing cold in the dark, on that strange and terribly uncomfortable bed, and I still could not cry. The light in the hall was left on all night, and it streamed through the wire-embedded window in my door.

I thought of my bear and my doll sitting at home on my bed where I had left them. I thought of my bed. It was warm, with flowered sheets and a quilt and a comforter. As I shivered under those thin, sterile-smelling hospital nightgowns and one thin, sterile-smelling sheet, I ached for my familiar and cozy bedclothes and companions.

I then thought of my Opie, my guinea pig. I could not

think of a time when I had not said good night to him. Would anyone feed him? Did he miss me? Oh, how I missed him! The smell of his pine chips and clean fur—even his ceaseless chattering and rattling his cage in the night—seemed ever so dear to me then. I tried to close my eyes and imagine him in the room with me. But it didn't work. The odor of cleaning fluid and stuffiness was too strong, and the silence all around was too loud.

My stomach gurgled for lack of food, and my chest ached for lack of more important things. My muscles, especially my jaw muscles, were hurting from being tensed against the day's events and the cold. I pulled my icy fists against my body. It was little comfort that my family also sat at home and I was the hell away from them. I wanted something to hold onto, anything.

I thought of what Biff had said: "You should have been good. And you wouldn't be here."

Then being here has nothing to do with being crazy. It has to do with being bad!

Unless, of course, being crazy is bad.

But I am neither one, am I? AM I? What is wrong with me if I am crazy? What did I do if I am bad?

I grabbed my pillow and began to sob at last, to release only a small portion of the terror and pain and frustration that was too deep to purge myself of completely in a lifetime. Tears and mucus soaked my pillowcase, so I turned the pillow over and soaked the other side.

I was so exhausted that I thought I might be able to sleep for a while. But then I heard my door opening, and saw a light dancing on the wall in front of me. I rolled over to see what was happening.

Someone was standing in my doorway in the middle of the night with a flashlight! The person called stiffly, "Tiffany? You need—to sleep—with your door—open—so we can check—on you—at night—do you understand, Tiffany?"

I blinked at the form in the doorway, not understanding

why it would talk to me that way and wondering how I
was supposed to answer. It didn't care about an answer anyway; it just backed away.

How does this strange person know my name? What other informa-
tion went along with it? And how can I get any sleep with the door
open and all this light in the room? At least when I didn't even have
a door, it was dark in the hall.

I rolled over and put my flat pillow over my eyes. I
couldn't cry anymore with the door open, knowing that
someone might see or hear me. A person came with a flashlight every two hours and looked in at me for some reason,
I didn't know what. I did, however, manage a few hours of
troubled sleep that night. I had been so deprived of it that
I don't think anything could have kept me from it.

I was awakened for the final time at seven in the morning
by a very fat woman wearing a white coat and carrying
a clipboard. She burst into my room and flicked all my
lights on.

"Good morning, Tiffy. You're going to get up now."

She had the biggest, fakest smile that I had ever seen
in my life. I could not tell whether her eyebrows were completely drawn in or just plucked really thin. They nearly
blended with her hairline.

I was horrified and embarrassed to be facing a fully
dressed stranger in nothing but two hospital gowns, the
shape of my naked and shivering body quite visible beneath. I groped desperately for the sheet as my sleep-
encrusted eyes attempted to regain their vision in the sudden light.

She was the second person to use my name without asking me what it was first!

Where do these people get it? I can make a wild guess—they ask
my parents. Just the way one asks the name of a dog from its master
because dogs can't speak for themselves.

The fat woman gave me no time to orient myself before
she gathered her coat in her hands and plopped herself
down on the end of my bed. I was humiliated to think of

how messy my hair must be and how I needed to brush my teeth.

"How are you this morning?" she wanted to know.

I wanted to push this obscene woman away with all my might and shout, "HOW IN THE HELL DO YOU THINK I AM? HOW IN THE HELL WOULD *YOU* BE?"

Instead, I offered as civilly as I could through chattering teeth, "Well, I'm freezing cold."

THREE

The large presence on my bed eventually introduced herself as Dr. Limband.

After "How are you this morning?" (the answer to which she did not even seem to hear), she told me that she and the rest of the "treatment team" had talked with my parents for a few hours yesterday after I had been brought to the ward. I didn't know what they had said, what they had accused me of that was so bad that they got away with committing me to the loony bin. I could not even imagine what I was up against.

Dr. Limband said that she had a pretty good idea of my "situation" but that she was going to ask me a few questions anyway.

She had already diagnosed me, had already made up her mind about me without laying eyes on me. Nothing I did or said made any difference to her. I sort of figured that at the time, and found the proof years later when I finally saw the papers she had filled out about me.

She was apparently in a big rush. She hardly took her eyes off her clipboard, which was turned exaggeratedly away from me, as she fired off her questions without allowing me to hesitate or finish.

"Have you ever experimented with drugs?"

"No." (In my entire, isolated thirteen years I had never even seen any illegal drugs.)

"How often do you drink alcohol?"

"Well, I don't, I . . ."

"Have you ever thought about suicide? If so, are you thinking about suicide right now?"

Of course I was thinking about suicide. Of course I had thought about it often for years and years and years. Who wouldn't have in my place? But I recalled the warning Sandy had offered me last night about not telling them I wanted to commit suicide because I would be in "deep shit then." So I said to this Dr. Limband person, "No."

"Have you ever tried to commit suicide?"

My face twisted as this question caused a sudden rush of painful memories.

I was in the kitchen brandishing a steak knife over my wrist in front of my mother. She just sat at the kitchen table with a cigarette and a clothing advertisement. I was frantic when she made no response. I cut my wrist a little, enough to make it bleed, but not very deep because it hurt, and I shouted at my mother, look at me, pay attention to what I'm doing!

It wasn't until I made another little cut that she took a long drag and said haughtily, without looking up from her paper, "This is exactly the kind of behavior your father and I are talking about. I have the right to take you to jail now, you know, for attempted murder."

I dropped the knife and ran upstairs crying . . .

Then there was the time I emptied a bottle of my mother's prescription painkillers and filled it with my own harmless anti-acne pills. Then I went to the living room where my mother, father, and brother were watching television. I began to swallow the pills from the clearly and dangerously labeled bottle, announcing loudly that I was going to take them until I died unless someone said they cared about me.

But they all just continued to watch their television program. It was a comedy too, I guess, because they laughed. They just laughed . . .

I didn't think any of these things qualified as suicide attempts, since I had never done anything with the intention of dying. But I could only imagine my mother's response to that question about me. She had probably said, with those big crocodile tears in her eyes, that I had tried to kill myself with knives and pills. I had to explain that. So I stammered to this Dr. Limband person, "Well, about three weeks or so ago . . . I took about thirty of these harmless pills . . . in front of my family . . . to see if they cared . . . but they just ignored me and I . . ."

I had to stop because tears were welling up and choking me.

Dr. Limband scribbled away on her clipboard, still smiling from ear to ear and nodding knowingly, as if I were a kindergartner telling her about my field trip rather than relating how my own family wouldn't care if I tried to commit suicide. She interrupted sharply to ask what kind of pills I took.

I stopped crying and straightened my back a little as I realized with a jolt that I was just humiliating myself in front of another person, a stranger, who didn't care.

"Tylenol." I lied, because it was the most harmless pill I could think of.

I decided I could not tell this woman about the acne pills in the painkiller bottle because the acne pills had not been completely harmless either. I had taken quite a few before I realized no one was going to stop me. They were certainly not fatal, but I was surprised to find that they made me sicker to my stomach than I had ever been in my life. I spent the night all alone vomiting over and over and crying with pain.

Dr. Limband waved her pen at me and chided, "That's no good, Tiffany. Tylenol can be very bad for your liver."

Then she turned back to her clipboard, making a note and announcing to the air, "We'll have to take a blood test and see."

I just stared at her.

After a few more questions, whose answers I no longer cared to try to be specific about, Dr. Limband stood up quickly. She had me follow her, in those awful hospital gowns and fuzzy blue socks, into the hall. She unlocked the big closet containing supplies for the patients and gave me soap, a washcloth, and a towel. I was then told to go to the girls' bathroom across the hall, take a shower, and report to the "dayhall."

All the female patients were supposed to share this large bathroom in the hall. When it was discovered that the private bathroom adjacent to my room had been left unlocked by mistake, it was immediately locked.

The large bathroom was drafty, and the slightest sound I made echoed. I couldn't cry until the water was running. I shivered and sobbed in a shower stall for half an hour, not even caring if there was a camera there to see me crying.

Eventually a woman stuck her head in the bathroom door and told me to hurry up. The towel was very small and thin, and reeked. I made myself stop crying, but I couldn't stop my teeth from chattering.

Behind that bank drive-through counter in the middle of the long hall was the ward office, where the patients' charts were kept. The office wall was half Plexiglas so that if the doors to the office were shut, the staff could still see the patients and the patients could not hear what the staff was saying. Patients were not supposed to enter the office for any reason.

Surrounding the office on three sides was the "dayhall." It was a medium-sized room with a television and a stereo on the left (which could be turned on only at certain times and with a staff member's permission) and a Ping-Pong table on the right. The back of the room had thick Plexiglas windows with window seats. A plastic couch and some pastel-colored plastic chairs were scattered throughout the room. At the front of the room was the "staff table," where two or three staff members would sit watching the patients on the dayhall and scribbling in their charts.

I learned in time that the second floor of the Magna Carta Psychiatric Building was where the adults were kept.

The third floor, where I was kept, was divided into two wards by that big blue door outside the elevator: the children's ward and the adolescents' ward. I was thirteen, just old enough to be on the adolescent side.

There was a "classroom" on the children's ward to which a few of the "adolescents" were escorted for a few hours in the morning and a few hours in the afternoon. Originally the junior high school I had been attending sent work to Magna Carta for me to do. Schoolwork was about the last thing in the world I cared about at the time, however, and the Magna Carta classroom "teacher" (I think she had a fancier title, but she let the patients think of her as a regular teacher) let me slide. Eventually she had me join in the activities she gave to the kids who didn't have schools on the outside to send them work.

Mostly we wrote different kinds of poems. The teacher had a large bowl of Jolly Ranchers on her desk that she gave out now and then. There were no strings attached, so I liked those Jolly Ranchers. She would also sometimes take us to look around the gift shop in the real hospital building on the Magna Carta Medical Center grounds.

The teacher was one of the few people in my early life to do a truly kind and helpful thing for me. After I had come to her class for a few weeks, she understood that I was terribly attached to my guinea pig and worried considerably about his being neglected. So she suggested that I have someone bring him to her classroom. She even arranged for someone on the ward to unlock the classroom when class was not in session so that I could feed him and give him water and change the litter in his cage. At least once a day I was in contact with something familiar and comforting, something that loved me. I don't know what I would have done if that teacher hadn't bent the "no-animals" rule for me. I am eternally grateful to her.

On the first floor of the psychiatric building was the "Occupational Therapy" room. Most of the adolescents, including myself, were escorted to this room and left for an hour every weekday with an "Occupational Therapist." "Occupational Therapy" turned out to be just a fancy term for sitting around doing arts and crafts.

For another hour every weekday the same kids were escorted to a small gymnasium in the basement of the building, where we hung out with the "Recreational Therapist" until he led us back to the ward again. He usually had us play volleyball, a game I quickly grew to despise. It still makes me angry that all the things so vitally important to a normal life—things like hobbies and exercise—are denied to so-called "crazy" people except in the horribly distilled and restricted form that these people have the nerve to call "therapy."

Patients were also assigned to different kinds of "Group Therapy." There was a middle-aged man in a suit who came to the ward once a week or so, and we had to go sit in the "family conference" room and listen to him preach condescendingly about some "teen issue" like "just saying no" or "abstinence," and then "discuss" it, using only the words and phrases he wanted us to. Not much help, that group.

All the patients on the adolescent ward were also gathered in a cluster once a week for a group that supposedly allowed patients to discuss their daily problems on the ward. This sounded good, but proved to be difficult when no patient was allowed to "complain" about a staff member or a rule. What other daily problems did we have? Just each other, sometimes. We would "elect" a new "president" and "secretary" and then sit around while the same two or three patients bitched about the same two or three others. And every once in a while someone would say they didn't like such-and-such about being in that place, and a staff member would tell the kid, "We don't always control what happens to us, we only control how we deal with it, and you need to discuss any problems you're having with a staff member on a personal level." Not that a staff member would ever take the time to talk with a patient; that phrase was just a way of shutting the kid up.

The day after I came to Magna Carta, Biff called his own little group on the dayhall. He told all the other kids to introduce themselves to the new patient, announce why they were on the psychiatric unit, and explain how they intended to improve *themselves* in order to be allowed to leave.

All the poor kids were sitting in a circle of those ugly plastic chairs that made farting noises when you sat on them. They fidgeted and squirmed with embarrassment. Some of them didn't even look twelve, even though I knew they had to be. One by one, they rattled off lines they clearly hadn't thought of by themselves and had said many times before: I have an "anger control problem"/I have "depression"/I ran away from home/I got pregnant/I didn't get along with my parents . . . I will take my "medication"/I will cooperate with my "therapy"/I will "control" myself . . .

Then Biff turned to me and demanded that I tell the group why I was here. I felt my skin burn with indignant humiliation.

I was there because my family had brought me and left.

It was obvious that I was supposed to say something like the already programmed patients, but I could not bring myself to do it. I said quietly, "I don't know. No one told me."

Biff narrowed his eyes at me and sneered, "Well, you had better figure it out, or you will never leave here."

A chart was posted daily on the wall outside the dayhall with all the adolescent patients' names down the side and each hour of the day printed across the top. Each patient was expected to ask the "therapist" or a ward staff person who had been watching them that hour to "please" write a grade in the appropriate box. The grade supposedly reflected a patient's "cooperation," "appearance," "attitude," and other such vague qualities.

It was hard enough to endure the presence of people

who were being paid to watch me and write things down about me behind my back. Every hour I had to force those humiliating words from my throat: "Will you please give me my grade?" Some staff members made a patient say it two or three times, claiming we didn't sound "sincere."

A patient's "grades" determined the "level" he or she was on. New patients started on "Level 1," but if they got good "grades" for a certain number of days they could be "promoted" to "Level 2." A patient had to be on a certain level to do or have anything more than food to eat and clothes to wear. Everything else was a "privilege" to be "earned."

On the weekends, patients did nothing but sit on the dayhall and eat their meals in the dining room. If a patient was on a good level, he or she could sleep in, but that was about the extent of the reward for total subjugation.

There was a half hour of Quiet Time after dinner when all the patients could go to their rooms and sit in peace. But during the rest of the day, when not at "school" or a "group," patients had to sit on the dayhall where they could be watched. Just sit—no standing around too long, no moving too much, no touching the other patients, no bothering the staff, no making loud noises. It was always noisy anyway, with twenty kids bored out of their minds crowded together in one room, and two or three staff people constantly announcing to them that they better be quiet and be still.

I can describe in this book all the horrible things that were said and done to me, but I can never even begin to describe the true horror of mental institutions, the never-ending, sanity-stripping monotony, the subliminal implications of this endless routine and always having some hateful stranger watching you endure it, or perhaps be driven mad by it, whichever the case might be.

I figured out pretty quickly that Dr. Limband was the "head honcho" of the ward I was on. She was the only person I saw there with a white coat. That meant she had nothing much to do with the patients or the daily goings-on. That was the job of those who worked under her. They gave all the stuff they wrote down about the patients to her.

She woke me up in the same unsettling way and sat on my bed for an approximate total of five minutes a day a few mornings a week, and that was all I ever saw of her. I hardly ever got a word in edgewise, and her face-splitting grin distracted me from my thoughts anyway.

Dr. Limband spent a lot more time with my parents and my grandmother in "family conferences." Sometimes I was actually included as a member of the "family" instead of just the teenage mental patient, but usually not. I noticed that Dr. Limband never listened to or spoke to anyone else in my family with that horrible, condescending grimace and tone she used with me.

Dr. Limband prescribed so many blood tests that at last I worked up the nerve to tell her that I was more squeamish about needles than anything else I could think of and that if she could just cut back a little I would appreciate it. Every time someone sticks me with a needle I feel the cords of my neck tighten and I hyperventilate. I always think of watching my mother inject herself with insulin, and the time she hit a blood vessel across the bed from me. Her bright red blood spurted across the white sheets and onto my face. I was five years old.

For the first three days of my stay at Magna Carta, I was so disoriented and stressed that I did not eat a single bite. I just looked at the food I had been told to take until I was told to take it back. The food certainly did not look tasty, or terribly nutritious. But the problem was that I just could not make myself eat anything, whether it was good or not. My stomach was knotted tight and threatened to reject anything I shoved into it.

One staff member who saw me put away an untouched tray told me crossly that "patients who do not eat food in a normal way have tubes shoved down their throats in a very *uncomfortable* way." When Dr. Limband heard that I was not eating, she simply told me with a smile on her face that she would order my blood taken after every meal until I did.

On the fourth day I woke up and found myself still in that chilly and frightening psychiatric ward with nothing but the clothes I'd arrived in, I was so dizzy and light-headed I could hardly stand. My stomach was twisted in terrible pain, and I was trembling from weakness. I knew I had to eat in order to endure the situation I was in and obviously wasn't going to be taken out of anytime soon.

It was so awful to force that food down my throat that morning. Dr. Limband and the rest of the people who worked there had decided that my not eating was some sort of battle of wills, and I wished there was some way I did not have to lose it.

By that time I was not being brought to the dining room after the other patients, but was ordered in with them. Patients were only occasionally allowed to talk in the dining room, but they sat around the tables and eyed me with curiosity and concern. They didn't need words to tell me, "I know how you feel." When at last I had choked food down to my protesting stomach, one boy dared to whisper to me, "See, s'not so bad. Jesus, I can't believe you hadn't touched nothin' for three days! I thought you were gonna pass out or somethin'!" And besides my conversation with Sandy, those were the first friendly words I had heard since I came to Magna Carta.

In contrast to Dr. Burns's description, I found that the Magna Carta adolescent psychiatric ward was not a place to go for a vacation, that there was not one caring person to talk to, and that I most certainly did not like it. The only thing he had not lied about was the fact that there were indeed some people my own age there.

Sandy had left the day after I came. But there was some-one else to take her place. Kids were always coming and going. The maximum stay limit was six months, but the average stay was between one and three.

Jake was the name of the patient who spoke to me in the dining room. He was fifteen years old, which was a pretty impressive age to me at the time. He had big, pretty blue eyes, dark hair, a round face, and a nice smile. He was of average size and build, and he asked me if I would be his girlfriend.

Never in my life had any boy wanted me to be his girl-friend, especially not an *older* boy.

It was against the rules at Magna Carta for patients to write each other notes, but Jake wrote me anyway. He even persuaded me to write him a note once. It was also more explicitly against the rules for patients to touch each other for any reason, especially *boy and girl* patients. But when no one was looking for an instant, or our hands were below a piece of furniture, Jake would take my hand in his. I liked this because his hands were always warm. How on earth he stayed warm in that constantly freezing place I don't know.

Sometimes Jake would try to touch me in other places. I would just push him away. He would look like that was rather amusing, but he would never try what I pushed him away for again.

During our joint stay at the Magna Carta adolescent ward we spent a lot of time in the bay window at the back of the dayhall together, talking. He said one day, "You don't belong here. If I ever saw your folks I'd give 'em what for. Can't believe they wouldn't want a nice kid like you. I'd want you. There's nothing wrong with you."

I didn't think there was much wrong with him, either. He was one of those kids in the dayhall group who was supposed to say, "I have an anger control problem." But that was hardly an explanation. I asked him how he had come to be at Magna Carta.

He sighed and stared out the window at the concrete and the tall brick buildings below and in front of us, at the crimson sun setting just beyond our Plexiglas prison. Then he told me, with as much distance between the words he spoke and the emotions behind them as possible, "My father drinks too much. He beats on my little brother, and me, and my mother. He came home one night about a month ago, drunk, and started hittin' my mother. Only that time I hit him back. With a wrench. I hit my father with a wrench so of course the court sent me here. At least it's only a first offense and it won't be on my adult record."

There was a long silence then. Jake's forehead pinched a little. I wanted to touch him, I wanted to say something comforting, but all I could think was, "If he were a stranger, instead of your father, if he were a stranger and he came up and attacked your mother like that, and you hit him back . . . they would have given you a medal."

Jake's mother, a hunched, shabbily dressed woman in a kerchief, visited him often. I never saw her smile; her expression was always pinched, worried, fearful. Eventually Jake went home with her, to his father and brother. He wrote me for a while.

His father never stopped beating his family, and his mother never stopped taking it, but at least the institution had "cured" Jake of his "anger control problem."

Jake had been good friends with a patient named David. David was thirteen and had blond hair and glasses. He had been driving around drunk without a license. When the police pulled him over they painted a white line on the ground and said, "Can you walk this white line?"

To which David replied, "No, but I can sniff it."

After juvenile jail, David found himself at Magna Carta. His story was pretty popular among the kids, and I must say I found it pretty funny myself.

Steve was supposed to have an "anger control problem," too. He was one of the nicest kids I ever knew. He was thirteen, but was about the size of a ten-year-old, and I didn't see how he could cause much damage to anyone even if he did have an "anger control problem." I don't know what ever happened to him. He was just gone one day.

Randy was brought to the psychiatric ward because he had a "weight problem." All I could think when I thought of his situation was, *If fat people belong in mental institutions, then why the hell isn't Dr. Limband incarcerated here instead of running the place?* The institution didn't seem to help Randy with his weight problem. When Randy came to Magna Carta he was twelve years old, about five feet tall, and weighed over two hundred pounds. When he left Magna Carta he was still twelve years old, about five feet tall, and weighed over two hundred pounds.

Randy's weight caused him a lot of trouble; he had to breathe through a tube a few times a day, and his knees were bad. But I almost wished I weighed two hundred pounds, because the staff did not pick on Randy. When he did not want to do something, he wasn't messed with, unless some particularly ambitious staff member wished to roll a limp two-hundred-pound body to wherever that staff member wanted it to be.

Tilly was a small, pudgy boy of thirteen, with soft brown eyes and hair. He was called "hyperactive." He did fidget more than most kids, and he had an annoying habit of flapping his hands so that his knuckles cracked constantly. He didn't seem terribly smart to me, but I think that probably had a lot to do with his being stoned all the time. He had been given so many drugs for so many years that his growth was stunted and he had breasts.

He wrote me love poems that were confiscated by the staff before he could give them to me. He hung around me a lot, which sometimes annoyed me because he had a grating laugh and way of speaking. But he was perfectly harmless. He kept me on a pedestal and didn't touch me. I felt sorry for him because he had no family or friends; he was a ward of the state. He was suddenly shipped off to a cheaper institution one day. I rather missed his adoring and entertaining presence even if he was tiresome sometimes.

There was only one patient on the adolescent ward at

Magna Carta while I was there who was not unhappy. Angela's complexion was rosy and her eyes were bright and laughing, although somewhat dilated from drugs. She was thirteen, but could have passed for eight. Her slightly freckled face formed a perfect heart. Her little pink lips were almost always smiling, and her hair was long and black. After her bath in the evening, some of the staff argued over which one of them would get to brush and dry that shiny, pretty hair.

Angela thought she was Batwoman, surrounded by comic book characters. She jabbered constantly to them in a language she had made up. She was always laughing, twirling around the dayhall, and ordering all her imaginary friends about. She was aware of the staff and the other patients around her; she just didn't find any of us very interesting, I guess.

Occasionally one of the staff members, who never bothered with the unhappy patients, would tell Angela angrily to stop carrying on with whomever she was having so much fun with because that person was *not real*. Angela would simply snap her fingers to shoo the staff person away, laughing and announcing with amused indignation, "Of course he is, you fool!"

I envied Angela's happiness immensely. I wished I could be the queen of a beautiful, entertaining fantasy world. I wished it could be real to me, more real than that damn boring ward. I wished I could wave the staff off like the peasants they were. I wished I were truly crazy. Since I was stuck in a mental institution anyway, it was the only way I could have tolerated it.

Toward the middle of my stay at Magna Carta, an Asian-looking boy was brought in from the street. His name was Tad. He was big and sullen, and they shaved his head because he had lice. His dark eyes took in everything and never offered anything back. He would sit on the dayhall and eye everything from a distance. He would do what any staff member told him to do with an air of humoring them. He always wore red and never spoke a word to me.

I asked a girl named Wanda, who seemed to know everything, what he was in for, and she said in hushed and scornful tones, "Drive-bys. He's a Blood." I obviously didn't understand, so she said, "Gangs, you know, Bloods, Crips, Folks . . . he's a Blood. He was involved in fourteen drive-by shootings."

"Shootings?" I repeated.

"Yes. Drive-by shootings. You get your guns, you get in your car, and you go by a house and blast it." She glared sideways at Tad, who was sitting at the opposite side of the room. "You gotta be fucked in the head to run the Gangs. You don't know who's in the house. *Babykiller!*" She spit the last word out through curled lips.

Tad coasted through his stay at Magna Carta better than any of us, doing what he was ordered silently and biding his time. The staff praised his "compliance," called him a "role model." But I wouldn't have wanted to be anything like him for the world.

When I first saw Wanda, she was sitting in one of the dayhall windows, picking at a place on her shirt where a button should have been. I went over to say hi to the new girl, but before I could say anything, she told me, "I wish my boyfriend wouldn't suck my buttons off everything."

Wanda was a foster child and quite willing to share with me what that was like. "I hope you get a foster home, honey. Sometimes, people just take kids for the money, and they don't take care of you none. But then you just go to your social worker and tell her that, and she'll move you."

"I don't have a social worker," I told her.

She said, "Well, you have to be in state custody to have a social worker, and sometimes social workers suck, too, but you just have to get a nice one that puts you in a nice foster home. Rich ones are the best, they aren't takin' you for the money, and they give you nice clothes and neat stuff. I had a rich family once, gave me my very own room, with lacy curtains . . ." Wanda leaned back against the Plexiglas dreamily. "They were nice too, let me do stuff like a regular kid."

I wanted to ask, "If they were so nice, why aren't you with them now?" But that sounded rude.

When Wanda cried, she sat in that window and let the tears roll silently down her cheeks. But she was pretty cheerful most of the time. I never even knew what was supposed to be wrong with her.

FOUR

One day, while I was being led with the other kids from the classroom back to the adolescent ward, I saw my stuffed bear and my mother's suitcase packed fat with my things on the office counter. I was very excited, but I could not have my things right away because they had to be searched. And a few things were kept from me, including my makeup kit.

I had been very self-conscious about not having makeup. I usually slathered it on first thing in the morning because I was so ashamed of my sickly complexion, teenage acne, and the chiseled rings under my eyes. But I was not on the right level to have makeup. I hadn't been at Magna Carta long enough to be promoted.

I never knew who brought me the suitcase and my bear. Various members of my family made the hour-long trip to Magna Carta to see Dr. Limband for those "family conferences," but they made a point of never coming just to visit me, like some patients' families did.

Besides being visited on the ward, patients on the right levels could be taken out on passes with "parents or other approved adults." I would have been happy never to see a member of my family again, but I was desperate for a pass for one reason—to get my diary out from between my bed and the wall. In the confusion of the six days between the time I had last been assaulted by my father and the day I was committed to Magna Carta, I had forgotten to move it from its temporary hiding place to the large blue trunk in the bottom of my closet, which I kept locked.

The contents of that locked trunk were the only bit of privacy I had in my entire existence. I have never liked store-bought diaries with only a few lines allotted to each day. In my trunk I had five or six spiral notebooks. Whenever I felt the urge to record the events of the day or write down one of the stories that were always floating around in my head, I grabbed one of those notebooks and scribbled for hours, starting on the next blank page. Even though my notebooks were a rather disorganized mix of fact and fiction, and hardly anything was finished before the next page was talking about something new, they were my most sacred possessions.

I told Dr. Limband that I needed to go home and get my diary, and she eventually told me that since I was on a good level, she would arrange for a pass.

My father arrived on the hour that my pass was supposed to begin. But he had no intention of taking me home with him. He had driven all the way from my hometown to the Magna Carta Medical Center just to see my face when he told me that he and my mother had changed their minds about being able to "handle" me. Actually, he boasted that *he* could handle me, it was my mother he was concerned about.

He also told me that my mother had taken my diary from under my bed. He said that the whole family had read it, and he had just brought it to the people here so that they might have a "little insight into the nature of my insanity."

Then he left.

I never went on pass to my home, or anywhere else, during my entire stay at Magna Carta.

On my tenth morning at Magna Carta, Dr. Limband barged in as usual and demanded to know how I was doing without really waiting for an answer. But this time, instead of turning and walking out, she announced that I would start taking the drugs she had prescribed today.

I was horrified. I told her that I did not want to take

any psychoactive drugs. She smiled and assured me cheerily that if I did not want to take pills, "injections could be
arranged." Seeing that I knew I had no choice, Dr. Limband
stood up, clutching her clipboard to the front of her white
coat, and told me that the antidepressants would make me
feel better.

I sat in my pajamas, shivering, after she had left. I did
not want to simply take pills to feel better without dealing
with the cause of my unhappiness—the abuse I had endured and would continue to endure, unless someone
helped me, until I was eighteen years old and suddenly
became a human being instead of the property of my biological parents. I knew that taking antidepressants without
dealing with the cause of the "depression" was as nonsensi-
cal and temporary as being stabbed and taking painkillers
without bothering to remove the knife.

The worst thing, though, was that the drug Dr. Limband
prescribed did not give me even artificial happiness. It
made me more physically ill than I have ever been in my
life. And that did nothing to lift my spirits.

Three times a day a staff member rolled out what they
called the "med cart." I was summoned, given a cup of water
and a pill, and expected to open my mouth so the staff
person could see if I had swallowed the detested little
thing.

After a few days, I was so weak and doped that every
little thing was a terrible effort—standing, sitting up, making my mouth form words and my mind grasp ideas. My
vision was blurry, and my sense of balance was off. I could
hardly walk in a straight line. I had to fight to stay awake
no matter how much I slept. And the headaches—I never
had, and probably never will have again, such terrible
throbbing headaches as that drug gave me.

To be incapacitated by drugs I did not even want to take
frustrated me no end. I was humiliated not to be alert and
quick in front of all of those people who watched and
judged me.

The noise of the crowded dayhall and the other rooms of the ward pounded against my head, making me want to scream in pain. I had little patience left for the monotony and meaninglessness of existence in that place, or the superior airs and insults of the staff. Every little annoyance was harder than ever for me to deal with. I thought of nothing but the end of each miserable day, when I was allowed to stretch out flat in the silence of my room. Too tired to sleep or cry, I just lay still and praised God that I didn't have to move anymore.

Dr. Limband explained blithely to me that I was just experiencing all the expected "side effects" and that I would "adjust." But as the days and weeks passed, I never did adjust.

Dr. Limband ordered that my blood be drawn almost every day to see how the drug was doing. (Of course she couldn't take my word for it.)

Blood was taken from patients in a little room on the children's ward, just past the big blue door. It had a doctor's table and cabinets full of vials and tourniquets and such. Sometimes it took two nurses to hold me still because I was shaking so badly. Even with a tourniquet on my arm, the room was so cold and my veins were so shrunken that whoever had the needle would usually have to stab me two or three times to get a vein. I always swore to myself that I would be strong in front of the nurse in the little room, but a moan or a whimper would usually escape me as the needle bit into the inside of my elbow. The needles were so large that I still have scars.

Although Dr. Limband always acted in front of me as though I were making a big, whiny, hypochondriac deal over how her drug made me feel, she knew from the blood tests that the effect it was having was very serious. It reached toxic levels in my bloodstream. It lowered my white blood cell count—my immune system—which would make anyone tired and weak. If she had given me a bigger dose, she might have killed me.

A girl named Melanie was brought to the adolescent ward a little while after I was. Neither her mother nor her father took care of her, or even wanted her around. She had spent a lot of time out on the street, just trying to take care of herself. Sometimes an older guy would take her in, and that's how she came to be pregnant. She was only fifteen.

Her swollen belly contrasted sharply with her sticklike limbs. She was only about my height, less than five feet two inches. Her white-blond hair was dry and shoulder-length. Her skin was thin and sickly from stress. She was not pretty in any way I can describe. Everything about her was just so sensitive and delicate, yet she emanated such unwavering strength that it was hard not to stare at her.

Her nose had been broken, by her father if I remember correctly. She was in the habit of holding her thin fingers over its crookedness. She laughed sometimes, and grinned, but usually she smiled with her eyes. Melanie's eyes were so faintly blue that they were almost clear. No matter how much misery she had seen and endured, her pure soul lay untouched behind those eyes.

The "teen issue" man had us all speak about child abuse once. When he asked me if I had been abused, I tried to explain that it wasn't so much physical abuse as emotional. When that wasn't good enough for him, I stammered about being smacked about the face and head and whipped with knitting needles. Some of the other patients laughed then—I guess they didn't think knitting needles were very dangerous instruments—and the old man moved on to the next kid for questioning.

I sat silently fighting back tears, telling myself it was a pretty unusual thing to be hit with. I hadn't specified that they were *metal* knitting needles, so thin that they cut and burned my bare arms and legs.

Maybe it's not even the bad thing I think it is to whip children. Maybe I shouldn't have let anyone know how naive I am to be sensitive to such things.

Then Melanie came to me when the stupid group was over and looked at me with those sweet eyes of hers. She told me, "There's all these fucked-up reasons why people won't admit certain things are abuse, y'know, like it's what their mamma did to them and they don't want to admit they were abused by their mammas. What your family did *is* abuse, and don't *ever* let nobody tell ya diffr'nt, okay?" She patted my hand and I nodded. When I said I felt guilty about being hurt by the abuse I had suffered when so many of the kids around me had suffered so much more than I had, Melanie told me, "If somebody's dog died, you wouldn't tell them they had no right to feel bad because some people's grandmas die, now would you?"

Melanie spent a lot of time stroking her belly and speaking to the baby inside. She would try anything she heard about to make her baby healthy, like drinking a lot of milk. She was so excited when she got her first sonogram. "Look!" she squealed to everyone, "My baby's sucking its thumb!"

Melanie so obviously loved her child that sometimes I forgot how hard it must be for her to have a baby all by herself at the age of fifteen.

She was often picked on by the staff for being so young and unmarried. Biff was always using the word "prostitute" around her. The "teen issue" man in the stuffy suit would always stare meaningfully at Melanie when he talked about how "teens should abstain from sex and, if they don't, it is very *stupid* not to use protection every time."

One week it was so bad that Melanie walked out of that damn group. I found her sitting on the dayhall with one hand resting protectively around her stomach and the other balled tight. Her head was tilted back, and she was blinking her bright, wet eyes.

She did not look at me as I sat down next to her. She banged her fist slightly on the arm of the chair and said quietly and waveringly, but forcefully, "I am not a *slut*, and I am not *stupid*."

It was not me she had to convince.

She licked her lip and continued, "I made a mistake. A *mistake* that I can't fix now. I can only go on, and make the best of this. It doesn't make the baby go away, to call myself a stupid slut."

"No, it doesn't," I agreed. "And anyway you're *not*. You're the smartest person I know."

That made Melanie smile as a little tear dribbled down her crooked nose.

Tasha was also fifteen. Her skin was a soft, rich brown, her features small, and her frame tall but thin. She had been raped, at the age of twelve, by her twenty-one-year-old cousin and had a child by him. She had originally wanted an abortion, as she certainly did not want to care for a rapist's child, and one that would be inbred at that. But her social worker denied her that decision, an abortion was refused her, and she was promised that foster parents would be found for her baby. She was put on a waiting list.

Her son had lots of problems. He was mostly deaf, had vision difficulties, and was epileptic. But Tasha grew to love him—to love him more than anything. He was three years old when Tasha's social worker popped in one day to announce that she had found foster parents. Tasha was horrified, and said that she had taken care of her baby for three years now and she intended to keep him. When they took her baby anyway, Tasha naturally fell into "depression," and was sent by her social worker to Magna Carta.

Tasha was the opposite of Melanie, crushed by life. She was quiet and patient and sweet. *Too* quiet and patient and sweet. She sat around with her hands folded listlessly in her lap. Her eyes were filled with silent, unbearable pain. She did everything she was told and never protested. She never raised her voice in all the time I knew her. I knew she wasn't too stupid to see that she was being treated unjustly; she just held all the anger and pain inside.

Just like mine, Tasha's muscles were always tense and

painful because of the strain of having no outlet for her emotions. She was subject to migraine headaches and stomach pains. Sometimes she just blacked out altogether from stress. She had with her a picture of herself from the year before she came to Magna Carta. Her arm was in a sling because she had fainted, fallen down a flight of stairs, and broken it.

Tasha had been allowed to visit her son at first, and she found numerous bruises on him. His foster parents were beating him.She told her social worker. Not only was no action taken to remove the child from the foster home, but the foster parents learned that Tasha suspected them of abuse and requested that she not be allowed to see her baby because they said it would "put false ideas in his head and make the transition more difficult for him."

And so, being a child whose wishes conflicted with those of adults, Tasha was denied visits with her own son.

She called her social worker again and again to beg piteously for just one look at him. I heard her one day at the counter on the office phone, sobbing into the receiver. "Please . . . he's my baby, my son . . . I have to see if he's all right, I'm worried sick . . . just let me see him, please . . . please . . ."

When she hung up, I went and stood stupidly next to her. She was slumped miserably, and her cheeks streamed with tears. She didn't even look at me as I stood there. My heart bled for her, but damned if I could think of a thing to do to comfort her. She squeezed her eyes shut and whispered so faintly that I could hardly hear what she was saying, "My own son . . . I can't help my own son . . ."

Then she stood suddenly, as if every last ounce of strength in her body had been gathered to achieve that one act. She walked to her room in a daze, and closed the door so that her crying would not disturb anyone else.

When a fat staff woman announced that Tasha belonged on the dayhall, I realized that Melanie had been watching Tasha too. Her eyes lit up and narrowed. She said in her simple but determined way that not even the staff could ignore, "She's lost her baby. You leave her the fuck alone."

And they did.

Matthew was brought to Magna Carta some weeks after I was. He was fifteen years old, and tall, but made of nothing but parchmentlike skin stretched around a skeleton. He always stood or sat hunched over, with his elbows clamped to his sides and his limp hands held out in front of him. Everything he did was stiff and in slow motion. And he never did much without being told. He usually just stared into space, his blue eyes dilated with drugs and round with fear and confusion. He had the worst shadows of any of us under his eyes.

I guess it was a good thing that the chairs on the adolescent ward were plastic, because Matthew wet his pants sometimes. I never heard what the people at Magna Carta said was wrong with him, and he was not asked to announce it to us. I always had the distinct impression that he had been born perfectly normal and then experienced something so dreadful that he had been thrown into a state of shock.

Sometimes I would look at him, into his round blue eyes, and he would be looking back at me, as if pleading with me to do something. It made me shiver to think how a normal person could stand being trapped in that wasted body and meaningless existence. I was sure there was some way to let him out if someone would just *try*.

But except for Coty, I never saw anyone who worked at Magna Carta do anything with Matthew except give him an order. Matthew would sometimes sit for an hour in his own urine before anyone did anything about it.

Coty had not been properly "trained" not to get "involved." He was the ward clerk—the secretary—and it wasn't in his job description to "interact" with the patients. So he did.

He was only twenty-one years old, tall and lean, with

long blond hair and a fuzzy mustache. He did his regular job all right as far as I can tell, but then he came out of the office in the evenings.

Sometimes a staff member would take some kids on the appropriate level down to the gymnasium-basement to play basketball. If you were on the appropriate level you didn't have a choice, so I usually had to go too. Coty would go with the kids when they were taken to play basketball. He was pretty good and liked to show off. He wore a bracelet that jingled as he dribbled the ball. I would stand around at the back of the court, annoyed about being there but amused by how much fun so many of the kids seemed to be having trying to take the ball away from Coty.

Coty never said much to me, but I damn near idolized him for being civil to the patients and especially for making friends with Matthew. Matthew perked up a bit when he saw Coty. Coty treated Matthew as though he were a regular kid, not like a freak, or even a fragile child, as some of the other patients, including Melanie and me, were apt to do. Coty taught Matthew, who hardly said a word, to sing (well, to whisper in a monotone) "Tutti Frutti." Matthew was very proud of himself. He even laughed, which was doubly amazing since I had never even seen him smile.

The presence of the staff, and the humiliation of being monitored twenty-four hours a day, always burned somewhere in my heart and mind. What made it a little easier for the patients to ignore the staff was that most of the staff tried their best to ignore us. Everyone who worked with the adolescent patients would introduce themselves to a new one. But that was all. Only a few ever held a conversation with me. Even fewer gave me any other reason to distinguish them from the countless bodies that hovered in and out of the spaces reserved for the staff alone. Our captors usually huddled around the staff table or in the office, breaking away only to make use of the private staff bathrooms. They preferred to gossip among themselves and rarely spoke to a patient except to "re-direct" one.

"Re-direction" was a fancy, humane-sounding word for punishment. Thirteen- to seventeen-year-olds were "re-directed" with a bad "grade" for the hour, "level drops," cancellation of family visits or passes, and, of all things, "Time Out." There were two chairs in the long hall across from each dayhall entrance. On the whim of any staff member, a patient could be told to go to "Time Out" and sit in one of these chairs for a certain number of minutes or hours. Just like preschool—except that the sentences were much longer, and if patients did not sit there until the staff member told them they could leave (never mind whether the prearranged time was up), if they fidgeted too much, or if they didn't have the right "attitude," then they were dragged bodily to "The Room."

An exception to the typical you-leave-me-alone-and-I'll-leave-you-alone staff attitude was Suzi. Suzi was only twenty-two years old, and she reminded me of girls I went to junior high with, the kind I despised yet envied for their shallow, protected existences. Suzi would bounce onto the dayhall with a box of Junior Trivial Pursuit cards and announce to all the seriously screwed-over and heavily drugged patients on the ward that she was going to "play a little game with us." She paused then, as if waiting for us to cheer or something. When no one looked very enthusiastic, she told us coolly that we didn't have to play, but if we didn't, we could go sit in the Time Out chair.

Suzi had us all scoot our chairs together in a neat semicircle and began reading questions to us one by one. I felt like a toddler whose bossy older sister had coerced me into playing school. Trivial Pursuit is a nice game, but this was *Junior* Trivial Pursuit, apparently written for very young children. I was humiliated by the simplicity of the questions and the way Suzi read them. I was even more aggravated by the fact that I was so heavily drugged that I had to think hard about those simple questions and struggle to get the answers out of my mouth.

At last, when Suzi asked, "What is the name of a four-legged mammal that you can ride and lives in a corral?" I couldn't contain myself any longer.

"A horse!" I exploded. "A *horse*, for God's sake! Don't you have anything that wouldn't insult the intelligence of a four-year-old?"

The other patients, who had been taking this insignificant little embarrassment patiently, looked at me in surprise. I had never so vehemently objected to anything before. Jake raised his eyebrows and looked away so he wouldn't laugh. Suzi lifted her little nose in the air and told me to go sit in the Time Out chair.

I sat and fumed, the drugs making it appear as if there were two Suzis, side by side, their words blurred together into one endless, meaningless torrent of patronization. I was so weary, so drained, that try as I might to preserve a shred of dignity, I broke down at last into sobs of burning humiliation right in front of the very people who had caused it.

There were several people on the staff at Magna Carta who were just college kids like Suzi. It had to do with some kind of training program. At first there was only one of those kids that I could bear—Tyler. Tyler was only twenty-one, and had been every bit as sheltered and spoiled as Suzi. He didn't have any real problems, and he didn't understand suffering, but what made him tolerable was that he admitted freely that he didn't have any big problems and he didn't pretend he knew how to solve mine.

He told me straight out that he was working at Magna Carta for school credit and that this sort of work wasn't his life goal—that he wasn't even very interested in it at all. He felt no need to "re-direct" or otherwise harass the patients all the time. And he certainly didn't insist that we play Junior Trivial Pursuit with him and then act like he was doing us a favor by associating with us.

But what he would do was something that no one else who worked at Magna Carta ever did. If I started talking to him, he would talk to me in return just like he would talk to anyone else. He would even let me sit at the almighty staff table at the front of the dayhall while he was working and talk to him. Patients were not supposed to do that. Patients were supposed to stay in their place.

I told Tyler about how hard I used to try to be perfect and how my family always found something wrong with me anyway, and Tyler told me all the bad things he did as a kid and how he got away with them. He told me about the times he had stolen his parents' car and how most of the time he got it back without their knowing it was gone, but one day he wrecked it. I was a little jealous, but fascinated by Tyler's stories. I don't think he ever noticed that if anyone should be classified as "bad" or "crazy" it would be him and not me, but at least he didn't care about my being labeled that way.

I let him read a story that I wrote. He judged it seriously, as a regular piece of writing instead of the product of the mind of a child, and a mental patient child at that. If he hadn't liked it he would have told me so instead of patronizing me. But he was impressed with it. He told me that I should send it in to magazines and that I would make a "load." I laughed at Tyler's idea of sending my story to a magazine, but I was very pleased to find the second person in the universe who took my writing seriously. (My Uncle Bob was the first.)

One day Tyler even broke the highest law in the patient-staff code and gave me a glimpse of a patient chart. He was looking at it as we sat at the staff table, and he said with a grin, "Looks like you have quite an admirer." When I did not know what he was talking about, he just turned the chart around, as if it were the most natural thing in the world, and let me see the love notes that Tilly had written but never given to me because he was caught with them.

I giggled.

The only other college-aged staff member whom I ever

liked had been on vacation when I was first left on the adolescent ward. It was two weeks later when he came back, a stranger that I took no notice of. But the patients who had been at Magna Carta long enough to remember the last time he had worked there clamored to him, begging to go outside. I did not know that a staff member was even allowed to take patients outside, because certainly no one had. But this stranger led those of us who were on good levels downstairs and out to a cement courtyard at the side of the building.

Two sides of the courtyard were tall buildings, and two were enclosed by very high fences. The floor was painted for tennis, and there was a tennis or volleyball net that could be set up. It was decided by the staff members present that the kids would play kickball with a red playground ball.

I was beside myself with the joy of being outside in the warm sun after being locked up and half frozen for two weeks. So excited, in fact, that I overexerted myself. I was the pitcher, and I was about to roll the ball when suddenly the concrete ground seemed to tilt. Objects took on an orangeish aura, and then the whole world was solid red. I put my hand over my eyes as I heard Randy shout, "Hey, c'mon, throw the ball!"

"Shut up!" I told him, which was an unusually angry thing for me to say.

Near-fainting spells had happened to me many a time, and just as I was about to lose consciousness, I told myself, as I always did, *If you fall down here on the ground nobody will give a damn, so don't set yourself up for embarrassment.* I walked as quickly as I could to a bench on the sidelines. I had been told once that it helped to put my head between my knees. But I couldn't see, I wasn't sure where my head was in relation to the rest of my body, and I certainly didn't know how to get it between my knees. I could hear noises of disgust all around me as I struggled to the bench and sat gasping and trying to regain my senses.

I had never known any staff member who wanted to do anything to help or comfort me when I was sick or about to faint. The last time it had happened, Dr. Limband's drugs had just been building up in my system while I sat on the dayhall. At first I thought that the ground had jumped up at me, but I quickly realized that I had fallen out of my chair and that I was bleeding from a small cut on my head where I had hit the table in front of me. Melanie and Jake stood up from their chairs, but were stopped short by a staff member's sharp,

"Leave her alone. She just wants attention."

I lay on the floor for a dazed minute until I could pull myself up and struggle across the room by myself for some Kleenex . . .

So I was very surprised when this time I heard a voice say kindly, "Why don't I take you in?" I felt a gentle but firm hand close around my arm and pull me to my feet.

The world cleared a little bit, and I looked up into the face of this stranger who had taken the kids outside. He had soft brown eyes. Instinctively I pulled my arm away from him, even though I already figured he must be okay as far as adult members of the opposite sex and employees of psychiatric wards go.

I didn't want to leave the warm outside world—I didn't even want to move—but this nice person obviously thought it was best for me to go inside. So I began staggering toward the door. The man followed me as I struggled to walk through the door and down the hall to the elevator. Since the outside was so bright and the inside of the building was so dark, I was once again blinded as my eyes attempted to adjust.

At first I thought I was imagining things, but I distinctly heard the man say, "Why don't I carry you?"

I couldn't remember the last time I had been carried by anyone. Long ago I had resigned myself to the fact that I would have to carry myself, no matter how badly I felt— I would have carry myself until my dying day, because no one else in this world would or could. But this man would not hear of my refusal. He simply leaned and lifted me in his arms as easily as I would lift my Raggedy Ann doll.

I was stiff with horror for a moment, feeling certain that he had misjudged my weight and would drop me, but I did not seem to even be a bother to him. A shivering sigh rose from the pit of my stomach to the top of my head and spread to my toes. I closed my eyes and went limp with relief in the arms of a stranger whose simple act of kindness I will never forget to my dying day.

I talked with that man once—and I call him a man, even though he was the same chronological age as Suzi, whom I call nothing more than a spoiled child. I was crying, and he took me out in the long hall to ask me why. I was crying about a movie, and I was ashamed of crying over a silly thing like that by itself, so I told him that the movie reminded me of my "older brother who had been killed."

I don't know if the man knew I was telling a lie, but whether he thought I had lost a brother or not, he saw a deeper pain than that in me, a deeper pain than could be caused by any movie. He saw what no one else would see even when I threw it in front of their faces. He saw that I was suffering from child abuse. That was what we talked about that day. I cannot remember any of our specific words, but the memory of his sympathetic brown eyes, old and deep, is etched into my brain.

When he told me quietly that his parents had "changed" between the time his sister was growing up and when he was born, I knew why he recognized my problem—he had had the very same problem when he was a child.

When we were finished talking, he hugged me. He was so tall that my face was mashed against the front of his shirt. He hugged me so tightly that I could hardly breathe, but I was glad. My mother was the only person who had ever gone through the motions of hugging me, but she was not hugging *me*, only the thing that she imagined was her daughter. For the first time in my life, someone had touched *me*, hugged *me*—Tiffany Blake—for myself.

I wonder, would he have reached out to me, could he have touched me, if he had not been through it all himself? Can a person truly sympathize with what they have never known? Or are there simply two kinds of people in this world—those that are deeply scarred and those that are not—who can never understand each other and get along?

FIVE

When the drug Dr. Limband was giving me reached indisputably toxic levels in my blood, she finally reduced the amount I was to take each day. Of course she never told me why she was reducing the dosage (I learned later when I finally saw my medical records); I was just unspeakably glad when she did.

A little while after the first cutback, Dr. Limband told me she was lowering the dosage again. She told me this with the first bit of irritation I had ever seen behind her mask of smiling perfection. As if it were my fault my blood didn't like her damn pills.

A little while after the third reduction I felt almost as well as I had before I came to Magna Carta. The stress of my situation still wore on me, as it always had. I was a lot weaker and paler and more weary than a thirteen-year-old who has not been subjected to complete restriction and constant abuse. But at least my vision was cleared, my head stopped throbbing, and I could walk down the halls without having to catch myself on a wall.

I knew the amount of medication I was taking then was almost nothing. Dr. Limband might just as well have taken me off it altogether, but then I would not have been swallowing three tablets a day like every other patient in the place, and that of course would have been unacceptable. The bleary, dilated, droopy-lidded eyes of the people around me, the heaviness and listlessness of their young bodies, were unpleasant indeed. But how else could twenty adolescents be controlled by a few adults? Our energy needed to be completely drained, our minds distracted from questioning and exploring and doing by being utterly overwhelmed by the sole desire to sleep. And even then we were not allowed to sleep, but were chastised for not doing what we were told as quickly as the staff wanted it done.

Although I was always disgusted with myself for not thinking of ways to protest the little absurdities and injustices heaped upon me at Magna Carta, I had been so well trained in my childhood to submit blindly to anyone labeled "authority" that I was not harassed as often as some of the patients. Since I usually did whatever I was told and accepted insult and humiliation quietly, I was almost always given good grades. Thus I was almost always on a good level, and just had to wait the required number of days to be promoted to the next one. I was sent to Time Out only that one time, by Suzi, and "The Room" was nothing more than words to me.

Melanie, who spoke out for herself and others, was dragged to The Room once, by Biff. I just barely caught a glimpse of her struggling against the hands that held her wrists so tightly that they were bruised. My fists clenched and my face burned with indignation, but I didn't have the courage to fight, even for Melanie.

When I saw Melanie again, released after hours in The Room, her face was drawn and white, her eyes wild with horror and panic. "My stomach!" she whispered to me. "He pushed me on my stomach! Oh, my God, my God, my baby!" Her trembling fingers stroked her bulging abdomen as she said the words "my baby" over and over. I stood, utterly lost as to what to do, when Tasha was suddenly at Melanie's side, holding her and telling her that babies were pretty tough and she was sure the baby was all right.

I had caught glimpses of the children's ward beyond the hideously institutional blue door because the "classroom" and the room where my blood was drawn were on that ward. One day the "good" little children were brought to the adolescent side to watch a movie with us. I can't explain why, but those younger kids gravitated toward me right away. They argued over who would sit by me until I suggested rotating at various points in the movie.

I did not initiate any friendship with these younger kids because of what my family had ingrained in my mind about "pedophiles." But when they introduced themselves to me, and talked to me, I would talk to them like regular people. I guess that must have been as rare and pleasant for them as it was for me when Tyler talked to me like a regular person.

Two of those little kids, Jenny and Elliot, made little pictures and notes for me that day. One of Elliot's said, "Wil you mery me?" I told him that was a nice offer, but that he was awful young for me.

Elliot was about seven or eight years old. He was painfully shy and pale, and he hung around me as close as he could without touching me for a while. Eventually he worked up the nerve to ask if he could hold my hand, and I saw no harm in that.

Jenny was nine. She had very long brown hair and big, all-seeing, hungry brown eyes. She apparently liked to talk, and she babbled away to me as if she had never had a chance to talk to someone and never would again. She drew me adorable pictures of Garfield, Odie, and Jon.

When the staff noticed how well the younger children liked me, they asked me if I would help the little girls get ready for bed at night. I thought I was supposed to be just a mental freak, too incompetent to run my own life, and here the staff wanted me to do their oh-so-specialized-and-hallowed work that took years of training for them to learn to do? But I had nothing better to do, and I liked those nice little kids who obviously needed a friend so badly.

I was told to go into the big bathroom in the girls' hall with the little girls while they took their daily showers, and just keep an eye on them and help them out in general.

A sullen faced girl with short, curly blond hair told me that she was shy and asked if I had to look at her naked if she promised she wouldn't run away. I told her I wasn't going to look at her if she didn't want me to because it was her body. Then I put my hand over my eyes and announced, "And if any of you want to run away stark naked that's not my problem anyway."

That got a few giggles, even from that poor, mistrustful-looking girl. She said to me, "Nobody ever listened to me before. Thank you."

I gritted my teeth as I thought about that.

Jenny wasn't shy. She always asked me to wash the spot in the middle of her back she couldn't reach. I liked to brush out her long brown hair. She chattered away at me the whole time. Most of the time she was smiling and telling me about what she did that day or about where she bought her pajamas. But one day her voice took on a subdued and serious tone. She told me of the long string of foster homes and institutions she had been placed in, and how no one anywhere had ever wanted to keep her.

She said I was one of the nicest people she ever knew, and seeing that she didn't have any family of her own, she wanted to know if it would be okay with me if she pretended I was her sister. Jenny always brought to my mind the image of that smiling pink doll lying neglected on the floor of Dr. Burns's waiting room. I always wanted to hug her and tell her that just because nobody wanted her didn't mean she was nuts.

Biff was the only staff person who said my helping the little girls was "inappropriate." He would sneer and glare at me as if I were a pervert when he saw me with them, but apparently his opinion didn't have much influence with the other staff, who continued to ask me to help.

The children's ward went on occasional "outings," and sometimes I would be asked to go with them to help the staff "keep an eye" on the kids. They would be herded into a rickety, full-sized van, and after arguing over who would sit by me, they would buckle themselves in and be off to the park for a few hours. I liked being out in the warm air immensely. One of the kids would usually be talking to me most of the time—even that blonde, sulky girl who didn't seem like she was used to talking to people. Behind her narrowed eyes and her pinched, downturned mouth was the fear and uncertainty that drove her to hide herself.

Her mother came to the park with the kids once. She had the sourest face I'd ever seen in my life. I didn't hear one word out of her mouth that wasn't a criticism or an insult or a threat to her young daughter. I don't understand how after meeting her mother, anyone could wonder how that poor girl came to be the way she was.

Every once in a while a field trip was arranged for a few of us on the adolescent ward too. The staff would take off their identification tags and pile us into the van. Once we went to a mall to see a sand sculpture. It was a nice sculpture, but I was rather embarrassed to be in a crowd, and so was every other patient there. Melanie threw her shoulders back and refused to hunch over to hide her "condition." She held one of Matthew's elbows and I held the other. He was quite frightened in the middle of all those bustling people, and he wouldn't move a step without being led. I don't know what he would have done if Melanie and I weren't there that day. People were staring unashamedly at us, and I felt my face turning red in spite of myself.

A couple of giggly teen-age girls in lots of makeup and designer clothes spotted our little mental patient parade. One of them pointed right at Matthew and said with a loud snort, "What's the matter with *him*? Is he a *retard* or something?"

I only hoped Matthew did not understand. I ducked my head and tried to pull him away from those little brats as quickly as possible. But Melanie stopped short, looked at me quizzically, and inquired loudly, "What's the matter with *them*? Are they *bitches* or something?"

The staff gave her a reprimand and refused to take her

on the next "field trip" because she couldn't control her "outbursts." She apologized, but I wished I had the courage it took to say things like that. The staff had no right to make her feel guilty for it.

The staff was extremely sensitive to the way the patients "acted" in the "real world." We got "re-directed" for behaving as normal kids do. I was irritated by the staff's obvious embarrassment about being seen with us. If I were not always on a good level and expected to go, I would not usually have joined the adolescent "field trips."

Occasionally, however, a staff person would skip the calculated "destination" and "purpose" of the trip, and instead of embarrassing us and themselves trying to "reintegrate" us into society, they would cruise the patients through the streets. If the patients were lucky, we even got to listen to what we wanted to on the radio.

One day a woman let us all out of the van by a big city fountain and let us cool our feet in it. I had rolled up my pants carefully, as some of the other girls had, but pretty soon everyone was drenched from splashing and frolicking. For a few glorious hours we were no longer the despised rejects of society, sitting pale and listless on our little ward as we were trained to; we were humans, young and free, laughing, flinging our limbs in the summer breeze and the swirling waters as the sun glinted off the droplets in our hair.

As we rode back to our ward in that rickety van, soaking wet, the radio blaring R.E.M., I saw Tasha smile.

That was all it took . . . to make Tasha smile.

For thirty days I was classified as seriously mentally ill and in dire need of institutionalization. For thirty days my parents' insurance company paid the people at Magna Carta for this institutionalization. But thirty days was the limit on the policy. So on the thirty-first day, when Magna Carta could no longer be sure of receiving payment for my "treatment," I was suddenly and miraculously "cured."

Dr. Limband flicked on all my lights that morning at

seven on the dot and announced with a face-splitting smile that I would be going home.

My eyes grew wide with horror. I clutched my thin sheet as I told her that if I had to go back to my abusive family, I would most certainly be driven to suicide.

Dr. Limband wanted to know what my suicide "plan" was.

This left me speechless. I hadn't known that my desperation was supposed to include a "plan" to be of importance. Dr. Limband smiled and made a note on her clipboard. My terror was no setback to her plan to send me home. The setback came when my parents refused to come and get me, claiming they couldn't "handle" me.

For two more weeks I sat at Magna Carta while it was decided behind my back what would be done with me. Naturally I knew nothing about the insurance or anything like that. All I knew was that after forty-seven unexplained days in a psychiatric institution, my parents arrived to take me home.

Dr. Limband informed me that day that my parents would be giving me hourly grades now like those I was given in the hospital, on a "point sheet," and that I would also be taking the point sheet to my teachers at school in the fall. I was to continue individual counseling (never mind family counseling), and I would need to learn to accept the "boundaries" that would now be laid out for me by my parents and my grandmother.

I don't know what on earth my parents and my grandmother said to cause Dr. Limband to believe that I *lacked* the very thing that I was being strangled by an excess of— *structure* indeed! But I was not really worried about more "structure" of the sort she was talking about being inflicted upon me. A point sheet? Are you kidding? My family would have to make one up, make copies of it every day, and instead of being able to throw vague accusations at my character, like "manipulative" and "lazy," they would have to find something specifically wrong with what I'd *done* each hour. And that was more work than any of them were willing to do.

I had more realistic things to worry about. I was frantic, crying and pleading and saying over and over that I wasn't just making up a *threat* of some sort, I was genuinely afraid that suicide would be my only way out if I were back under the control of my irrational and abusive family.

At last Dr. Limband turned to me with the second hint of impatience behind her glued-on grin that I ever saw. She told me crossly that she would report my *alleged* abuse to the state child protection service and have a social worker check up on me. Not having much of a choice anyway, I agreed under this condition to go home with my parents.

I was driven home under the same blanket of silent hate that I had been driven away from it under.

Of course the conditions of my home had not changed at all while I was gone, except that my mother had taken advantage of my absence by moving from that uncomfortable little room in the garage back to the one upstairs. Her bed and mine were now situated on opposite sides of the same room. The only good thing about that little situation was that of course my mother wasn't going to live in a room without a door, and it had been put back on.

I had my fourteenth birthday a few weeks after leaving Magna Carta. I received in the mail the usual nice presents from my father's parents and my grandmother's aunt and her daughter. These were people I had exchanged letters with all my life. When I wrote to any of these people, I never mentioned the abuse and loneliness I endured. I told them about all the good things that happened to me. Still, I resented the fact that they just *had* to have some idea of what I was living with, and they never mentioned it. Why did no one say anything to me when I was committed to a mental institution? Did they honestly think I was crazy or something?

I don't know why I never had to see Dr. Burns again,

but suddenly I was supposed to go to a psychiatrist my mother had been talking to for a while instead. His name was Dr. Kern, and he worked at a "family counseling" place called Kid Counsel. Kid Counsel had an inpatient clinic that my parents had me on the waiting list for, but I never saw it. I guess my guardian angel was looking out for me *that* time.

There wasn't a single thing to like about that Kid Counsel place. Their slogan, "Support for parents. Solutions for kids." was printed on their business cards and posted on the wall over a picture of a little hunched-over stick-figure-like representation of a kid. Don't parents ever need "solutions," and don't kids ever need any "support," for heaven's sake? Of course, but that would be the slogan only if kids had the money and the power to drag their *parents* to little "family counseling" places and demand that they be "fixed."

Dr. Kern's hair stood straight up, and it wasn't a buzz cut or anything, it was long. He smelled so bad I could hardly stand being shut up in his tiny office with him for an hour a week. He was as condescending to me as Dr. Limband had been, but at least he didn't smile. He gave me all kinds of tests to take home and fill out. At first I thought, *Ah-ha, now I can prove I'm not crazy, I just have all the symptoms of a child experiencing abuse.*

But the tests weren't made for children, much less abused children; they were made for adults. For example, a large part of one test was meant to determine whether I had a normal sex life. Obviously the expected answers included a regular amount of and degree of comfort with sexual intercourse. The people who made up this test didn't take into account fourteen-year-old virgins.

I quickly realized that any answer I wrote to any question could be construed in any way that anyone who read it wished. Since I am not a perfect being, the slightest of my faults could be picked out and used as evidence that there was something dreadfully wrong with me, as my family had been doing all my life. Even if I *was* perfect, I could then be accused of being "anal retentive" or something like that. So I just wrote what I thought sounded best and filled out the bubbles on the multiple choice tests at random.

Dr. Kern never shared what he thought was wrong with me, what he thought of the answers on the tests, or even what he thought I would have to be like in order to be considered "good" enough or "normal" enough not to have to see him anymore. Not that I asked. I had given up asking people like him things like that a long time ago. My mother was perfectly delighted to tell me over and over what she thought he thought anyway.

According to my mother, Dr. Kern said I had one or many of the following (depending on what sort of mood she was in at the time): multiple personality disorder, borderline personality disorder, borderline schizophrenia, behavior disorders of all sorts, a pathological lying problem, sociopathy, etc. My mother also filled me in on what Dr. Kern had "told her" about me: that I was clinically depressed (as opposed to being disheartened about real problems), that I had a vague chemical imbalance in my head brought on by adolescence or inherited from my uncles, that I would be "sick" for the rest of my life, that I needed years of institutionalization, blah, blah, blah . . .

And how could I know whether what she said was true or not?

Dr. Limband had Dr. Kern continue to prescribe the "antidepressants" I had been given at Magna Carta, and my mother was supposed to give them to me once I was home.

But she didn't know she was supposed to check my mouth.

When the drug had completely left my system I had more strength and energy. Dr. Kern and my mother even noticed that I suddenly felt and acted "better," as I had hoped they would. They commented often that my body had finally "adjusted" and that the drugs were doing me "a lot of good now."

When I had a little bag full of spit-out pills, I showed

them to my mother and said that psychoactive drugs, especially this particular kind, were bad for me and that not
taking them anymore was what had "improved" me. Although the label "uncooperative" was then added to the
long list of my character flaws, psychoactive medications
were never prescribed for me again.

I can't express how relieved I was.

A couple with a four-year-old daughter had moved into
the other half of our duplex a year or so before I had
been sent to Magna Carta. The mother had asked my
mother if I was available for baby-sitting. She was smart
to do this, because if I had asked, my mother would have
said no, but my mother never refused a stranger. I had been
nervous around Lilly, the little girl, because of the whole
you're-a-pervert-if-you-like-kids thing, but we got along
quite well. She adored me, as most children do for some
reason. Her parents never complained, and they asked me
back time and time again.

After I got back from Magna Carta, Lilly's parents never
asked me to baby-sit for their little girl and her new baby
brother again. When they needed a sitter, they asked my
brother. What on earth had my mother told those people?

I looked for another job because I knew I would never
survive a summer not seeing anyone but my family and not
being allowed out of my house except on errands with my
mother. Eventually I volunteered to work in a local Civil
War museum. It took a struggle with my mother to be allowed to take the job and be provided with transportation,
but for some reason I lucked out that time.

I was absolutely delighted with my job. I got to wear a
Civil-War-era costume and give tours and help preschool
classes that came to make old-fashioned crafts. These were
all things I enjoyed immensely. I took care to memorize
my tour and read all the information that was given to me
on the museum and the period it was recreating.

The only thing that made the job hard was my mother.

She had worked at the museum and had made friends with my boss. Suddenly my mother was visiting my boss all the time, and I could only imagine what she was telling her. Having no idea what my boss must have thought of me, I assumed the worst, and I was painfully humiliated to be in the same room with her. I kept trying to assure myself that if my boss did not think well of me, I would not be working with her customers and her valuable antiques. But it didn't help. My confidence was shattered. When I got home from work, I would cry as I did when I got home from school, because I was so sure I wasn't "good enough." And when I expressed this fear to my mother, she said it didn't matter because not much could be expected of a person with a mental illness anyway.

When the summer was over, and my job as well, I started ninth grade—my last year of junior high school. I had no classes with my friend that year, so I saw her only before classes. It was just as well, because I was terribly uncomfortable in the presence of anyone who knew where I had been.

One day my history teacher, one of the few teachers I have had that I admired, was saying something about "civilization" that upset me. He was the sort of teacher who actually encouraged his students to express their opinions, so I raised my hand and gave a little speech starting with, "What is *civilization?* Do you have to eat with a fork to be civilized? The word doesn't have a meaning, really. It's just one of those many words people use to say that they are better than someone else. White people came and said the Indians were uncivilized, and that made it okay to take their land and kill them . . ."

I went on like that, not mentioning that I thought the present-day equivalent of "civilized" and "uncivilized" was "normal" and "mentally ill." If you are labeled "mentally ill," it's okay for "normal" people to lock you up and mistreat you the way it was okay for "civilized" people to slaughter and enslave the "uncivilized."

The teacher liked my enthusiasm, but I stopped talking

when I realized the other students were snickering at me. When the class was over, the boy who sat behind me made a grand gesture, rolled his eyes, and exclaimed passionately, "What is civiliza-*shon!*"

He did this for a few days after class until one day I realized that unlike the other kids who mocked me because they thought I was a nerd, this boy had been impressed by what I had said.

We talked sometimes. His name was Jeff. He probably never imagined that he was my only pure comfort in the miserable few months between my release from Magna Carta and my inevitable reimprisonment.

S I X

    A little while after I started ninth grade, my parents suggested to the school that I be tested for placement in the BD (Behavior Disorder) class on account of my "psychological history."

    I did not know until years later that the school had nothing to do with the shame of being taken to the BD room and asked questions like, "Why do you feel it is not your responsibility to do well in school?" Nor did I know that the school refused to put me in the BD class because they had never had any problems with my "behavior" in school. My parents told me there was "no question" that I needed to be in that class, and that I would be attending it as soon as there was "an available desk."

    This lie that I had no way of knowing was a lie added a lot of fuel to my all-consuming desire to escape my family and go somewhere, anywhere, that was not under their influence. Each day I went to ninth grade, I thought I would die from the shame of everyone knowing that I had been to the loony bin, and that I was going to be put in the BD class with the kids who threw desks across classrooms.

    I prayed harder than I have ever prayed for anything in my life for the social worker from the state child protection service to arrive as Dr. Limband had promised she would. The idea that she would not understand my situation, or not care even if she did, never entered my head. I told myself that if I could just talk with her first, she would put me in a nice foster home, the kind Wanda had always talked about.

Long before I ever saw a social worker, however, a woman named Heather Williams began arriving at my house every week from an organization called Family Matters, Inc. If I had thought that going to Kid Counsel for individual "counseling" once a week was the most horrible experience in the world, it was just because Heather Williams hadn't come to my house yet.

Dr. Limband had recommended "family counseling" for the sole purpose of helping my family "cope with the seriousness of Tiffany's illness." So of course Heather had the opposite of an open mind about my case. And while Dr. Limband believed that the best way to deal with "crazy" children is to smile constantly and patronize them, Heather's theory was that if she just made it clear to me that I wasn't going to "get away" with my "behavior," then I would "shape up." She gave me the most hateful stares I have ever received from anyone not related to me. She always spoke sharply and forcefully to me and never paid any attention to anything I said, not even my constant protests against being called "Tiffy" instead of "Tiffany." I have always hated that nickname.

Heather spent an hour or more each week with my parents, and sometimes even my little brother, apparently believing whatever they told her, just as Dr. Burns and Dr. Limband and others before her had. I guess it makes sense for a stranger to believe the word of three adults over that of a child, especially if the child has just been in a mental institution. I couldn't even begin to defend myself because in the first place, I had no idea exactly what I had to defend myself against. It was all said behind my back.

I never had a chance.

When at last a social worker from the state child protection service arrived at my house—the savior to whom I had attached the last hope for my life and sanity—she said hello when introduced to me and then commenced to spend over an hour out on the porch alone with my parents.

Once again I could hardly fathom what my parents must

have said to Marjory Nelson, and I had no idea how many
reports she had received from the various other people who
had "worked with" me. I just knew I was utterly without
hope when the first words out of her mouth when she came
into the room with me were, "Well, Tiffany, I understand
you have a little problem with honesty, eh?"

I begged and cried and told her about everything that
had been done to me that I could think of, the constant
torrent of emotional abuse, the occasional physical abuse,
the fact that I was the scapegoat for all my family's problems, including my mother's physical illness, which was
most obviously irrelevant to me, and didn't even that alone
prove my family had a problem?

But it was no use. Marjory nodded now and then and
scribbled on her clipboard. At one point, when I was telling
her about the time my father hit me in the face and
knocked me into the washing machine, leaving a large
bruise on the back of my head, she said, "You know, Tiffany, I am not here to take away the rights of parents to
discipline their children."

Even though my parents could obviously get away with
anything they wanted to do to me, they were a little more
careful after the social worker came, at least in the physical
sense. While they continued their emotional torture, they
stopped hitting me.

And that was the worst thing that could have happened.

I didn't really give a damn about being smacked around
or whipped. If I bore the pain without crying, I had my
dignity, and that was all that mattered to me. But physical
abuse is the only kind of abuse that gives a person something to show for it. What proof did I have of emotional
abuse? None. All I had was my hair-raising story of being
treated like I was insane when I was perfectly normal,
against my family's perfectly reasonable-sounding story of
my being treated like I was insane because I was insane.

So I did a desperate thing. I cracked a bottle on my jaw
to give it a nasty bruise and claimed my father did it.

The first person I showed my bruise and told my fib to was my mother. I don't know why I did that when she already knew damn well that my father beat me anyway, whether this particular time it was the case or not.

She had been peeling carrots once, in the corner of the kitchen, when I was about nine years old. Until then I had told myself that my mother did not rescue me from the physical abuse of my grandmother and my father because she never actually witnessed it. But that day she asked me to wash my hands, and as I walked to the sink I heard my father coming home.

Suddenly the sink seemed to leap up and bite my hands. I whirled around and my father was there, gnashing his teeth and making his eyes big and crazy. He hit me again and snarled in a rage, "SPIT IT OUT!"

I had no idea what on earth he was talking about, so I stood stupidly as my father backhanded me across the face. I turned to my mother, who was watching as my father yelled the same words and accentuated them in the same way again. I had bitten my tongue and the blood was hot in my mouth. At last my mother held out the trash can to me and said with a little smile,

"Your father doesn't think young ladies should chew gum, Tiffany."

And indeed, my father left when I had spit out the offending grape-flavored substance. For a minute I just stared at my mother, who was humming as she continued to peel the carrots over my bloody hunk of gum in the trash.

All my mother said when I showed her the bruise I had made myself was "I don't believe that," and at least that time she was justified.

The next person I showed it to was Glenda, my new individual therapist at Kid Counsel. Somebody had apparently noticed that I didn't have much to say to Dr. Kern and thought I would "relate better to a woman."

She said, "Mmm-hmm, I see."

So I was back where I had started, only with guilt for

having lied and a painful bruise on my jaw. I began to despair after that. I even began to doubt myself very seriously.

Maybe there is really something wrong with me. Maybe all these things I believe are abusive, that I should not have to tolerate, are not so bad after all. Maybe I am too sensitive, or too nuts.

Or maybe even if the way I'm being treated isn't normal, it's still okay, because I don't deserve to be treated normally; maybe I'm not normal. Maybe all those things I've heard about me are true, and I'm crazy after all. Why would my whole family and all those strangers believe such a thing if it weren't true? Wouldn't my family protest the idea that their own flesh and blood is nuts until it was a completely unavoidable conclusion? Crazy people don't think they're crazy, so it makes sense that I don't believe it if I am, doesn't it?

Oh, why won't anyone tell me anything straight out? I can't stand all this guessing what people think and what people have heard and said. If I were just informed of the general consensus on what my problem is, maybe I could fix it . . .

I began to dwell continually on everything I had ever done wrong, or that I knew someone somewhere thought was wrong, and wondering which deed or combination of deeds made me deserving of my lifelong loneliness, of my sudden institutionalization, of being analyzed by all these strange and hateful people, of being placed in those classes at school, and of the general disgust that hung over my head wherever I went.

By about five months after leaving Magna Carta, I had fretted over the dilemma of whether or not I was crazy or bad for as long as it was humanly possible to do so.

One night in my bed I began screaming. I don't know if it was dreaming or being awake that caused me to start screaming, but I could not stop. I flung myself out of bed, my body shaking with emotion, muscles jerking from lack of use and being tense always, always, as long as I could remember.

My mother came up the stairs and flicked on the light. I was still screaming.

My father and brother came and stood in the doorway and stared at me. I guess it surprised them to see me in a frenzied state they hadn't just driven me into purposely.

My mother took me to the living room couch and had me lie down. I was still screaming, my eyes were wild, and I just kept twisting and jerking my body, trying to stretch my atrophied muscles, trying to struggle away from the unbearable pain in my heart. I felt as though someone was pulling a steel band around my chest, tighter, tighter, and I was screaming for help as my breath, my life was squeezed out of me.

My heart was racing at a truly alarming rate, and I could barely gasp between the screams that spewed endlessly from the agony inside me through my raw, dry throat. My mother flung her body over mine in an attempt to quiet me.

Heather arrived a few days later and found me sitting on the couch in my pajamas, my hair loose in my face and a desperate, crazed look in my eyes. I was talking to my stuffed bear, trying to convince myself it could hear.

I had decided to let myself go crazy for two reasons. One, if I were to lose all touch with reality, I might be happy, like Angela, the girl at Magna Carta who thought she was Batwoman. I might find comfort in an imaginary world if I could just immerse myself completely in it. Two, maybe they would put me away again. As terrible as it was, I had decided it was better than being at home.

Heather was absolutely infuriated by this attempt of mine to "make people feel sorry for me." When I refused to make any coherent responses to her sharp questions and demands to "look at me when I am speaking to you," Heather turned to my mother and said to her, with great sympathy for her having to deal with such a child, "Well, she's been on the waiting list, it should be any day now."

If I had only understood that remark, if I had only known that my family had been steadily wading through the drawn-out process of having me committed to a state institution even before I had left Magna Carta, then I wouldn't have had to go to all the trouble of making myself nuts.

I soon found myself in the back seat of the car again, hunched over and yellowish-pale as parchment. I had packed a suitcase this time, and made damn sure that every last one of my notebooks was locked tight in my trunk. I cuddled and whispered good-bye to Opie, my best friend in those past months, and tried to push from my mind the possibility of never seeing him again. I had even remembered to bring something to hang onto for dear life—my large, stuffed bear.

I thought myself very well prepared. It never occurred to me, however, that the place I was being taken to this time, Wilson State Hospital (WSH), was a damn sight different from a private clinic like Magna Carta.

It was October 15, 1991. I watched the red and orange and yellow leaves of trees whiz past my window, trying to concentrate on their beauty and not on any thoughts or feelings about my present situation.

Don't think, don't feel, it doesn't do any good, be good, and quiet, don't feel, be happy, be separated, be numb, don't feel anything, don't feel anything, what will you do if you feel it, Tiffany? Showing your rage and your pain is what got you into this mess in the first place . . .

There were many buildings scattered around the few acres of WSH, some very old and some abandoned. I was taken to the admissions building, where, since I was not old enough to be human, not legally responsible for my own life, my father signed me in on "volunteer" status. The admissions staff asked my parents numerous questions while I sat quietly in a chair with my bear. I watched a little fly that buzzed around the stuffy office for a long time.

At last they took my photograph. It was an automatic thing for me to force my face into a less-than-enthusiastic smile as one should for a picture. I have since wondered if anyone else in the world smiled for their mug shots.

My parents could have left then, but my mother insisted on going with me in the security vehicle to the building for "adolescents." It was a grotesquely huge, ancient, brick-and-cement atrocity called the Smith Building, after some doctor. It was three stories high and seemed infinitely long. There were pigeons and pigeon droppings all over the place. On each end was a porch enclosed with rusty chain-link fencing.

As the driver of the security vehicle led us to a locked door in one of those porches, the hideous building towered over me more ominously than anything I had ever seen. I stood still, trembling violently. I licked my dry lips, stared at the porch, and whispered, "It's like my guinea pig cage."

This sent my mother into a frenzy of sobbing about "her poor baby" and lamenting the "necessity" of leaving me here for the rest of my natural life. I did not protest her carrying on as I had in Dr. Burns's office six months before. I hadn't the strength anymore to push her away when she wound her arms around me and dribbled her crocodile tears all over me.

Inside the cage was another locked door that led inside the building. As that door clanged shut behind me, I was met by such a stench and such horribly anguished and hateful "vibes" that I clutched my bear in terror.

My parents went, as usual, to a separate room to discuss me with their new friends, the staff of Wilson State Hospital. I was left on the dayhall, a large, square, dingy white room with one rounded end, which contained huge rectangular windows crisscrossed with bars. In front of the windows was a television, surrounded by plastic chairs as if it were a shrine. There were four card tables set up, and two locked cabinets stood in one corner with a little mirror hung next to them. There was nothing else in the room except heaters and the ever-present "staff table" in the front of the room. That table and its chairs were, of course, the nicest pieces of furniture there.

A woman sat at the staff table. She had tight, immaculate curls arranged on her head like rows in a meticulous garden, a hard face, and a sour, pinched, downturned mouth. She sat with her arms folded. The only other person in the dead-silent room was a heavyset black girl who was drugged so heavily that she struggled to keep her head up. She was wearing a thick leather belt on top of her shirt. She gazed at me with curiosity struggling beneath the dope-induced haze.

I was drawn slowly to the windows at the back of the room, the only thing in the room a little better than hideous to me. I ignored the white bars that were built into the window, leaving only little rectangles of thick glass. I reached my hands up and tilted my face toward the sun that streamed between the bars. The beams danced across my fingers.

Then I noticed that I no longer held my bear. Where was he? I turned and looked around to see him sitting on a heater by the door. The woman at the staff table decided suddenly to shuffle some papers. The girl was watching me; she obviously had nothing better to do. I looked at her belt, there was something weird about it . . .

My God! There are cuffs on that belt and her hands are locked in them!

I felt my eyes grow wider, as if that were possible, and I stared up into the girl's face with horror. She glanced down at her bonds and looked away with embarrassment.

There are few things as unsettling as seeing a person physically bound against her will for the first time. A person, sitting there in the place of the dogs you see tied to trees all the time. And she didn't look more than my age.

I turned quickly to look at my hands in the sunlight again. I turned my back on that poor girl, on that hateful-looking woman at the table, on that room so bare and ugly that it burned my eyes.

I concentrated, I concentrated hard on my slender little

fingers stretched out in front of me in the rays of sun that streamed brazenly through the bars.

Years ago, was it really years? I had thickly callused palms from climbing trees and swinging on monkey bars. Physical activity was one of the only things I had to combat the debilitating influence of my family. It gave me strength, a rush of adrenaline, a sense of accomplishment. I found comfort and joy in the big sky I played under, the fresh air that filled my lungs, and the natural beauty that surrounded me even on a city block. When that was taken away, it hadn't been long before my hands were soft and pale, skeletal, with the nails at the ends bitten down to the quick.

I reached higher into that sunbeam, my heart pounding with terror and my breath catching in my throat, and I wished with all my might that I could feel the beam's substance under my fingers, that it would turn solid and I could climb up it and away from there. Because no matter how hard I tried to be crazy, to escape from reality, I could not. My dilemma, my horrid surroundings, were always perfectly, painfully obvious, and I could neither create something pleasant nor shut anything out.

I was eventually led to another room, a minuscule office, and asked questions like Dr. Limband's. To most of these questions I answered the craziest thing I could think of, "The yellow rabbits." That was the closest I could come in my situation and condition to saying, "Fuck you and your questions. You don't take my answers seriously, so why shouldn't I do the same with your meaningless, degrading interrogation?"

In the evening I was led just off the dayhall to a room on the left side of a long white hall. The room was a tiny cement cubicle containing a set of drawers, a barred window, and a metal prison bed. My suitcase was not given to me, it had been sent away to be "searched and inventoried and marked." All I had was my bear and the large accordion folder I brought with me. It contained my most

important stories and drawings, ripped out of my notebooks just in case the lock on my trunk didn't hold.

I was told to empty my pockets, and then my head was
searched for lice. The woman who did it looked as if she
expected vermin to jump out at her any minute. This attitude was mystifying to me as well as irritating, because I
was clean, of course, my hair brushed and pulled back and
my makeup tastefully applied. I wore a nice flower-printed
turtleneck and almost-new jeans.

I was given two top sheets and a perfectly flat plastic
pillow, a pillowcase, and an extremely thin, patched blue
blanket, all stamped "PROPERTY OF WILSON STATE
HOSPITAL." As if I would steal them or mistake those
wretched things for my own.

I didn't sleep well, if for no other reason than the fact
that right over my head on the wall was a long smear of
dried blood. I was checked at night with a flashlight, roused
in the morning, given a towel and washcloth, and allowed
into the shower room. I was informed that any patient who
wanted to shave her legs could be given a razor as long as
a staff member was supervising its use. I noticed patients
didn't shave much.

Every morning I was supposed to go to a little room
down the hall where there was a sink and a bunch of mops
and buckets. I had to get a mop, fill a bucket with water,
and go to the dayhall to receive a squirt of cleaning solution (it was considered too "dangerous" for patients to
squirt their own cleaning solution). Patients mopped the
concrete floors of their cubicles every morning, and then
their rooms were "inspected."

I was told that I was not to go back to my room until
bedtime and that I was to remain on the dayhall in the
daytime, where I could be watched.

There was nothing to do on that dayhall except sit or
stand. Even the television (which I would not have been
interested in anyway if I had something better to do) was
not to be turned on till evening. While the other patients

went somewhere else to eat, my food was brought on trays to the dayhall, where I picked at it gingerly.

If I had had something else to do, then maybe I would have put my hands down. But day after day I just wandered from one window to another on that dayhall, with my back to my bleak surroundings, watching the sunbeams waver over my wasted hands. It occurred to me that I looked a lot like Patty Duke in a movie about Helen Keller that I had seen lately, waving my arms about in front of me as though I were blind. And indeed I was blinded, not physically but emotionally. I was wounded, blinded, lost, and abandoned, pacing my cage with nothing do or look at but my own hands.

The other patients on the dayhall would eye me strangely. None of them were sure if I was worth trying to communicate with. Most of them seemed to think I was the oddest thing they had ever seen, walking continuously back and forth in front of the windows with my hands stretched toward the sun and a dazed, frightened, pleading look in my eyes. I was more hideously and startlingly sickly-looking than I had ever been before.

Three boys sat at a card table one evening studying me. They did not bother to lower their voices as they discussed me. I guess they thought I couldn't hear them. It was interesting, really, to hear what people thought of me when they thought I couldn't hear them, so I never bothered to tell anyone I could.

One boy said, "You know, I wonder what the fucking hell is the matter with her?"

"Yeah, never seen nothin' like it. She must be way off her rocker."

The first two had excited, childish voices, but the third boy had a low, serious voice. He paused a moment to look up from what he was doing to gaze at me. My ears burned as I felt his stare behind my back. He said solemnly,

"No, she's not off her knot. I've seen it before. Shock. Somethin' happened to her, somethin' real bad. Did you see those two that brought her in? Must be her folks. Bet you anything they had something to do with it. Assholes. Bet they did that to her. Damn shame . . . bastards."

"Yeah, bastards," one of the first two boys chimed in. "It's too bad. She looks like a nice little thing."

SEVEN

Over the next few days, I continued to sidle back and forth in front of the curve of windows at the back of the dayhall, stretching pathetically for the sunbeams that streamed through the crisscrossed bars. Occasionally a large black man would call me over to the staff table. His lip would curl and his eyes narrow as he ordered me to put my hands down now and act like a "human being." Other than that, I was utterly and completely ignored by both the patients and the staff members who surrounded me continually. I turned my back on them anyway.

The immense windows I hovered before were made to open just a tiny crack. The bottom panes swung outward over concrete attachments on the outside walls. It was so horribly stuffy and fetid on the dayhall that I wondered if I could get any relief by mashing my face between the slanted pane and that block. I gulped air through the tiny crack and was lost in the bliss when a woman shouted my name so angrily that I started and cut my head on the window frame.

I could always feel the muscles in my neck, so tight and tense it hurt to turn my head. My heart pounded and my breath strained. It was my body's way of pleading for a way out of this dreadful situation. But I would not even let myself think about my situation. I would start to, and the rush of hate and pain and panic that followed frightened me. I could not cope on my own.

One day a woman called my name out and asked me to come with her. Turning, my elbows locked out straight and my hands spread before my face, I followed her silently to a little room right off the dayhall, next to the front door. It was the "family conference" room. There was a ratty cloth couch there, and she had me sit next to her. Then she did the oddest thing. She put her arms around me, held me close to her, and cried. I was horrified. I felt guilty that she would cry over me. I was relieved when she never did anything like that again.

At last, after more than a week, someone attempted to talk to me for the first time. A woman had come in and was watching me from across the room. The boy that had said it was a shame I was in shock because I seemed like a "nice little thing" went to her and asked quite plainly, "Can she hear us?"

The woman, without looking away from me to the boy, said, "Yes."

Oh, damn her, now no one will talk about me as if I weren't there.

"Is she blind?"

"No."

"Then why does she hold her arms out like that?"

The woman responded shortly, "Why don't you ask her?" Then, suddenly disinterested, she got up and left the room.

The boy began walking toward me. I could see him out of the corner of my eye. I was frightened. Would he be mad because I had let him think I couldn't hear him? Would he make fun of me for acting so dumb? I sidled away. The boy stood quietly behind me, watching me for a moment.

In each window a dying purple plant was hung in a pot. I stood on my toes and stretched my fingers up to one of these until I could barely touch the leaves that hung down. The boy said,

"Hi. I'm Daniel. What's your name?"

I said nothing, I couldn't think what to say. I just took a sideways glance at Daniel. He was of average height and weight, just a little taller than me. He had an upturned nose, blue eyes, and black hair that was obviously well combed but stuck out every which way anyway because of cowlicks. He wore a clean T-shirt and jeans and sneakers. He didn't look different from any of the kids I had grown up with.

He waited for my answer, and when he didn't get one, it appeared that he would go away. Not wanting him to leave, I gazed up at the plant as meaningfully as I could and blurted out the first thing that came into my head,

"Wandering Jew."

Eight days. I had not spoken in the entire eight days since I had been brought to that bare and nauseating hell. My voice was clear and soft, but the shock of hearing it again made me wince. Daniel wrinkled his forehead for a moment and then brightened.

"Oh, that's the name of the plant!"

We both looked at the deeply purple plant above us for a moment. Then Daniel said, "You're pretty smart. Guess you're not so crazy after all."

In the days that followed, my conversations with Daniel distracted me from acting out my shock. I left my window vigil to sit across from him at one of the rickety card tables when he was on the dayhall. I don't remember much of what we said, except that they were the same things we would have said to each other anywhere else. It was a while before he explained to me that he had been left at WSH a few days before I had when his foster parents moved out of town.

He introduced me to the other patients around us. The girl who had been on the dayhall when I came was named Diana. She was still strapped in that wide, heavy leather belt with the "padded" leather cuffs and metal lock. It was hard to look at her sitting there like that, but we talked with each other the way Daniel and I did. She asked me once to scratch the top of her nose, which I did, horrified at the thought of being purposely rendered incapable of doing such a simple thing for myself.

I learned from Daniel that the ward we were on, called

Smith 1, held twenty kids aged twelve to fourteen. There was another ward set like a mirror image of Smith 1 that was called Smith 2. It held twenty kids aged fifteen to seventeen. There was a Smith 3 above Smith 1 that held twenty kids aged eighteen to twenty-one. Smith 4 (above Smith 2) stood empty for the time being so that asbestos could be removed. I heard often what a day it had been when they had had to get rid of the twenty kids on Smith 4. Children who had been forgotten for years were rescued by that stroke of luck.

There were many other buildings on the grounds of Wilson State Hospital, most of which I hardly ever saw even from the outside: the admissions building, the building with the wards for adults, a correctional facility, a gymnasium, an auditorium, a library. There was a dining room for all the patients, adjacent to the drug rehab and old people's wards. There was also a building where the kids on Smith 1 and 2 went to "school."

Daniel explained that whenever someone new came to the Smith building, they were kept on the dayhall all day long for a week of "observation." His week was over and so was mine. He was sent to the school and the dining room. He said he couldn't imagine why I was still kept on the dayhall, with my meals brought on trays. I didn't know either. I told him I didn't care. A longer chain is still a chain.

After more than two weeks, the woman who had cried for me, named Pam, took pity on me again and asked me if I would like to ride with her in the van to get the kids from the school building. We drove down a winding bit of pavement to a small, square, two-story building made of dull-colored brick. Pam had me climb out of the van and meet the "principal" of this "school," who was standing in the entrance watching the other kids pile into the van.

"This is Tiffany," she said. "It looks like she won't be coming to school."

I had been standing quietly, nervously, eyeing with uncertainty the building towering over me in the sharp October wind. It was as dingy and cold as everything else I had seen lately. It hardly beckoned me, but this was where Daniel and the other patients went during the day, and I wanted to be with them. Quick as a wink, before I lost my nerve, I drew myself up to my full five feet two inches, focused my eyes up into the eyes of this "principal," and announced, "Yes I am. I'm coming to school tomorrow."

The principal, a little middle-aged man in a sweater vest, gave me a politician-smile and said, "Well, that's nice."

The next day I was handed a "schedule." I was to take my morning shower between 5:00 and 5:15. After I mopped the floor of my cubicle, I was to go to the dayhall, where I was allowed to apply my makeup. (Thank God I didn't have to "earn" it like I had at Magna Carta; it was just kept in a tub with my name on it in one of those locked cabinets on the dayhall.) Then I was to be taken with the other kids to breakfast and to "school."

Instead of being listed with all the other patients on a chart on the wall every day, like I had at Magna Carta, I was given a "point sheet" with the hours of the day down the side and categories like "hygiene" and "respect" and "responsibility" at the top. I was supposed to ask to be graded every hour, and was given a number from 1 to 5 in each box, 1 being the worst. The average of all these points at the end of the day decided what level, 1 through 5, I would be on tomorrow. That level decided how much of a human being I was going to be treated like that day. My name was stamped on each point sheet given to me, but I was acutely aware that my case number was always stamped *above* my name.

I had to be in line to be escorted to breakfast at seven. After roll call and a lot of being told to be quiet and blah, blah, blah, the patients were led to the end of the hall. There we were to stop and be told once again. We stopped at the end of the next hall, too, and then in front of the rickety, puce-colored van that waited outside the building.

At the dining room we were halted outside, and again in the entryway, where we waited for the other wards to get through the line. Inside, we were never allowed to sit with or socialize with patients from other wards. The food was disgusting and unhealthy—mostly grease and salt. But in the dining room, patients used metal utensils. Patients "on trays" back on the dayhall were given plastic ones. I hadn't realized those plastic spoons had sharp edges until I put one in my mouth for the first time and was suddenly drooling blood all over my instant potatoes and mucus-colored gravy.

I could not eat in the presence of the old people and their stench. They meowed and barked and cried endlessly. They went to the bathroom on themselves and threw things and took their clothes off during breakfast. One woman whose face seemed to have imploded threw a glass of tea all over me from behind. I left the dining room shaking from the whole experience.

After breakfast the patients from Smith 1 and 2 were driven, one ward at a time, to the school building. I entered for the first time clutching my schedule with clammy hands. My wide eyes absorbed the little entryway, which contained green stairs and a large portrait of the founder of the school.

I took my slip of paper to the "office" for directions and was told to go to the room at the end of the hall around the corner. In that small, dark-paneled room were two boys sitting at a table with a film projector on it. In the corner was a gray desk, on which a hard-faced man in a faded red sweat suit was propping his feet.

"Sit somewhere, we're watching a film and taking a quiz on it tomorrow," was all he said.

I sat as far as I could from the two boys, with my shoulders hunched and my thin hands clasped together so tightly my knuckles were white. I was quivering all over, and as the film began, tears bubbled out of my eyes and down my cheeks against my will.

One of the boys turned to stare at me. He had very blue eyes and an angular face. His nose was thin and straight, and his cheekbones stood out. He was exceptionally thin but wiry-looking. His hair was dishwater blond and cut close to his head so that his little ears stuck out. I put my chin down and let my hair hide my face from him. My crying made not a sound.

I was trying to sneak a wipe at my eyes with my sleeve when suddenly a Kleenex materialized under my nose. It was held out gently in a very large, very bony hand. I looked up at the owner of this hand, and he was still staring at me, quite sympathetically. I took the Kleenex silently, not knowing what to say. The boy reached out his long, thin arm behind him and picked up a box of Kleenex, whispering, "Do you want some more?"

I nodded. He pulled a few out of the box and held them out to me.

"What's wrong?" he wanted to know.

Suddenly the hard-faced man said crossly, "William, you leave that girl alone."

William, who had been speaking very softly to me, suddenly exploded to the sour-faced man, "Jesus Christ, she's crying!"

The man, whose eyes were small and beady, said loudly, "I can see that. Now turn around and mind your own business and you better not say any more swear words or you're going to the office!"

And do you know what William said to that?

"I don't give a fuck about the office! You just want me to let her cry? You're some kind of stone-cold snake."

My mouth fell open. I had never heard a kid speak that way to an adult.

"That's it, you go to the office and I'm calling security," said the man.

Then William stood up. If my mouth were not already open, it most certainly would have been then. William was the tallest person, much less kid, I had ever seen. He faced the man, the Authority, and said with a sneer, "Oh, you do that. I'm real scared. You know what? You're fucked in the head."

He turned to me as if he hadn't just bellowed the most wonderfully disrespectful words I had ever heard, and held out the box of Kleenex for me with the softness he had had in his eyes before. When I took it, he strode on his long, thin legs out the door. The man followed.

I was left alone with the other boy, who took a moment to study my bewildered expression. His features were almost indistinguishable through his acne. His dark hair was parted in the middle and greasy. He said, with a slight speech impediment, "Don't pay any attention to them. They do that about every day." Then he turned back to the film, which was droning to a nonexistent audience about "peer pressure."

That was "Health Class." Next was a weird class called "Music Video," which consisted of watching old musicals. It was "taught" by a bitter-looking, middle-aged woman with a sharp tongue. A very tall, large-boned, but rather soft-looking boy was in that class. He was intelligent and sensitive, and obviously no one had ever appreciated that. He was always kind and willing to talk freely with me, which was funny since with almost everyone else he kept to himself. He tried to scrunch down all the time and looked at the ground. I thought he looked like Cary Elwes and I told him so.

Next was "Science Class." The man "teaching" it was very tall and about as quick and light as lead. He always wore suspenders and boots, which earned him the nickname "Elmer Fudd." There was one boy in that class. He was of average size and wiry-looking. He sat with his arms folded and always had a sullen expression.

Mr. Hurst asked me if I knew any science. He was the first of any of the "teachers" to be interested in knowing what I knew. I told him I had a good background in science, especially biology. Mr. Hurst then went to a shelf, and pulled out a yellowed and dust-coated textbook. He said, "The boys are studying planets, but that might be too easy for you, so study this book."

And that was all. I didn't cry that hour because I had never seen such an old textbook, and it was rather interesting. I was to discover the next day that William was also in this class, but had been sent back to the ward earlier that day because of the argument in health class.

Next was "English Class." The "teacher" was Ms. Rivers. She was tall and had permed blonde hair, a tan, bright eyes, and a big smile. She was very different from the others, but I still wasn't sure if I liked her. Her room had desks instead of tables, and the walls were decorated instead of somber and Spartan. I felt like I had left the Dark Ages to step into a modern kindergarten.

After this class the teachers left for their lunch break, and staff members from both Smith 1 and Smith 2 came to drive the kids separately to the dining room. After lunch it was "Quiet Time" in our cubicles on the ward.

Then we were taken back to school, where I had "Drawing Class." A small man with a pleasant but unchanging face told me his name was Mr. Davis. He gave me paper and explained that I could use any of the pencils in the box in front of me, and that their leads were of different hardnesses according to the numbers printed on the sides.

I knew that already, but he did not explain it in a condescending way, so I listened politely. I sat and stared at the blank sheet of paper. It was so white that it seemed to dare me to mark it. I did so love to draw, but I couldn't that day. There was no inspiration in me.

Mr. Davis asked if I would like some colored pencils. I shook my head, venturing to explain, "I . . . I can't think of anything to draw." There was a long, suffocating silence. There were two boys and the largest girl I had ever seen in my life in that class. They stared at me shamelessly until I was quivering again. At last Mr. Davis said from across the room, "So what did you do?"

To get committed is what he meant. It was obvious that he didn't think I looked like I had done the usual sort of thing a kid does to get committed to the worst place in the state. The other kids held their breath for the answer. I stared at my paper, not knowing the answer myself. But I knew that the last thing I had done that caused everyone to sneer that I just "wanted attention" was to go into shock, so I suggested softly, "I guess because I pretended to be crazy."

I could not read Mr. Davis's expression, but I was suddenly afraid I had not given the correct answer. I began to cry silently.

Last of all was "Math Class." A tall man with a reddish beard "taught" that class. He asked me what math book I was in, and when I said I didn't remember, he gave me a test to take. I sat at one of the two tables in the room and sobbed. There were two boys in that class. One was blond with glasses and was usually too cross to speak to me. I soon learned that the other boy was named Jim.

Jim was only fifteen and had a full, black beard. His nickname was "Ape Man." His blue eyes were strikingly bright and pleasant. He made an effort to be friends right away. He was short compared with all these giants I was meeting, but he was built like a fire hydrant. His hands fascinated me; they were so square and amazingly strong. Jim was at WSH only until his trial proceedings could be taken care of. He soon went to jail on charges of assault and battery.

After that class all the kids from Smith 1 and 2 were led back to their separate dayhalls to sit around until dinner. Although we did it elsewhere anyway, the dayhall was the only place patients were allowed to talk with each other. Just like at Magna Carta, there was absolutely no touching allowed, especially between boys and girls. You had to wait until you were sure no staff were looking to poke at someone in a friendly way, or to touch them when they were crying. And if you weren't careful, you would get sent to one of the "Time Out" chairs for up to a few hours or have restrictions placed on you, such as having to stand "Arm's Length" or sit one "Chair Away" from any other patient, or just patients of the opposite sex, depending on your crime. Sometimes a patient would even be sent to "the Side-Room" or be put in those God-awful shackles.

I think if it were financially possible, the unfortunate children dumped in mental institutions would all have separate little "dining rooms," "dayhalls," and "schools" as well as cubicles, and no patient would ever see anyone but their keeper. They would give it a nice term like "One-to-One Treatment," or something like that. If it weren't for the misfortune of overpopulation and shortage of money, I would probably be pacing in front of a row of windows all alone in my cage to this very day. I might even still be curled up on that bed at Magna Carta, wondering if I were the only person left in the universe.

It was Daniel, as it had been Sandy before, who brought me to my senses by acting toward me in a normal, adolescent fashion in the midst of the insanity all around us. When I had someone to talk to or play with, I was distracted from the cold, gray walls around me, from the noise and confusion, from the bars and locks and shackles, from the endless demeaning rules and the sharp presence of those who enforced them.

I was not choosy about whom I sought friendship from, but I was especially drawn to flirting with boys, the art of which I was just discovering. The boys in WSH, like boys everywhere, I guess, were usually quite concerned with how "tough" they were and whether or not so-and-so was any more or less tough than they were. It was all-important to them to climb the hierarchy that had been formed among the boys of the ward.

Zach, who was neither the biggest nor the tallest patient around, seemed to have won the title of the toughest on Smith 1. He had lived at WSH for a year by the time I arrived. He reminded me of Tad from Magna Carta in that he seemed to be watching life instead of being affected by it, and seemed to find all the chaos around him slightly amusing if not utterly dull. His eerie eyes took in everything, and his mind seemed sharp as a blade, but neither his face nor his mannerisms ever gave the impression of anything but boredom. I think he was some sort of Asian-Caucasian mix. He had dark skin and hair. His face was rather flat, and his eyes were slanted. The oddest thing was that his eyes were also yellow.

Zach was only thirteen years old and just a fraction under six feet tall. He was broad-shouldered and large-boned. He grasped my wrist one day and held up his palm against mine to compare. My fingertips barely reached past the middle knuckles of his fingers.

"Jesus," he said, "you're small."

And I guess I was a bit on the small side, at about a hundred pounds. But I said, "Not really, it's just that you're *gargantuan*."

As the time passed, I ventured to ask him a personal question or two, and discovered that he was not ashamed to answer me anything. He told me in a solemn but steady voice about his father and how he hanged himself in prison. Zach's mother had never cared what he did with himself, so he had grown up on the streets, sleeping under bridges and such.

He wore a lot of red, the color of the Bloods, a gang that practically overran parts of his hometown. I never asked if he was a member; it seemed unlikely that a street kid would have much choice but to turn to a gang for acceptance and protection. But Zach seemed an independent sort, and it was possible that he had wanted to make it on his own.

Having to steal and such to survive, Zach had had numerous brushes with the law, and that was what brought him to WSH. He also had a long, white ridge of scar across the soft flesh of his stomach, where the owner of a car stereo he had been ripping off had cut him with a knife. There were little scars on Zach's face, and his hands were crisscrossed with various scars.

It was easy for me to forget that he was a year younger than me chronologically. He had grown so much older in a lot of ways in thirteen years than I had in fourteen. I would ask him what the new words I was suddenly hearing all around me meant, and I trusted his solemn answers. I knew the basic swears, like *shit, damn, fuck,* etc., but I had no idea until I came to a state institution of their innumerable variations and all the other words that have been made dirty in this world.

I leaned over to Zach in the dining room one day and whispered, "If I ask you something will you promise not to laugh?"

He nodded.

"What does the word 'slut' mean?"

Zach's usual poker face cracked into a grin, then he laughed out loud and announced to everyone else at the table, "Crazy Girl don't know what a *slut* is!"

But he told me what it meant: "A girl who will fuck anybody for the hell of it."

When he asked me if I would be his girlfriend, I didn't know any better at the time than to say yes.

Of the kids on Smith 2, William, the boy who could not stand to see me cry the minute he saw me, was the most fascinating to me. I adored him, though I wouldn't admit it, the way one adores an older brother but wouldn't let him know it for the world.

William was six feet three inches tall at the age of sixteen. Besides being rather unmistakable-looking anyway, he was a hick and insisted on wearing clunky cowboy boots (his shoe size was 14), big belt buckles, and a black cowboy hat. He had a bit of a drawl and told big stories, some exaggeratedly true, some obviously not. He cursed no end, and most vividly, I might add. I liked to watch him talk because his face was wonderfully mobile, his large, bony hands demonstrated everything he was talking about, and his deep blue eyes were mesmerizing. It was obvious that he fancied himself pretty tough, and in a lot of ways he

was, but his eyes were never cold and bored like Zach's—
they never hid a thing.

William was exceedingly thin, as I mentioned before. I
had never heard of anorexia or bulimia plaguing a boy before, but when I was told he suffered from a combination
of both I didn't disbelieve it. I rarely saw him eat anything,
especially when something was troubling him. He looked
sick and about to vomit most of the time, and I knew that
people get that way when they purge themselves enough.

I asked him once if it was true that he didn't eat and
that when he did he gagged himself. He looked down, his
ears slightly pink, and said yes.

"But you're so thin!" I exclaimed, "How much do you
weigh?"

"A hundred and forty pounds," he said, ashamed of it.

"Good Lord, you don't think that's fat, do you?"

William suddenly glared at me with anger flashing in
his eyes. He stood up so forcefully that I flinched a little.
He spit out the word *"Nunya!"* (which meant "That's none
of your God-damn business!") as he stormed away.

He was still very tall and large-boned, quick, and amazingly strong for weighing so little. I was never sure whether
to be afraid of him of not. He towered so high above me
and was very easily angered. His face and hands were
scarred, and the rumors of what had led to his being institutionalized ranged from just fist-fighting too much to actually shooting someone.

He would be sent back to Smith 2 or kept there at least
once a day for "acting up," and sometimes I wouldn't see
him for days at a time. He was kept in "the Side-Room"
during those times. Usually when I saw him again, he was
paler and thinner than usual, with some of the spark beaten
out of him, and his wrists bruised and cut from the "humane
restraints." I felt no fear of him then. I just wanted to reach
out and hold him.

E I G H T

I had heard that Tilly, the boy at Magna Carta who had written me the love notes I never got, had been sent to a "cheaper institution." I didn't know it was WSH. He had deteriorated so badly in that miserable place that he didn't even recognize me when he saw me again.

Poor Tilly, who at Magna Carta was always squirming and cracking his knuckles and saying silly things he thought were pretty funny, just sat on the dayhall of WSH, motionless and lifeless from the obvious increase in the drugs they gave him. Those drugs had made him short and flabby, with breasts, made him so that the other kids made fun of him and picked on him.

I hadn't thought much about him before, he was harmless enough, annoying sometimes, but so small and pudgy with such soft brown eyes. He had never hurt a soul, and there he sat, abandoned and destroyed for being "hyperactive." How could that God-awful stupor and the listless despair in his eyes be considered preferable to a few nervous habits and a little more energy than most kids have?

There were two halls leading from the dayhall, as there had been at Magna Carta. Since only the so-called "most uncontrollable" kids were abandoned at WSH, there were always three times as many boys as girls (and the majority of all the kids were large for their age). So the boys' hall was twice as long as the girls', and the girls' hall contained all the offices of the top dogs of the place.

The kids that the staff most wanted to "keep an eye on" were put in the cubicles closest to the dayhall, the ones right after the Side-Rooms on each side of the boys' hall. I was put in one of those cubicles that first night, with that horrible streak of dried blood, dark red against the bleak cement walls. The next night I was told to move to the room next door to that one. It was a few weeks before I was told to move to the girls' hall, to the room on the very end that was the only one on the ward big enough for two patients.

That room was like all the others, with exactly the same furnishings except that there were two of everything: two of those metal bedframes (which I was told were donated by prisons), two cheap little chests of drawers, one heating unit bolted to the floor under the window, and one barred window. The walls were the same, foot-thick concrete blocks, painted over and over in a color not quite gray, not quite white. The door was metal, painted dark blue. In the places where the half-inch accumulation of paint was chipped, you could see that the door had also been yellow, beige, and red at one time or another.

My roommate's name was Shirley. She was only thirteen and was about my size, only a little pudgier. She loved to talk, and made up incredible stories about herself. Since none of the patients at WSH had life stories that contained anything but misery, abuse, and drudgery, it was quite common to make up more interesting ones. Shirley's and my favorite subject was our "family on the outside." I had a brother in the army and a brother that had fights with me with corn tongs and a sister that was a beautiful fashion model, and of course there was that brother who had died. Shirley collected pictures and pretended they were of her children. I never knew the true story of her life or the specific reason she was dumped at the age of thirteen into a miserable hell of an insane asylum. I never asked. And she never asked me.

One evening I was sitting cross-legged at the head of my fully made bed while Shirley sat at the foot with her feet dangling above the floor. We were chatting and laughing. Eventually Shirley clasped her hands behind her head and leaned back on my bed to stare at the ceiling. Suddenly a woman named Charlotte flung open the door to our room and gasped.

"What are you doing on her bed?" she demanded of Shirley. I didn't understand the implications of Charlotte's shock. Shirley did, and she giggled. Charlotte informed the two of us that *that* sort of thing was not allowed, and Shirley obligingly moved away from my bed. When Charlotte was gone, Shirley continued to giggle, "She thinks we're lesbians!"

"We're what?" I wanted to know. Shirley sank onto her own bed, laughing uncontrollably. "You know, lesbians, women who have sex together."

If I had ever heard of homosexuality in my little bubble of a childhood, the idea had never registered. I thought it over and said with surprise, "But, I don't see how women can *do it!*"

Shirley fell over in hysterics.

I was glad to share a room with someone. Shirley would jabber at me every night until she fell asleep. I liked to hear her breathing and know that I was not alone under the especially heavy blanket of night that smothers child-inmates at mental institutions across our country.

Then one night I awoke to feel hands wrapped tightly around my throat. The moon was not strong that night. I could barely see Shirley in front of me, trying in vain to choke me. I knew she wasn't mad at me; she was either hysterical or still asleep. Being about the same size as Shirley, I managed to roll into a sitting position and pin her arms down. She struggled for a minute, and it was very hard for me to keep holding her, but eventually she slipped quietly back to her own bed.

The next day I asked Lorri, the ward psychologist, if I could be moved to a single room. Instead, a staff member came by later and told Shirley to move to the room across the hall. The patient in that room was told to move in with me. Her name was Grace. She was twelve and made up even more incredible stories than Shirley. They were sick stories, her way of talking about the feelings that sexual, physical, and emotional abuse had caused her without having to reveal the actual, painful events to me.

She was a shockingly neglected child. Her clothes were old and ugly. She didn't know how to take care of herself, how to keep herself clean. Annoyed by her blue eye shadow and the clown dots on her cheeks, I pulled out my own makeup one day and offered to give her a makeover. Her eyes widened as she looked hungrily into the tub with my name on it and all my personals inside. As I applied the final touch to her eyelashes, I noticed she had tears in her eyes. I felt like crying myself as I realized her life must be even lonelier than mine. She had never hurt a flea, she was only a child, and all she needed was a little attention.

I shared a room with Grace for nearly two weeks before she suddenly started snoring. After a few nights of sleeplessness and a few days of grogginess, I requested again to be moved to a single room. And again my roommate was moved instead. I had the double room to myself only until another female patient arrived. I wasn't sure if I anticipated or dreaded that day.

It was an evening in mid-November when she came. I helped her make her bed because there were no fitted sheets at WSH and you had to tie a top one to the plastic mattress in a tricky way that never really worked. I told her my name and asked hers. It was Brittany.

Brittany was not the stereotypical child mental patient, neglected and beaten down by abuse and an ugly, mechanical system from which there was little hope of escape. She did not evoke pity—quite the opposite. She was tall and thin and straight, like a fashion model. She held her head up at all times and walked with a nonchalant stride. She wore brand-name jeans and a soft brown leather jacket. I stared at her hands as they quickly spread out the sheets. They were long and pale, with long, long red nails like I had never seen in person before. Except for the fact that her face was so pale and exhausted, she looked just like one of the spoiled rich girls who had made fun of me at school.

I blathered at her nonstop. When she sat down on her made bed with her arms around her knees, looking like she might vomit at any moment, I wondered if I should shut up and leave her alone. But if I were in her place (and I had been twice already), I would have liked to have had someone to talk to, to distract me from my terror and confusion. So I asked her if she minded if I kept talking, and she said it was all right. Then I asked her if I looked like a dork in my Super Mario Brothers hat, and she said that it was all right too.

After a while, she told me her story. She came from a wealthy little suburb adjacent to my hometown. She had a little brother just like mine. She told me she had never been close to her father until just before he died suddenly. She and her mother did not get along. She had run away from home to stay with an older boy who was into crack. She said most of her friends were involved with drugs and made a lot of money that way. After three days the police came to the house and arrested everyone there. They took Brittany to JDC (Juvenile Detention Center) for a night before she arrived at WSH.

I asked her about JDC and she told me what a strip search is like and how an officer sticks a finger up your ass. Then she said that at JDC you always go straight to solitary for at least your first couple of days. She described the little cell with a toilet and a security camera and a crack they shove a tray through. She was only fourteen and had never been in any legal trouble before.

Having never seen an illegal drug in my life, I was very interested to know what crack had felt like and all. Brittany said it made her throat numb and that even though it had been two days since she had taken it, she still felt like shit. I wasn't surprised; I had always thought that the minute you tried an illegal drug you would turn into a junkie or something.

I had more in common with Brittany than with any other patient. We were good friends from that first night. However, a lot of the time I felt inferior to her because she had more than I did. Sometimes she rubbed it in, too.

Since our room was at the end of the hall, the other ward door (besides the one in the cage) was directly to the left. When it was left open, as it sometimes was for air, you could see into the extremely large room that held the elevators and main visitors' room, a drinking fountain, and the huge double doors to the outside. Beyond this room was the girls' hall of Smith 2. At the end was their dayhall, but you could see only a tiny sliver of it from our room, and anyone standing in our line of vision was barely recognizable.

Soon after we had met, Brittany asked me to peer down the hall during Quiet Time one day. "Who's that?" she wanted to know, her expression rather dreamy. I peered out excitedly, although cautiously, because it was against the rules to stick your head out of your room during Quiet Time, to see who it was that Brittany liked.

Leaning his ungainly six feet three inches way over the Smith 2 drinking fountain, in his ridiculous cowboy boots and a yellow-and-black-checked flannel shirt, was William.

"Are you kidding? Him!" I was surprised. Brittany and I pulled our heads into our room quickly, as I probably had attracted attention with my outburst.

"Yes, why not? He's not really crazy or anything, is he?" Brittany wanted to know.

"No, no, he's not crazy, it's just that he's . . . he's *William*."

"William." Brittany sighed the name. "Well, you don't have a crush on him or anything, do you? I mean, you're Zach's girlfriend, aren't you?"

"Yes. And *no*, I do not have a crush on him. You can have him if you like. But I must warn you, he's got a mean temper."

I thought it was funny enough for a girl like Brittany to take to a boy like William, but even funnier still was to see William so smitten with Brittany that his ears turned pink and he didn't know what to say when she was around. I was glad that they each had someone, but I was also very jealous. I was jealous that William spent so much time with Brittany. He was my friend first. I came up and kicked him in the shin once for it. It didn't hurt him; I knew it wouldn't. He just yelled, "What the hell is your problem?" and gave me the silent treatment until he caught me crying about it.

J onathan was a very heavy, roly-poly black boy of four- teen. He had had such a horrible life that he was terribly emotionally impaired and confused. When he was not even in kindergarten yet he witnessed his mother murder his older brother with a knife. She was in prison for a while (I mean, you can beat your kids and all, but it is sort of frowned upon to kill them). I don't know the details, and I don't know what happened to his father. He probably never even had one; he never mentioned one. Jonathan grew up being shifted from abusive foster parents to shit- hole institutions like WSH and back again. He had been at WSH for nearly two years already when I first arrived.

One day he took a dollar's worth of quarters from my room. He stole just about anything that was left out. Every- one knew he had done it, but there was nothing I could do about it. The staff did not concern themselves with things stolen from patients, and anyway I was not a nark. I figured he might as well keep the money because I had more and Jonathan had nothing. I had nearly forgotten about the whole thing a few days later when Jonathan came to me privately, in hysterics.

"Oh, Tiffany, please tell Zach not to beat me anymore, I promise I won't take anything, I promise!"

I could hardly understand what he was saying and asked him to explain himself. Jonathan explained that Zach had sneaked into his room in the night with a belt and said that if he ever stole from me again, Zach would beat him again. Jonathan showed me the welts across his back, about ten pink streaks.

Jonathan blubbered, "I wasn't supposed to tell you, please tell him not to do it anymore, he'll listen to you, I'll pay you if you tell Zach not to beat me anymore!"

And then Jonathan held out fifty cents of the dollar he had stolen from me.

He seemed to be carrying on more than necessary, enjoying the drama of the whole situation. I told him to keep the money and went immediately to Zach on the other side of the dayhall. I sat across from him at a card table and eyed him for a minute. Jonathan weighed a lot more than Zach, and he was two years older, but Jonathan was awfully slow and was cowed psychologically by Zach.

I demanded that Zach tell me if he had put those stripes on Jonathan's back, and he admitted quite freely that he had. He seemed not to feel particularly sorry or proud of himself, either. There was a silence until Zach glanced up and noticed my stricken expression.

"I didn't hurt him much," he said blandly. "Jonathan's thick."

"I know!" I cried out. "But it doesn't matter! You can't just hurt people like that! You frightened him, he came crying to me!"

"He did?" Zach lowered his eyebrows.

"Look," I said, reaching out and forcing myself to put my hands on Zach's. "It isn't right. I'd rather he steal from me. Please, please, promise me you won't hurt him anymore."

Zach withdrew his hands from mine and sighed, "Whatever."

It was only a few nights later that a shrill scream woke us all up. Although screaming was common enough in the daytime, it was not often heard at night. All the patients rushed to our doorways to look out through sleep-encrusted eyes into the bright hall. Jonathan was rushing out of Diana's room and back to his own. Diana arrived in the hall quickly afterwards, panting in terror, her nightshirt ripped open and her right breast bleeding from deep teethmarks.

The only staff member to witness all this from his vigil at the staff table was that nasty black man who had picked on me during my first few days at WSH. His name was Tyrone. In response to Diana's frantic cries, he sneered and told her she deserved it, that she must have been leading Jonathan on because "black girls are all the same."

I was utterly shocked by the whole situation and did not even know what to say to poor Diana the next morning. I thought then that maybe Zach had done me a favor by making it clear to Jonathan that he was not to mess with me in any way. Everything was so complicated in that place; I didn't know whose side to be on anymore.

Two weeks later, I was getting my mop and filling my bucket in the mop room, muttering to myself about the foolishness of mopping every single day when the rest of the place was filthy anyway. I turned and Zach was there. He said not a word, but put his hand around the back of my neck and put his face to mine and his lips on mine. I was horrified, petrified, rooted to the floor as Zach's tongue forced its way into my mouth.

I had seen kissing on television and read about it in books. I had imagined it would be very romantic and dreamy; it was something I had looked forward to. But this was not at all what I had in mind. The damn closet they called a "mop room" was stuffy and it stank, and it had one of those awful windows with the built-in bars too. Zach's fingers bit into my neck hard, and he pushed me against a sink that was moldy and wet. The taste of him made me gag. I wondered how long it had been since he had brushed his teeth.

When at last he let me go and stepped back, I clasped both my hands over my mouth tightly, wiping the saliva away as quickly as I could. I stared at him in horror. He stared back at me in his expressionless way for a moment, then turned and left as silently as he had come.

I gathered my bucket and mop. I had to walk past the staff members on the dayhall. I had to get a squirt of cleaning solution from them because it was "too dangerous" for patients to do it for themselves. I burned with shame; I felt branded. It was torture to take every step as slowly as I normally would have, my head thrown back and my teeth gritted. I was afraid I wouldn't make it to my cubicle in time, but I was just inside the doorway before I broke down and cried bitterly. I had a dreadful vision of my grandchildren asking me what my first kiss was like, and what would I tell them?

It was dirty.

It was a little over a week before the next occurrence. It happened in much the same way, except that this time Zach slipped his hands down my pants. He started sneaking into the mop room more often and doing the same thing, and he grew bolder and began touching me on the dayhall and at the school and even in the line to the dining room. He never hurt me—he was actually rather gentle when he touched me—but it made me feel sick inside. I hated it. I wasn't ready for it yet. I learned to stand still, frozen, and numb myself, my body, my feelings.

I let him do it. I never fought him, never protested in any way. I never even told anyone about it, and not just because I didn't want something said to me like what was said to Diana. I was afraid that if I didn't let Zach do whatever he wanted, he wouldn't be my boyfriend anymore, and I would be alone.

He left me eventually anyway. We were sitting across from each other at a card table as usual. Just before time for him to turn in, he looked hard into my eyes and asked abruptly, "Are you afraid of me?"

I was startled and unable to answer. But he knew the answer. He was staring at me in a way that made my flesh crawl. He stood up, and something rather like anger burned behind his yellow eyes. He said loudly and coldly, "If you are, I don't want you no more," and then he walked away.

I tried hard to get him to come back to me, but it never worked. I was devastated until another boy, named Kevin, asked me if I would be his girlfriend now. I said yes. And after him, I had another boyfriend, and then another. I was almost never without one, not just because I wanted protection (not many of them attempted to protect me anyway), but because being someone's girlfriend was the only way I felt I mattered to someone.

I was constantly torn between my need for attention and the feeling that having that kind of relationship with boy after boy made me that word Zach had taught me—a slut. That was what the staff at Magna Carta and WSH called me in my chart. Well, they had a fancier word—"seductress"—but it meant the same thing. In my records they called me this because I flirted, because I touched boys, because I talked to them, and because I had once "waited in line for a boy to catch up." I was called a slut to my face by a male staff member. I was given "Arm's Length" and "Chair Away" restrictions, which meant if any staff member saw me sitting in a chair next to a boy, or standing within arm's length of one, they were to send me to the Time Out chair for a few hours, or to the Side-Room.

In such primitive places as mental institutions, girls are still made to feel shame for expressing their sexual side in any way. I was not the only one picked on for being normal, but I was picked on a great deal. I rather think that this treatment stemmed from jealousy on the part of the staff. I believed it when I was told I was ugly, but the truth was that I was a damn sight prettier than any of them.

Around Thanksgiving, 1991, just a little while after Brittany had arrived at WSH and befriended me, I was called from school to the ward, where I was told that a visitor was waiting to see me. It was quite unusual for a patient to be allowed to leave school for any reason, so I immediately understood that something was up. And indeed, when I entered the dim, dingy family conference room, I saw Lorri, the ward psychologist, and my father seated on the ratty furniture, looking grim. I hadn't seen or heard from a member of my family in over a month.

When I sat down, my father simply said, "Tiffany, your mother has run off."

"Really?" was all I could say.

"Yes." My father explained that her clothes and insulin were gone and there was a note saying she had gone to Florida. He also said she had stolen two hundred dollars from his account. He told me he just thought I should know.

"Oh," I said, and then I was told to go back to the dayhall while my father stayed and talked to Lorri for a long time. He left the ward without saying good-bye.

Two days after my father's visit, my grandmother made the drive to WSH as well. She told me not to listen to my father, that my mother had not "abandoned" me like he wanted me to believe. My grandmother insisted that my mother was very, very ill and that my father would not let her go to the hospital (because he said he "couldn't afford it"), so she was trying to take a vacation, relieve a little stress, and maybe she would feel better. She said my mother had left a note for me saying that she would be back again in two weeks, but that my father had taken it away and disposed of it.

Then my grandmother turned to Lorri and said that she always tried to stay out of my family's business, but that this time she made an exception because she thought I should know the "truth." My lip curled at her lie. As if my grandmother had ever done anything *but* meddle in our family business.

On Thanksgiving Day my father took me on a visit to my own home. The heavy drapes were drawn; there was little light and much smoke in the house. Long ago the walls and everything else that was once white had been stained yellow by my chain-smoking parents. The scruffy furniture and decorations in dark wood and colors that surely could never have been thought any prettier than the contents of one's stomach, even in the seventies, added to the suffocating atmosphere.

Trash overflowed the trash cans. Every dish we owned was scattered throughout the house. Bugs crawled and flew around in abundance near uncovered food. The whole place was as big a mess as it would have been if the police had gone through on a drug raid. It was a bad, bad sign for the house to be in such disarray.

Every Thanksgiving before, the family had gone next door to have dinner at my grandmother's. But not that year. She wouldn't have anything to do with us all of a sudden. My brother tried cooking Thanksgiving dinner himself. He burned the frozen turkey and burned the edges of a frozen pie while the middle stayed frozen. We ended up eating ready-made rolls.

I eyed my brother questioningly as he moved about the kitchen and ate his roll in silence. His face was pale and pinched. What had happened to my aggravatingly spoiled and hyperactive eleven-year-old sibling? Why wasn't he going on about some wild story he had obviously made up, or at least embellished? Why wasn't he telling me with a smirk that he was glad I was in the loony bin where I belonged?

With my mother gone, no one fixed his meals for him anymore, no one washed his clothes, no one listened to him ramble on and praised him to the sky for every silly little thing he did or said. With me gone, there was no one around to compare himself with and feel good about himself in comparison to.

At first I thought he was just sulking. But he asked to talk with me in private, something he had not done in years. I guessed that he really needed someone to talk to, since our father sat around watching television all day, acting like neither my brother nor I existed.

I closed the door to the room my mother and I had shared when we were both home, and sat on the edge of my bed. My brother pulled up a chair. He was quiet for a moment, then blurted out, "We can't let Mom come home, because Dad says he will blow her head off if he ever sees her again!" He reminded me that our father had lots of guns in the basement where he lived. Then my brother said, "Dad has gone off the deep end. He's been yelling and swearing about Mom, smashing her stuff and all. He threw her stool by the stove down the stairs and everything. I'm scared."

My poor little brother's eyes were big, and he was shaking a little with emotion. I think it was the first time in his life that he had admitted to himself the Big, Ugly Truth—that our family was not stable, to say the least.

When my family was together, my brother had fared pretty well—he was the baby and the favored one. Not that either of my parents or my grandmother could really care for anyone, but my brother considered them better than nothing. He had ignored, even denied, any abuse or neglect inflicted upon him, and he had turned against me when I did not do the same, all in the interest of "keeping the family together." Now it was falling apart anyway. Where did he belong now? What was he supposed to do?

I said a few comforting words and gave him a hug. I did not know what else to do. At least neither of us was alone with the knowledge that complete upheaval was right around the corner.

He told me that he had been feeding my guinea pig, but that he did not know how to change the litter in the bottom of the cage. Opie was suffering from the heavy stench under him that he could not escape. He lay in the corner of his cage, panting hard. I scooped up the old newspaper and pine chips and arranged a fresh layer. Then I cuddled Opie until my father came and said it was time for me to go back to the institution.

When I was returned to WSH that evening I sat at the staff table and vehemently related the things I had observed that day. I begged for advice as to what could be done for my guinea pig, and especially for my brother, who was all alone with a father who had completely lost it. The three women present were not interested in my "ravings;" all they wanted to know was whether or not I had "behaved" myself on my first pass.

A little more than a week after Thanksgiving Day, I was called from school for the third time, and found my mother in the family conference room with Lorri. My mother announced that she had filed for divorce.

Her story was that when she had come back into town from Florida, she had called the house to say she was coming home, and my father had said that if she did he would blow her head off with his shotgun. She then called the police and filed for divorce. Since she was the one who filed, she received temporary custody of the house and my brother and me until the divorce hearing. She told me with glee about how the sheriff had gone to the store where my father worked and told him that she had filed for divorce and he was not to go home. She wished she could have seen the look on his face!

Suddenly she burst into noisy sobs and tears. She wailed

that the whole marriage had been such a nightmare, right from the honeymoon, when my father preferred watching a disgusting gangster movie to being with her. And it had gotten worse from there. He was always calling her names and putting her down. She claimed he had come to her in the hospital when she was first diagnosed diabetic and told her that he couldn't love her anymore because she was a "worthless cripple." I had heard all this before, but the next part was new. She clutched the arms of her chair in horror, and whispered hoarsely that he had raped her and held a gun to her head, saying that if she ever told anyone he would kill her.

"Oh!" she cried, grabbing me and dribbling tears on my arms, "how dreadful it must have been for you children to see your mother mistreated so! I could have left long ago, but what would have happened to you children then?" She was speaking in a voice that would carry to the very back rows of her imagined audience. "As long as I was there he took everything out on me. I protected you."

I nearly choked to death when she said that. Of course she had been mistreated, of course I had always pitied her, but where did she get off saying that the worst thing that ever happened to my brother and me was witnessing *her* pain?

I reminded her of the last time I had been beaten in front of her and asked if that was her idea of protection. My mother squirmed visibly as she said, "I don't recall anything like that ever happening."

"Oh, really. You don't recall him ever hitting me at all?"

"If he did, and I'm not saying he ever did, I must have been in shock. My therapist says I have been experiencing a lot of shock, a lot of denial."

When I continued to appear quite disbelieving, my mother drew herself up angrily to shout, "You have no idea the things I've done for you! Your father is a voyeur, a pervert!"

I asked her what she meant. She told me my father was a man who "liked to look at little children naked." She "had to insist, at great personal risk," that I be allowed to put clothes on and shut the bathroom door as I became a modest age.

I was stunned into silence. I couldn't have had a better teacher than my mother when it came to making up preposterous stories to get attention. The only difference between my lies and hers was that she actually seemed to believe hers herself. Also, I outgrew my storytelling, but she only did it more often as she got older.

My mother then turned to Lorri with a defiant gleam in her eye. "He always told me that no judge in his right mind would give two children to an unemployed cripple woman, but we shall see about that!"

She had only one more thing to tell me before going home. My guinea pig, having been neglected for more than a week since I had last cleaned his cage, now had mites. He would need to be washed once a week for six weeks in a diluted sulfur mix. It dyed him orange and made him stink like rotten eggs. It burned him in the places where the mites had bitten him, and he squealed till I thought my heart would break. I figured that the person who had promised to take care of Opie while I was gone and then left him to get mites should be the one who had to wash him, had to listen to him shriek. But my mother brought me home on a pass once a week for six weeks just long enough for me to do it myself.

And so ended my parents' miserable seventeen-year "marriage." It was my dream come true. Separately, the members of my family were all a little less crazy than when we were all together, feeding off each other's dysfunction.

My father began visiting me on a regular basis. It was the first time he had ever taken any interest in me. He brought me candy, food from my favorite place to eat, and packs of the movie cards that I collected. He would ask how I was doing, and I would launch into passionate, long-bottled-up descriptions of the ward and its people. During my monologues my father would nod off to sleep in one of the upholstered chairs in the main visitors' room.

My mother, however, could take me on pass, could take me away from WSH instead of just visiting. (My father could not because of her restraining order.) She began taking me out about one day a week. She never failed to remind me, each time I saw her, of what an awful man my father was and how she was the only person in the world who had ever loved me. When I talked endlessly to her, she stayed awake. Because of these things, she won the little "suck up to Tiffany" contest my parents were having and recruited me to her side.

How was I to know that she was doing something worse than simply ignoring me? She was writing down a skewed version of everything I said to her and giving it to WSH as "proof" that I needed to remain institutionalized. She never once admitted to my face that she wanted me kept in that place. She always claimed that my being there was beyond her control. I believed her because even though I knew she was a liar, I assumed that she was only a confused, attention-starved liar like myself. I have only ever lied in attempts to gain something I needed desperately. I have never lied just to hurt another human being. Just before writing this book, when I saw my psychological records for the first time, I discovered that the nastiest things ever written about me were in the photocopies of the letters my mother wrote. She accused me of lying maliciously, of being two-faced and expert at play-acting and manipulating people. She claimed that I abused her and had a vendetta against her. Clearly, since this was the way *she* operated, and because she hated me so much, it was beyond her comprehension that I could possibly be any different, that in spite of the way she treated me, I wanted desperately to love her.

If I sound like an angry person as I write this book, it is only because I was not angry enough as I lived it.

A few days before Christmas, Brittany was sitting on her bed while I lay on mine and stared at the ceiling during Quiet Time. She asked me why my mother hadn't taken me out on an extended Christmas pass yet. I told her my mother felt that she "couldn't handle" me for more than just Christmas Day itself.

I was rather glum, thinking about how every single time I visited with my mother we got into an argument about something. I wasn't too thrilled about spending time with my cousins and all my other relatives, either, who knew nothing about what was going on with me except that I was currently residing in a mental institution.

"But you are going home for a little while?"

"Yes." I was a little confused about Brittany's sudden interest. Brittany's mother refused to see her, so I assumed that passes in general were an uncomfortable subject for my best friend.

"Would you like to get us out of here?"

I shot up into a sitting position, "What? Would I?! Oh, how could I do that? It's impossible!"

Brittany explained that she had friends, she had *drug-dealing* friends who kept their identities and activities as quiet as possible. She knew someone who would come and pick us up from anywhere if she asked him to, and she also knew someone with whom we could live until we thought of what to do next. All I had to do was get to a phone.

Patients were not allowed to make private phone calls on the ward. There was a pay phone directly off the day-hall, and you had to ask a staff member to dial a pre-approved number for you (the "treatment team" decided who would go on your "list," and it was only adult members of your immediate family—no friends). Then you had five minutes to squish the receiver into one ear really hard, put your hand over the other, and scream your conversation over the ruckus of the ward.

Brittany held out a piece of paper with the number of a man named E———— on it. "Give him directions and tell him to come the Monday after Christmas. He'll take us to L————."

I ran to snatch up the number.

When I was five years old, I used to think I could sit in a bus station and fake amnesia until someone felt sorry for me and took me home. I even planned to put superglue on my fingertips so the police couldn't find out who I really was.

Even when I was old enough to know no one was going to take me home with them like Paddington Bear, I thought endlessly of escaping. But how would I live? I wasn't old enough to have a job; that left stealing and drug dealing and prostitution as the only means of survival.

I had learned from Melanie that older men take in girls, but what if I ended up pregnant like her?

I asked Brittany what we would have to do in return for these young men's help. Brittany eyed my babyish prairie boots, my sweatshirt with a koala on it, and assured me that I was "not their type." I told Brittany I wasn't quite comfortable associating with drug dealers and that I didn't want to be one myself. She said, "Look, would you rather stay here and go crazy?"

"But what about the police?" I insisted. "I don't want to be arrested."

I, a harmless fourteen-year-old, would have to slink away from everyone in a uniform and cringe at the sound of every siren. And policemen are our friends, ha ha ha!

Brittany said, "That's the last thing we have to worry about. Once we're gone, our families would have to press charges to get us back, and it's not like either of ours would give a fuck."

I was silent a long time.

"So do you want to come?" Brittany asked patiently.

"I'll call for you," I said, "and think about going myself."

Brittany leaned back, satisfied. Then she added, "And I bet I could get William to come too. That might help."

Christmas that year was like it was all the years before, which made it more of a farce than ever. My brother and I woke up and opened the presents under our tree. Then we went next door to my grandmother's house to open the presents under hers. The family was all hugs and smiles and jokes as they sat around the lavish Christmas dinner like a Norman Rockwell painting. My mother's siblings were there—my Uncle John with his wife and two kids, and my Uncle Bob.

My grandmother had brought Uncle Bob with her when she moved next door eight years ago, and kept him in the basement. He was the only person I grew up around who didn't hit me or insult me (well, hardly ever insult me). He had a desk in the garage that he would let me sit at sometimes and use his markers and such. He liked the fact that I drew, and he loved the fact that I wrote. To others, my stories were not "practical," and the ones about abused and lonely children were only "proof" of how "sick" I was. But Uncle Bob was always wanting to help me copyright my work and try to sell it. He scraped up all his money once to get me a large hardback book about the writer's market.

I was never sure what to think of my Uncle Bob. I knew that no one else liked him. I understood very early that he was a taboo subject, something my family was ashamed of. I was not to ask why he had no family, no job, no home of his own, why he hid in the basement most of the time, or what that funny stuff was that he drank. Since I had grown up around him, I wasn't too curious anyway. I settled for the whispered, scornful snatches of conversation I heard now and then as an explanation—"was a genius . . . burned out . . . clinical depression, chemical imbalance . . . in and out of mental institutions since he was thirteen . . . needs medication, constant care . . ."

It wasn't until Christmas Day, 1991, that I understood what phrases like that really mean. I sat surrounded by lovely gifts from people who were gadding about so cheerily that no one would ever guess they had abused me for years, had turned myself and the world against me, had ruined my life. I looked over and saw my Uncle Bob sitting in the middle of his gifts from the very same people. He looked obviously uncomfortable, as if he didn't want to be there and wasn't sure what to do with himself. His body was scrunched up small, and his hands trembled. He breathed heavily, with effort. His medicated eyes were dull, sunken, and old. He looked as bad as . . . as bad as me!

Forty-some years ago an intelligent, sensitive little boy had lived basically the same twisted, cruel, loveless childhood I had. Then, to top it off, he was committed to a mental institution for no better reasons than that his family was tired of him and the institution would make money. He was further neglected and oppressed, given drugs to subdue him, and probably even electroshock "therapy" and God knows what else that they did to children like that in the '60s. These abuses were justified by calling him "depressed," by saying he had a "chemical imbalance."

Did he ever even know how he was wronged? Or did he break under the torture at some point? He seemed to have assimilated their opinion of himself, or at least found it too difficult to argue. Even after he turned eighteen he let someone else say that he was not capable of taking care of himself, he let someone else control him, and he will probably be controlled all the rest of his life.

I sneaked to a phone the instant I got back to my house. Ordinarily it would have been difficult, but the place was abuzz with Christmas activity. It was easy to get hold of E———. I blurted out, "Umm . . . you-don't-know-

me-but-I'm-a-friend-of-Brittany's-and-she-is-in-some-big-
trouble-they-busted-her-in-a-crack-house-and-now-her-
mom's-keepin'-her-in-a-loony-bin-will-you-bust-her-out-
next-Monday?"

I didn't know how else to say it—what would Amy Van-
derbilt suggest as the proper way to relate that sort of information? Apparently I did all right, because E——— said,
"Oh, man, that sucks big dick. I guess I can come get her
. . . Monday you said? Gimme directions to the place."

I instructed him as Brittany had told me to, and even
told him what time would be best and what parking lot to
go to. I warned him to be careful.

I had believed firmly until then that Brittany was seriously overestimating the simplicity of a break from a mental institution. But E——— sounded as though he were
being asked to take her to a movie. As I hung up the phone,
my stomach churned and my hands trembled at the ever-
nearing reality of getting into this total stranger's car and
being driven out into the unknown. But I had decided that
I had to try anything to escape the fate of my poor
Uncle Bob.

I t is stated quite clearly on the rather short list of "patients'
rights" posted in various places at WSH that "Physical
restraints and/or seclusion shall not be applied unless ordered by a physician to prevent substantial bodily harm to
self or others."

"Seclusion," or "the Side-Room," are words used by institutional staff to improve the sound of what the patients
more realistically call "The Cell" or "The Hole." On the
Monday after Christmas, the day E——— was supposed
to pick us up, Brittany had been found in possession of a
cigarette and was ordered to the cell for twenty-four hours.
Never mind that she was not causing "substantial bodily
harm to self or others;" never mind that it was a clear viola-
tion of her rights and the law to tell her to go there. What

could she do about it? If she refused, they would drag her in and lock the door.

I sat close by William in our last hour class, when our rescue vehicle was due. Our regular "teacher" was ill and we were given a substitute "class" in the woodshop building. The teacher there had William, me, and a second boy watch a film about the fighter jets in the Persian Gulf War. I wasn't interested in debating the educational value of such an activity, as I usually did. All I could think of was how to get another good look out the window at the parking lot without arousing suspicion.

I was upset about Brittany being sent to the Side-Room for no good reason, but doubly agitated over the fact that now I did not know what to do when our rescue vehicle came.

Would it even come?

I was perfectly white, even my lips, which were pressed tightly together. I had hardly slept a wink the night before, and this was obvious from the purple under my eyes like bruises. Every cord of my body was stretched tight with emotion.

William had his long, thin legs stretched out casually in front of him. He was as sickly-looking as usual, but no more so. He picked absently at the brim of his hat, which he held in his lap. I could feel his piercing, steady gaze on me, and at last I turned from the window and looked up at him. After a minute, he whispered with contempt, "You're the shakinest thing I ever saw."

I looked down at my hands on my lap. They were indeed shaking visibly, and I supposed the rest of me was trembling just as obviously.

"Yes," was all I could say.

William was not a touchy-feely person, to say the least. He was quite uncomfortable being touched, and it was quite impossible for him to display physical affection himself. I didn't know how he and Brittany got along as boyfriend and girlfriend, and it was none of my business; all I knew was that he had certainly never touched me.

So what he did then was doubly amazing. He reached out slowly, determinedly, as if he had to force himself a little, and placed his huge, skin-and-bone hand on mine. His fingers curled over and enveloped my entire hand. He looked at me for a moment, fearing that I would pull away, repulsed by his touch, but I didn't. My trembling quieted a little.

William squeezed my hand and observed, "Your hands are damn cold."

To which I smiled a little. After a long while he said in a different tone, almost apologetically, "I can't leave without her."

I responded with an emphatic, "I know that, neither could I."

It strikes me as funny that the substitute teacher never noticed that William had his hand placed over mine. To anyone who worked at WSH, that was a sure sign of demon-induced bodily lust that must be "corrected" immediately. I guess that guy was just as observant as most of the people there, and although he could never believe in such a thing as friendship between two mental patients, he would hardly notice if we were fucking on the table, either.

I felt a slight, sudden movement from William and looked up quickly toward the window.

A black car—Brittany had said to look for a black car. And there was one now, a sleek, shiny black car such as I had never seen before, with darkly tinted windows, creeping slowly around the parking lot. It was a far cry from any of the beat-up relics that the underpaid staff of WSH drove. It was him, our bust man! He came!

The excitement of the car died quickly, however, as there was nothing left to do after merely viewing it. I held my breath as it circled slowly, slowly, once . . . twice . . . and again before it finally pulled away.

When it was gone a pair of tears dribbled from my eyes.

"Oh, now, don't do that." William pulled his hand away from mine and used it to reach into the back pocket of his jeans. "Look, how would you like to see my wallet?"

It was well known that I liked to look at boys' wallets, especially if they contained a drivers' license or something else of interest. William was offering me his now as one might offer a stuffed toy to a crying child. And it worked, I guess.

I found to my amazement that William kept every letter and every picture ever given to him by any family member, friend, or girlfriend stuffed into his nice leather wallet. He let me read them, one by one. I didn't see how they all fit, there were so many!

William grinned at my surprise and interest. "Ha, I got a wallet to top any lady's purse, more junk than any of 'em."

The night before E——— drove by in his James Bond car, Brittany and I had prepared for our escape by stuffing my many-pocketed winter coat with our most por table and necessary or prized possessions. Among these things was a bubble gum case filled with about two dozen of my anti-acne pills. It was dangerous for me to have them since it was against the rules for patients to have any medi cation on their person or in their rooms. Medication was only given out one dose at a time by a member of the staff. I had gone to great lengths to get hold of some extra pills lying around my house during my Christmas pass and sneak them into the institution through the after-pass search of patient and belongings.

It was a little more than a week after our failed escape attempt. I had called E——— again when I was taken on my next weekly pass, but he told me he didn't believe that Brittany was really there anymore. Brittany asked me one night if those pills I had weren't actually antidepressants of some sort. Having a slight case of acne herself (as more than two-thirds of the teenage population does), and being relatively accepting of it, I am sure she didn't understand why it was so desperately important to me to have acne medication. She did not know how I had been made fun of for having acne, how my family told me I only had it because I was dirty. She thought I was really so attached to a more serious kind of pill that I was just ashamed to admit taking.

I insisted they were really just acne pills, and she dropped the subject and rolled over to face the wall. I simply went to sleep, never thinking to take them from the drawer where she knew they were, never imagining how desperate my poor best friend was feeling over there across the room in the darkness until it was too late.

I awoke in the middle of the night to the sound of Brittany going out. A few minutes later the lights flicked on, and staff members gathered around my bed demanding to know what "they" were and where I got "them."

Brittany had taken my pills from the drawer and swallowed them, claiming she was trying to commit suicide. They were hardly fatal, to say the least, but I remembered overdosing on them that one time and that they had caused the most excruciating stomach pains and vomiting I had ever endured.

They simply put her in the Side-Room for taking those pills. Even if she wasn't serious about wanting to die, she obviously needed some attention. Instead she was forced into a little cell to writhe in agony and vomit up those pills over and over and over again all alone.

I know all this because they put me in the cell across the hall.

I held during my interrogation that I had simply forgotten to turn my pills in after my Christmas pass. I don't think anyone who worked at that place was observant enough or cared enough to suspect that my story was not entirely true. Two of the women who had come in left rather quickly. Only Charlotte—that woman who thought Shirley and I were lesbians—stayed to tell me angrily that having pills in my room was a matter of life-and-death seriousness. She told me that I was completely responsible for whatever my pills did to Brittany, and that if they killed her, I would be her murderer.

Then she ordered me to go back to sleep to be "dealt with" in the morning. She flicked out the light and shut the door so quickly that for a moment I could have believed I had dreamed the whole thing. But the bed across from me in the moonlight was still empty, and the terrible claws of guilt dug deeply into my chest. Naturally I did not "go back to sleep." I lay all night in my bed too horrified to even cry.

In the morning I was allowed to dress and use the bathroom privately before I was led to the cell. Outside the thick blue door I was ordered to remove my "shoes, belt, hair fasteners, and everything in all pockets." Then it was explained to me that for now I was in "Unlocked Room." If I did not "conduct myself appropriately," the door would be locked until it was decided that I could "handle" Unlocked Room again.

The steel door of the cell shutting behind me made a

small echo. I stood just inside it and stared at my new surroundings.

Like every other room at WSH, this one had a window. In addition to the built-in white bars, however, there was a thick metal "security screen" bolted over it. This meant that only enough of the world could be seen, only enough light could enter, to give you a hint of what you were missing. It was a maddening tease.

There were three objects to accompany me in my isolation: a brown plastic mat tossed haphazardly on the floor, a convex mirror in the right corner of the ceiling (so that anyone peering in the window in the door could see the patient even on the door side of the cell), and a naked light bulb in a small white cage in the middle of the ceiling (the switch for it was outside the door).

Mat, mirror, light bulb. Light bulb, mirror, mat. My eyes ran over these things again and again, searching them for some clue as to what I was supposed to do in this room.

Slowly the answer came, though I tried not to believe it: nothing. There was nothing to do. That was the point. I remained standing in the center of the cell, aware of the seconds passing with the beating of my heart. My lungs began to expand and contract with increasing force and difficulty without the help of any air moving around me. My hands were trembling like white birds shaking their feathers. My muscles stiffened, my scalp prickled, my knees began to wobble. I grew so dizzy I hoped I might faint.

I knew already that any human being can be driven mad in a cell. But I had no idea that it began so early. I clenched my fists in an effort to contain my overwhelming desire to scream, to flee, to fling my body against the walls. Those walls, those four, bare, white, close walls that bore the marks of hundreds, maybe thousands, of children who had already lashed out at them in vain with nothing but their bare hands and feet and heads and nails. There were desperate claw marks everywhere. There were huge chips knocked out of the paint. There were even angry dents in the thick screen and the steel door.

Nearly every day since I had been brought to WSH I had heard the screaming and banging of some poor kid in one of the cells. The staff then had their pick: cuffs and shackles? Straightjacket? Or the bed? Every last one of the beds at WSH was a prison bed; they had metal loops built into the frame, through which leather straps could be threaded and tied around the prostrate patient's hands and feet. Two staff members would stand outside on the dayhall so the other patients could see them roll up a sheet and know they were going to tie it around the chest or head of the child in the cell. Patients in restraints were given injections of heavy sedatives in their stripped rear ends, the door was locked, and their sentence doubled at the very least. My stomach knotted at these thoughts.

I strained to peer out the window in the door, a six-inch square piece of wire-embedded Plexiglas with its frame bolted into the door. All I could see was the cell on the opposite side of the boys' hall. The door was open for some reason, and I saw a plastic bucket in front of Brittany's feet. In an instant I saw a flash of hair over that bucket, and the sounds of retching floated under my cell door.

I turned around quickly with my hand clamped over my mouth at the sight of her vomit. The cell became blurry and red. It then seemed to lurch upward, but only because I had collapsed onto my knees. In another instant I found myself flat on my back, struggling with all my might to breathe regularly.

Without my usual barrettes, my hair flowed out over the cold floor. Strands of it stuck to my sweaty face and neck. Strain had given me a fever that rattled my teeth.

Brittany, my dear friend, you are always so cool and composed. Why didn't I see that was just a show, that you feel just as bad as me inside? I should have guessed, I should have wondered why you questioned me about my pills. I should have gotten you to talk to me.

Even now I'm just lying here leaving you alone when you have finally made it clear that you need someone.

If I had any courage, I would go to you, I would swing open this unlocked door and hold your head, give you a cool washcloth for your face and speak comforting words to you until they laid their hands on me and dragged me away and locked this door! But I have no courage. Forgive me for having no courage . . . forgive me for being no better than the assholes who work here!

I banged my trembling fist on the floor and put the other hand over my face as the tears bubbled up and choked me.

The assholes who work here. The assholes who are paid to care for you and still do not. The assholes who treat you like shit and tell me it is my fault when you do something desperate. Oh, I can see them now, sitting and gossiping as usual around their sacred staff table. They put those two bad mental patients in cells and all is right with their world. Business as usual. Oh no, nothing more required of them. Assholes, bastards, how could they? How could they?

At last I put my mouth to the crack under the heavy metal door and screamed. At first it was a scream of pure, primal anguish and rage. Then, between the choking and sobbing, I was more specific,

"HOW CAN YOU SIT ON YOUR FUCKING CHAIRS AND ACT LIKE NOTHING IS GOING ON? WHAT THE HELL IS THE MATTER WITH YOU PEOPLE? WHAT UNDER HEAVEN COULD RENDER YOU SO PERVERTED AND CRUEL?"

"BRITTANY? BRITTANY! DO YOU HEAR ME! HOW COULD YOU DO THIS? WHY DIDN'T YOU TALK TO ME? WHY DIDN'T YOU TELL ME? I WOULD HAVE CARED! DO YOU THINK THESE MOTHER-FUCKERS CARE? THEY THINK YOU TRIED TO KILL YOURSELF AND THEY DON'T CARE, DO YOU HEAR ME? THEY DON'T CARE! I COULD HAVE TOLD YOU THAT BUT YOU HAD TO DO THIS! NOW DO YOU SEE THEY DON'T GIVE A FUCK? I THOUGHT YOU WERE SMART! HOW COULD YOU BE SO STUPID? WHY DID YOU HAVE TO DRAG ME

INTO THIS? NOBODY GIVES A FUCK ABOUT YOU
OR ME AND WE WOULDN'T SUFFER THIS IF YOU
KNEW THAT!"

A bald farmer, who worked at the institution when his crop wasn't doing so well, came and peered down at me through the window in the door. He ordered me to "lie down on the mattress" as if I were a dog barking at the postman.

"FUCK YOU!" I screamed. "THERE, I SAID IT! I SAID FUCK YOU! HA!" In the middle of my misery I found a stab of joy and liberation in the fact that I had said to a deserving adult what I had never in my life had the courage to say before.

For fourteen years I had hardly ever even said "damn." Now, after only three months in a state mental institution and two hours in a cell, I was an avid potty mouth. For fourteen years I had strained with all my might to live up to what I thought other people considered "good" or "sane." But those people, for one reason or another, simply didn't care about me no matter what I was. I ended up in the same place I would have if I had never even tried to befriend the system. So why should I refrain from saying what I thought of that, from yelling, using "bad" words, expressing rage, criticizing "authority," and doing whatever else was considered "bad" or "crazy" by a bunch of people who didn't give a rat's ass if I lived or died? Since I couldn't think of a single reason, my speech continued to burst forth from the most anguished depths of my soul,

"GOD PUT YOU HERE, IN THE MIDDLE OF THE GREATEST HUMAN MISERY THERE IS, IN THE MIDDLE OF THE SUFFERING OF ABUSED AND ABANDONED CHILDREN! AND HE GAVE YOU THE POWER TO DO GOOD! TO UNDERSTAND! TO HEAL! AND WHAT DO YOU DO INSTEAD? WHAT DO YOU DO? YOU SIT AT YOUR TABLE LIKE OVERSEERS, LIKE GODS, AND YOU REVEL IN YOUR POWER AND YOU ABUSE IT AND YOU ABUSE THE CHILDREN, THE HELPLESS CHILDREN!"

I gasped with terrifying difficulty, my body shaking almost spasmodically as every fiber contracted in agony,

"AND WHEN YOU DIE YOU WILL GO TO GOD AND HE WILL ASK YOU! HE WILL ASK YOU WHAT YOU DID GIVEN THE POWER TO EASE THE ULTIMATE SUFFERING AND WHAT WILL YOU ANSWER? I SHOULD LIKE TO BE THERE WHEN YOU ANSWER! WHEN YOU ANSWER TO GOD!"

I was prepared to continue speaking my mind until they came and tied me up, until their mind-controlling drugs put me to sleep, but when the heavy door opened, it was only Lorri, the ward psychologist. She gazed down at me lying stricken with stress-induced fever and frenzy on the floor. Then she squatted beside me. There was a momentary crease in her forehead, a slight indication of the fact that she was human, as she spoke these words:

"I have nothing to do with lock-up. I used to, but it got to be too much. I . . . I can't anymore, there are so many things . . ."

So she at least knew what I was talking about, she knew that what was going on all around her was wrong. But unlike me at that moment, she had more to lose if she spoke up—her job, her professional friends, her reputation.

I stared up at her with glazed eyes. My crying stopped as I contemplated the fact that here was a woman so tortured by her conscience that she would go to a fourteen-year-old mental patient for help. I could not tell her I understood and accepted her silence, because that would not be entirely true. But I did not know what to tell her to do about it. I said nothing, my head throbbing and swimming, my body quivering, and my eyes burning from fever and having nothing to look at but those painful white walls. Lorri looked at me a minute more, and then, seeing that I was not the one who could give her what she came for, she said in her usual tone, "I don't think you want to lie on the floor. I came in here once, to see a patient, and I was about to sit on the floor when it was pointed out to me that I would be sitting in something else."

I lay paralyzed. Now I knew what that dreadful smell was—remnants of human waste. But the worst thing was that there was nothing I could do about it. I was so drained by the events of that morning and the night before that I could not lift a finger.

My crying had ceased somewhat, but it soon began again. The sobs tore at my chest and the tears came so thick and fast that each one seemed to stretch from my eye to the floor.

Lorri reached out to where my small, pale, and trembling fingers lay on the floor, and she held my hand in hers.

Touch, human touch, and energy. I could feel Lorri's sympathy and comfort flow into my hand and spread slowly through my arm and body. After a long time, my crying slowed again and I found the strength to move myself from the floor-toilet to the plastic mattress that stank so bad I didn't see why Lorri thought it any better than the floor. She left me there, no longer frenzied, but still feverish, trembling and completely emotionally and physically exhausted.

They let Brittany out hours before me because she had been too busy vomiting to scream like I had. They told her to move her things to another room, and that she and I were not to be together anymore.

When I heard this news I had been lying for countless hours on that horrid mat. My eyes were red-rimmed and swollen. Even when I realized I had just lost the best friend I ever had, I had no tears left.

At odd intervals a staff member's face appeared in the window in the cell door. He or she inspected me like a faulty bit on an assembly line and scribbled something in my chart. If my eyes were closed, I was reminded sharply that patients are not allowed to sleep until nighttime. Sleep is an escape.

I discovered the only way it is possible to survive in a cell without going mad. I fell into a stupor. I barely, barely moved or thought or felt. I stared at the wall, still aware of my surroundings, but they seemed more like the horrid surroundings of nightmares than reality.

Trays had been brought to me for breakfast, lunch, and dinner. I had picked half-heartedly at them and kept the sugar packets that were supposed to be for my iced tea. I had put them in my pocket to eat later. But then I thought of something better to do with them.

When that bald farmer came to the window for the next fifteen-minute peering, he did a double take at what he saw. I had rolled my sore, aching body away from the wall and poured my sugar along the floor in two-foot lines to form the words, "FUCK YOU."

Staff members from other wards came to peer through the window in amazement. Their surprise stemmed from their idea that mental patients are no better than dogs. When a dog is hurt it is expected to howl, but imagine the reaction to a dog that writes "FUCK YOU" on the floor with sugar.

Unable to deal with, and therefore anxious to get rid of, any evidence that mental patients are just as human as anyone else, Tyrone sneered at me and spit the words, "You think that's funny? Well you clean it up and see how funny it is then."

After I had mopped I was released to go sleep in my assigned room.

All signs of Brittany having ever existed in that room were gone. I quickly prepared for bed in the dark and crawled between the stinking, cold sheets with a raw, throbbing wound in my middle that has never fully healed.

Another girl soon came and was put in the room with me. Her name was Loretta. She was slightly smaller than me, slightly younger, blonde, and obviously still interested in being what a young girl is "expected" to be in this society. As I had, she arrived at WSH armed with stuffed animals and a doll. She also had her own blanket (quite a luxury) and various other cute little-girly things. She was pretty and intelligent and soon became a favorite of the staff and other patients on the ward.

Like me, she had a totally screwed-up home life, but had lived sheltered from the rest of the world. Like me, she had lost her true identity in her efforts to get others to care about her. We had so much in common—perhaps too much, because we despised each other; we were in competition.

I tried very hard to be nice to her, because I recognized that I didn't have a very good reason not to be. But I guess I didn't do very well, because she put in a request that I be moved.

I had expected to be able to hold out until Loretta left and then perhaps convince someone to let Brittany move back in with me. I was horrified at the prospect of being moved out of the double room. I refused to move my things, and when they were moved across the hall for me and I was banned from Loretta's room, I sat in the hall, protesting.

A fat black woman who insisted on wearing spandex all the time told me that she was real tired of me "acting like you're the queen of the double room, thinkin' you can kick people out when you please."

I just wanted to be with Brittany. I had no attachment to any little cement excuse for a room in a lunatic asylum. Hadn't I asked to be moved out of it twice before? But before I could remind that woman of this fact, she ordered me to get into my new room or she would have me dragged to lock-up.

So I went into cubicle 170, the room across the hall. It was the room they had moved Brittany to when she had taken my pills, and now they had taken her out of it and put her back in the double room with Loretta. I was devastated when she and Loretta became good friends. There was hardly a night I did not cry myself to sleep in the silence of the single room.

Soon after all this, William was bragging about his "rodeo" days to me during science class. The things he said were always plausible, but I wasn't sure if I believed him. I questioned him about what he was saying until he demanded sharply, "Are you calling me a liar?"

"I don't know," I said, looking down at my hands on my lap. I had always backed down when he became agitated, and then he would cool off and we would go on with our conversation.

"Well, you had better not."

Since my time in the cell, I had been less willing to remain silent about anything I thought was unfair. "And what if I do?" I asked, although I still had my eyes lowered.

William looked thoroughly disgusted. "Just shut up, okay, before I kick your ass."

"Oh, you really scare me," I muttered.

"What? I mean it now, I'm gonna whup you with my belt."

I had heard of William cutting other kids. I thought of the welts on Jonathan's back, and I quivered inside. To this day I cannot explain exactly why I suddenly narrowed my eyes at William and said in a low, steady voice, "I dare you. I dare you to do just that."

He was up like a shot and cried out to Loretta, who was sitting next to me,

"Do you hear her? She dares me!"

Despite the fact that William was very loud by now, Mr. Hurst still snored in his chair, as was his habit while his "class" watched a film.

William unclasped his belt buckle and pulled his belt from his belt loops. Very slowly, menacingly, he folded it over so as to hold both ends in his right fist. He towered above me, all six feet three inches of him quivering with emotion. His eyes flashed, and the wirelike tendons in his forearms swelled against his skin. When looking intimidating didn't work, he hesitated.

"Do you know what this feels like?" he wanted to know.

"Yes," I responded solemnly.

"Do you know I can make you bleed?"

"Yes," I said again.

"Would you like me to make you bleed?"

"No."

"Then why don't you take it back?" Something a little like amazement was creeping into William's eyes.

"I won't," I announced matter-of-factly. "I don't care what you do, I won't."

The momentary bewilderment vanished, and William's face burned with renewed anger. He jerked quickly into a fighting stance and flung back his fist with the belt in it. I grasped the sides of my chair and went rigid with both determination and absolute terror. William brought the belt down with all his force—onto the table in front of me. The terrible *thwack* caused me to flinch and jerked Mr. Hurst out of his sleep. The belt slithered from William's hand onto the table like a black snake. He flung himself back down in his chair and folded his arms hotly, the veins still throbbing in his neck. He looked away from me and said crossly to Mr. Hurst, who was glancing around in confusion, "Go on back to sleep, ain't nothin' goin on."

Mr. Hurst made some remark about not being a smart mouth and to stop screwing around and watch the film. William sat silently, and Mr. Hurst went back to sleep.

I was petrified in my chair, my heart pounding, my breath shallow, and my body quivering. Loretta stared at me and remarked to William, "Hey, look what you did to her."

William turned sharply around and I looked away. Across the classroom was a mirror, and I could see I was dead-white. I tried with all my might to keep tears from gathering on my eyelashes. William stared at me until I turned red with shame, and he said, seething with disgust, "Cry."

I tilted my nose up and pressed my trembling lips together defiantly.

"That's what I thought," William sneered. "Next time I'll beat you to a bloody pulp, so don't fuck around with me."

But I knew by then that his threats were idle. Pretty soon everyone in the Smith Building knew too, thanks to Loretta. He only had to hit me once to save his reputation, but now he was jeered at for letting a girl get the best of him. Some kids told me I was brave to stand up to William like I did. I must admit I liked to be called brave. But victory over one of the last people in this world I wanted to fight with was bitter.

During Quiet Time I sat on the metal bed of the lonely, one-patient cubicle 170. I had lost Brittany, my best friend. I had failed to befriend Loretta. And William had not acknowledged my existence for two days. I would rather have been hit than pass by him in the hall and have him turn away.

Warm tears dribbled out of my eyes as I wondered if he would ever tell me his muskrat story again, or make the veins in his arms swell up until I shrieked for him to stop it and Mr. Hurst told me to settle down while William grinned innocently.

Oh, why didn't I let him say what he wanted? Why didn't I just shut up when he got mad? If he wants to look like such a tough guy what's the harm in letting him? What have I won by calling his bluff? I have only wounded his pride. What's so brave about doing that to your friend? It was mean and I'm just a bitch, I always have been, and that's why I'm sitting here all alone.

In a moment of weakness, in a single moment of betraying my own rationale and thinking what those who despised me would wish me to think, everything they had ever said or believed about me rushed in and attacked my mind.

You like to hurt people, don't you?

You have no conscience, no feelings, no remorse.

You're a sick, twisted little girl.

You have no respect for anything, not people, not nature, not God . . .

And in a frenzied moment of self-hate I flung myself face-first into the concrete wall of my cubicle. I pounded my face against that wall until the pain was too great for me to stand, and I collapsed onto the bed that always reeked of cleaning solution.

But I was not done yet. My writing clipboard lay nearby, and I grasped it and began banging my face against it. Soon blood streaked across it.

I don't know how or why, but the realization of what I was doing suddenly pierced my senses like a knife. I dropped my clipboard in horror.

Oh, no! No, I mustn't do this to myself. It won't make the guilt go away.

My left eye was swelling. I reached my hands up to my face to see where the blood was coming from. It was my nose. Blood rushed thickly through my trembling fingers and dribbled onto my shirt.

I realized that I couldn't just sit there and bleed all over my clothes. With my hands cupped over my nose, I peeked out of my door. Loretta was there. She took one look at me and hurried down the hall to tell the staff that I was bleeding rather profusely. A woman named Doris came into my room with washcloths and told me to pinch my nose.

She was initially concerned, and asked in a rush, "Who did this to you? Did Zach do this? Did one of those big boys on Smith 2 do this? Tell me who did it! Don't be afraid, I won't let them hurt you again!"

I just shook my head until at last Doris saw the blood-streaked clipboard on the floor. She asked incredulously, "Did you hurt yourself, Tiffany?"

Tears of shame flowed over my cheeks. I nodded very

minutely. Doris looked at me as if I were the boy who had just cried wolf when there was no one there. All sympathy and concern in her voice and eyes vanished instantly. I soaked one wet washcloth with blood and Doris quietly motioned for Loretta to get another one. The bone all around my left eye throbbed. I could feel that the lid was beginning to swell shut.

When the bleeding stopped, Doris led me out to the dayhall so that I could be placed on SP (Suicide Precaution).

SP simply means having to remain on the dayhall twenty-four hours a day for as many days as Dr. Bizaldo, the one guy a patient almost never sees, decides. I had to sit there all day and have my "meals" brought on trays, as I had when I was first brought to WSH. If I had to go to the bathroom, I had to wait until a staff member felt like taking me and standing outside the stall. A plastic mattress was dragged out onto the floor in front of the staff table for me to sleep on at night. No grown man had ever seen me in my pajamas before, but I was not allowed to sleep in my clothes. I burned with humiliation.

I lay under the bright lights the first night and looked up at the staff members present—two fat, vague-looking women, one makeup-caked woman in a skirt-suit with tightly curled hair, and Tyrone, who never said a nice word to anyone and was rumored to beat his wife and children. They paid no attention to me, only shuffled their endless papers and paused now and then to threaten the patients who stuck their heads out their doors to gossip with each other at night.

I thought of Brittany and Loretta whispering to each other as Brittany and I used to do. I thought of how much better even dark, solitary cubicle 170 looked compared with the bright dayhall with those horrid people I could not cry in front of. My loneliness was sharper than ever. I would have been content to keep the fact that I had recently felt bad enough for the first time in my life to beat myself up a secret. But since it was all over the building, I wished someone was with me who gave a God-damn.

I suddenly rolled over and leaned out on my elbows over the cement floor. I looked at it a minute, closed my eyes, and cracked my face onto it. I didn't do it very hard, since my face was sore, but when no one made any move to stop me, I did it again, and again.

Tyrone watched me with his arms folded listlessly across his chest. There was no expression in his dull, arrogant face. Just as I had suspected, it was procedure to punish any patient who hurt themselves with the humiliation of SP, but if a patient was already on SP, then no one had to do anything more about it unless they cared, which they didn't.

I raised my fingers to my nose to see if I had made it bleed again. I had.

"I think I need a washcloth," I ventured.

"Too bad, stop picking your nose," sneered Tyrone. His lips twitched and his head jerked at his own little joke.

The blood was starting to dry on my clenched fists before one of the fat women took pity on me and told me I could get some Kleenex.

When I lay back down on my mattress I stared at the blood that had spurted onto the floor when my nose had made violent contact with it. The pattern it made reminded me of a toy I had played with when I was a child, the one that spun a piece of paper while I squirted different colors of paint on it. Any dumbass could see there was no way that "picking my nose" could have done that.

For the next few nights I barely managed to collect a few restless hours of sleep. During the days I hardly ate anything they brought on the trays. The staff kept reminding me that it was against the rules not to eat, and said pretty soon they were going to strap me down and force a tube down my throat.

Once I took a particularly yucky slab of salami a woman was trying to force on me and threw it against the wall.

All the kids got a big kick out of the fact that it stuck there for three days, and when it finally fell off there was a dark, permanent grease stain.

I hardly spoke to the other kids as they sat around the dayhall after school and meals, only Brittany. The strain of being watched without a moment's peace paled me and dug the purple trenches under my eyes deeper. But my physical misery was nothing compared with the shame and the isolation that tore me apart inside.

No one ever talked with me about my hurting myself. No one ever asked why I had done it.

The other patients knew without my saying a word how badly I felt about what had happened between William and me. They found nothing unusual in my hurting myself about it. Self-abuse is shockingly common, especially among people who have been conditioned to believe that they are to blame when things go wrong.

As for the staff, they either didn't care, or they had their own notions as to why I did it, so they didn't see why they should bother to ask.

ELEVEN

After three and a half days and two nights of SP, Dr. Bizaldo called me over to the office counter before he left to go home. He said, "How are you feeling today?"

"Fine." (The universal lie.)

"Well, Tiffany, do you feel like hurting yourself anymore?"

"No, I guess not." I was still ashamed of myself, still thought myself a stupid bitch, but I wasn't about to bruise the hell out of my face in front of these callous assholes anymore.

Dr. Bizaldo looked skeptical and said, "Hurting yourself and drawing attention to yourself will not bring your parents back together."

I was so startled by this statement that my hand slipped on the counter and I nearly fell over.

"What?" I exclaimed, "You think I hurt myself over my parents' divorce? That's the best damn thing that ever happened to me!"

Dr. Bizaldo did not listen, but continued condescendingly, "Perhaps you do not think it bothers you, but divorce is a very scary thing for an adolescent to deal with. Since you have no previous record of hurting yourself, if all goes well I will take you off SP tomorrow morning."

I was weakened and frustrated by this, but by concentrating on the arrogance and stupidity of the rest of the world, my intense self-disgust was lessened a little.

When I returned to school two days later, the welcome

of the patients from Smith 2 was very reassuring. My current boyfriend, Drew, even let me wear his watch. It had been his grandfather's. My eye was open by then and my cheekbone bruise gone, as well as the bruise on my forehead where I had banged it on the floor. A yellowish-purple lump remained over my left eye.

Mr. Davis, the art teacher, told his class that day about all the patients he knew who had hurt themselves and said that sometimes those lumps don't go away. He spoke of a patient whose whole face was deformed from self-abuse. He made it sound as grisly as he could. That was his way of showing he cared about me. Also, he reveled in storytelling.

Finally I saw William in the hall. I shied away from him, expecting him to still be angry, and perhaps even angrier if anyone had blamed him for what I did to myself. Just as I was passing him he grabbed my arm with his left hand and wrapped his right around my jaw. He swiveled my face to the light and inspected the bruise over my eye. His jaw muscles shifted as he ground his teeth together slightly.

Instinctively I put my arm on his chest and tried rather lamely to push him away. I was more startled than scared. He turned my face again so that he could stare down into my eyes and said, "God dammit! Don't you ever do that again, do you hear me? If you deserved that I would have done it myself!"

I knew then that he wasn't angry anymore, that he had been worried about me. He made me swear that I would never hurt myself like that again.

It was arranged that I would see Lorri, the ward psychologist, once a week in her office for an hour-long "one-to-one." It was the only thing Wilson State Hospital ever did that, instead of being detrimental to my well-being, actually resembled help for any "problem" I was supposed to have.

Once a month the "treatment team" (Lorri, Dr. Bizaldo, and the ward social worker) made up a little "review" of my situation, what was supposedly still wrong with me, and how WSH was "helping." This was sent to my parents. Every fourth session with Lorri, she would hand me one of these reviews for me to look over and sign. Problem was, I couldn't read the handwriting. But that didn't matter. Whether I understood what those reviews were saying, and certainly whether or not I agreed with them, was totally irrelevant. I was just ordered to sign them. Then Lorri and I could talk about what was really going on with me.

Lorri didn't look like all the other stuffy women in administrative positions, with mime makeup, big hair, and little skirt-suits with heels and lots of accessories. She didn't wear any makeup or seem to put anything in her hair. She usually wore just plain old shirts and pants. Her mouth wasn't pinched together, either, and she didn't perpetually stare down over her nose at me as if I were a loathsome little insect.

Unlike any other psychologist or psychiatrist or counselor I had ever been made to go see, she let me talk about what I wanted to and she didn't interrupt me. She actually even seemed to take me seriously, and acted as if what I said was important, not just the ramblings of some crazy child.

I spent all my time with her sorting out all the bad things that had happened to me in my life out loud. I told her that my father had grown up in a family with outdated, stereotypical roles—man goes out and makes money, woman stays home and takes care of house and kids, kids are to be seen and not heard, etc. I told Lorri I didn't think my father was very smart about people, and that he just couldn't find a way to fit into a family that wasn't like that. He was frustrated, so he took it out on me. I explained that my mother had been seriously psychologically abused in her childhood by her obsessive, controlling, tyrant mother.

She had been so emotionally fucked up that she would never have been a good mother even if she hadn't gotten so physically ill on top of it all.

My mother had been convinced in her childhood that she absolutely could not be less than perfect. When she was not a perfect mother to me, when she was not even a good mother to me, she could not ask for help, she could not admit that she was not perfect; she had to cover her tracks. She had to make it seem as though the way she treated me was justified because there was something wrong with me. I told Lorri I didn't think my mother was even consciously aware of what she was doing. She had convinced herself more than anyone else so that she would not feel the insufferable guilt that comes when you realize you have abused and betrayed your own children.

I told Lorri that the eternal cycle of parents abusing their children because they had been abused would continue for as long as society did not discourage it. As long as friends and teachers and psychologists and social workers know or suspect that a child is being mistreated and say nothing, that child will grow up thinking that what happened to them was not child abuse, that it must have been okay or someone would have said something. And if it was okay for their folks to do it, then why wouldn't it be okay for them to do it to their own kids?

I pointed out that it isn't any coincidence that most people with psychological problems were victims of child abuse. The same with criminals—the more violent the crimes they commit, generally the more violent their childhoods were. If no one cared that they were beaten and molested and raped and cheated, what a surprise it must be to them to find themselves in jail for doing those things to other people! Not that having been treated badly is a good excuse for treating others badly. The point is that it shouldn't come to that. Society shouldn't wait until kids are totally fucked up and then simply lock them in jails and mental institutions and claim that the only reason they are there is because they are different from other people, because they are possessed by the devil, or have a chemical imbalance, or whatever the catch phrase of the decade is.

Lorri agreed with me. That was all she needed to do. That was the thing that comforted me. I had figured everything out for myself a long time ago; I just needed to know that I wasn't the only one in the world who saw things that way. Then I knew I wasn't crazy, then I knew I wasn't bad, then I knew I didn't have to bash my face against a wall. I talked to Lorri when I started to doubt myself, which usually happened right after I visited my mother.

I asked Lorri one day if it was too late for me, if I was completely crazy. She asked me what made me think I was crazy. I reminded her that I had faked seizures to get attention; that I was completely paranoid about being watched by people, recorded, and judged; that I was perpetually sick and weak with stress; that I was deeply confused and frustrated and often despaired; that sometimes I wanted to kill my family or the people who worked at the institution, or kill myself.

Lorri told me that my circumstances were confusing and frustrating and would make anyone despair. She explained that because my family and the people at the institution caused my unfair circumstances, it was completely normal to want them out of the picture. My childlike subconscious was afraid that nothing less than death would keep them from hurting me. As for wanting to kill myself, I didn't really want to die, I just couldn't see any other way sometimes to escape my intolerable circumstances. Lorri reminded me that every child needs attention, and that I had actually found a more ingenious and less harmful way of obtaining it by faking seizures than the average kid who beats up other children or something like that. Lorri explained to me that it was not "paranoid," as my mother called me, to be afraid of being watched and recorded and judged, when patients in a mental hospital are in fact being watched and recorded and judged nearly twenty-four hours a day.

I told Lorri that I had been treated that way long before coming to a mental hospital. I told her how my grandmother used to hide tape recorders in order to catch "evidence" of my insanity. I told her about my parents babysitting me and taking my door off the hinges and reading one of my most sacred notebooks. I told her about the time I had gone down into my father's basement and found a notepad with the word "Tiffy" and then some notes, the word "friend" and then some notes. I hadn't looked at it very long before my mother snatched it away, but it was obvious my father had been listening in on my phone conversations and recording them for God knows how long. I started to cry as I explained that I had no idea how many other times and in how many other ways my privacy had been violated. Every time I saw a movie or read a book about hidden videocameras and microphones, one-way mirrors, or mind-reading machines, I had no idea how plausible it was for things like that to be tracking me at that very minute.

Lorri told me that it was her firm opinion that the technology for reading a person's mind would not be developed anytime soon. As for cameras and microphones, they were increasing in use and popularity. However, as she smiled a little and lowered her voice to say, "A cheap, run-down place like this could never afford such a system."

"Are you sure I'm not paranoid?"

"Yes, I'm sure."

"Are you sure I'm not crazy?"

It was then that Lorri told me a story, a story as simple as my long-winded speeches about abuse and children and society were complicated, but just as profound.

"A woman sleeps naked in her house. One night her house catches fire. She runs out naked and screaming for help. If someone were to see her, and the burning house, they'd understand why she was naked and screaming, and her reaction would seem normal. But if the house of fire were not in plain sight, if it seemed that the woman was running around naked and screaming for no reason, they'd think she was crazy. Tiffany, if you were acting in the ways that you do in normal situations, you would be abnormal, but you react quite normally to abnormal situations. Do you understand?"

"Yes." I understood. I have often been unable to believe it, to refrain from being so down on myself anyway, but I have understood it for as long as I can remember. No one told me this, no one ever even agreed with me for fourteen years, but that answer just came to me and made sense to me whenever I thought about it.

I would sometimes sit and talk with some of the staff members, just to try to understand them and their prejudices. A few of the people who worked at WSH seemed to be all right except that they didn't think about things much. They accepted everything that went on around them without wondering if it was right or wrong. They would let me sit at the sacred staff table if there weren't any charts out and talk to them.

But state institutions don't pay much, certainly not anything like private clinics, and there isn't much "opportunity for advancement." WSH was out in the middle of nowhere, and so most of the people who worked there were struggling farmers and small-towners who could do nothing else. The narrowness of their lives caused the narrowness of their minds. They were bitter and frustrated and took it out on the one group of people around who were lower on the social scale than they were.

One of the sorriest-looking women was Anita, the woman who had been on the dayhall with Diana when I was first brought in. She sat rigidly, stiffly, as if she were made of iron rods. Everything she ever did or said was purposeful, to the point, and forceful. She usually wore jeans and a plain shirt. Her clothes were cheap, but she kept them starkly void of stain, wrinkle, or wear, except the seat of her pants. Her eyes, small and round and cold like my grandmother's, glared out from behind the glasses perched on her hawklike nose. Her mouth was a perfect upside-down U. When I looked at her I thought, *Well, if people get no other punishment for being nasty, self-righteous, judgmental bitches, at least they always pinch their own lips off.*

When Anita filled out the patients' point sheets, she never gave anything higher than 3s, telling us all with seething disgust, "If you were a 5 you wouldn't *be here.*"

Sometimes I almost felt sorry for her, thinking what a barren, loveless life she must have. I asked her once if she had been abused as a child. Her outraged retort was, "No, most certainly not!" (as if being abused was shameful). "And if I had I would not let it affect my behavior as you children do!"

"So you admit that is our sin, to be abused! To be wounded! You know about it!" I gasped.

Anita snapped, "Don't you take that tone with me. You know you're not supposed to sit at the staff table. You go sit with the other patients where you belong."

I stood up. "And what if I took this chair and smashed your face, what sin would it be of yours to bruise?"

"That's it, you go to Time Out now and not one more word like that or I'll call security for your threatening."

Brittany came up behind me and tugged on my arm. "Save it," she whispered fiercely, "for someone with half a brain to understand."

"But what sin is it to bruise?"

"Go to Time Out, Tiffany." Anita was indignant, yet slightly bored because we disgusting little patients did this sort of thing to her all the time.

Brittany pushed me toward the chair, whispering, "Go on, she's just a stupid old bitch, don't let her get to you."

Anita told Brittany to step away from me. "Patients aren't supposed to touch each other." I looked back at them as

I went to the Time Out chair in the hall, tears of frustration and insult spilling over my cheeks.

But what sin is it to bruise?

I went up to another particularly hateful-looking woman once and asked her as politely as I could how things like having a cigarette or being a "pest" could be used to send patients to the Side-Room when the rule stated that only causing "substantial bodily harm" could do that.

She just snarled, "Get away from me or you'll find out."

This time I was expecting such a reply. This time I understood that a conversation with a little mental patient wasn't going to cause anyone with such deep prejudice and hate to have a revelation. I looked into her eyes. She had the same flat, cold eyes as Anita, as my grandmother, as that Heather Williams from Family Matters, Inc. They never showed a spark of life, love, joy, understanding, or sympathy. They were completely empty, like the Side-Room.

And I thought how fortunate I was merely to be imprisoned by other people instead of by myself.

Mr. Davis told me once that he was glad that he didn't have very strong emotions, that he wasn't very easily upset like I was. I told him that the more pain and rage and misery people allow themselves to feel, the deeper their souls, and the more capable they are of feeling wonder and love and joy. I told him that even if it meant that I suffered more in a place like this, I wouldn't trade my sensitivity and passion for anything. I told him it would be a sorry day when everyone in the world goes to their doctor for pills to keep from feeling anything but continuously "normal."

I don't know how much Mr. Davis agreed with me, or even how much he understood, but he always let me talk. I talked all hour long every day I came to his class. The longer I was kept at WSH, the more I talked, in Mr. Davis's class and everywhere. When I had nothing interesting to say, I made something up. Most of the other patients liked to listen to me; they were lonely and thought I was interesting. Some of the staff would allow me to prattle on, but some sent me to the chair for it, or reported it as a sign of my "insanity." But I did not shut up.

I had always known, as most everyone does, that it is not a good idea to express your opinions everywhere you go because you might end up in the loony bin. Only in the loony bin did I understand why. Expression of ideas promotes change. As long as no one else knew what life was like for me and other children in the same situation, it wasn't going to change. But if I told enough people, someone somewhere would demand that it be improved. When mental institutions are not allowed to keep anyone who is not truly mentally handicapped, their business will be cut by more than half. When only caring, educated people are allowed to work in mental institutions, a lot of people will be out of jobs.

Like Angela and Matthew at Magna Carta, at WSH there was at least one kid who actually had a problem with the functioning of his brain, instead of being called crazy just because he wasn't acting like a normal child in spite of being treated abnormally. Samuel was in the late stages of Huntington's disease. He was not expected to live to be twenty.

He was nothing but skin and bone, standing five feet eight inches tall, weighing in at just a hundred pounds, and losing. Technically, at fifteen, he should have been on Smith 2, but everyone knew he wouldn't be very well off surrounded by kids ten times his size. His eyes were like Matthew's from Magna Carta, large and blue, dilated from drugs and staring dazedly, but there was something more in those eyes. A person was still in there, a person who had to deal with the slow disintegration of his own body and mind all by himself.

He wasn't considered "well enough" to be sent to school (funny how when a patient was considered "well" they were merely sent to school, rather than released). He was only occasionally sent to the dining room. He stayed on the dayhall day after day. A teacher came to the ward to work with him for a little while on weekdays, and he occasionally went to the gym or on an outing with the other patients. Other than that, the three years he had spent at WSH were even more empty than everyone else's.

Samuel was in constant motion; he couldn't keep still. He would rock back and forth in his chair and shift his weight back and forth while standing. He was always licking his fingers and wiping them on his shirt. His coordination was bad, and he couldn't take care of himself. Since it was apparently the job of the employees of mental institutions to boss around and punish normal kids instead of taking care of mentally ill ones, Samuel usually smelled from lack of bathing. His teeth were rotting out, his dirty hair stuck out all over his head, and his wrinkled clothes were dribbled with the food he could never quite carry to his mouth.

Poor Sammy immediately attached himself to me, as I would put up with his perpetual motion and babbling. He could not talk very well; he stuttered and slurred his words. I am not sure how much of this was due to his disease and how much was due to the numerous drugs he was being forced to take.

He would tell me three things over and over—what a good friend I was, how neat his older brother Skip was, and that this was his green bear, Limey. Samuel's stuffed companion was as ratty as he was. It was eyeless, stained, and quite glaringly green. But Samuel loved it and had it with him most of the time.

Sam was like a parrot, copying all he heard. Therefore it was not uncommon to hear him sputter such things as, "M-mthr . . . fugger . . . muther fugger . . . Hee, hee!"

When he said something like "muther fugger" or anything else a staff member didn't like, he was expected to go to the chair or the cell. And if he didn't understand or obey, then security was called.

The first time I saw Samuel "taken down," some fat man in a security uniform hurled himself on top of Sam, and Sam crashed to the floor while a few more people ran in with restraints. I waited in horror for the sound of Samuel's frail, protruding bones snapping in two. His flailing limbs were grabbed and cuffed. He was beet red from lack of air and screaming pitifully. The security man said, "Ew, he's spitting on me!" (which Samuel was as he gasped and cried), and the ward clerk, not even trained in the "art" of restraint, grabbed a towel, knelt on the floor, and wrapped it right around Samuel's whole face.

I had come to be able to disconnect myself from the daily occurrence of some child patient being taken down in this manner, but when I saw them do it to poor, dying Samuel, I had to go to the toilet and vomit.

Sam would emerge days or weeks later from the cell, having hardly eaten or slept, his face drawn and white and the rings under his dilated eyes as thick as my finger. His hands would often be strapped to his sides in a cuff belt. He would squirm and writhe until the leather cuffs bruised and cut his bony wrists, trying pitifully to get his fingers to his mouth to lick them.

I would sit by him while he chafed against his bonds and begged for his green bear Limey, looking so utterly miserable that I wanted to scream.

I used to wonder if Samuel's family, the only family with a truly mentally handicapped child on Smith 1, actually cared for him. Perhaps they lived too far away to visit and did not know how badly he was being treated in this institution. Maybe they thought it was offering him better care than they could give him. Then one day I saw what looked to me like cigarette burns on Samuel's chest. I asked him if that was what those scars were, and he explained with much difficulty that they were chicken pox scars. I then said with relief, "Then your parents do not abuse you, they love you and you love them?"

Which sent Samuel into a terrified, squirming frenzy, licking his fingers and stuttering, "No . . . no . . . no . . ." until he could find the words, "Sexually inappropriate" to describe his parents.

It was only later that I understood that cared-for children with mental disabilities are usually kept at home in this day and age. A professional visits them, or they are sent to a day school for handicapped children, or both. As a last resort, they are sent to far more sophisticated places than state institutions. Only if no one loves them do they end up like poor Sam.

One Saturday afternoon, when all the patients were sitting around the dayhall in typical abject boredom, Zach found a plastic stick attached to a flat rectangle, less than one-half inch by one inch at one end. Goodness only knows what this odd bit of equipment was originally intended for, but Zach and the other boys immediately made use of it as a weapon.

The plastic was very tough, and it took a certain amount of strength to bend back the end with the rectangle on it and then let it slap back down on someone's flesh. It left a hideous-looking welt in the shape of a rectangle with a tail. Several boys, including Zach's best friend Derrick, gathered around closely just in case someone on the usually oblivious staff was watching. Then anyone who wished to prove his "toughness" could hold out his arm for Zach to inflict a welt upon.

I rolled back my sleeve and scooted my chair over to Zach's. The last person hit was trying very hard not to let the tears in his eyes spill over. I held out my arm, palm up, over the arms of the two chairs. He looked down at me without the slightest hint of an expression and said simply, "No. Next."

It annoyed me in the first place to have nothing better

to do than join the boys in their little game, and I was much more annoyed when they wouldn't even let me. "Why not, you bloody bastard, just because I'm a girl?"

Everyone was silent except Derrick, who said, "Damn, you not just any girl, you a crazy little girl."

Zach looked at me again in the same expressionless way. He took hold of my wrist and turned the softer side of my arm under. He bent the plastic rectangle back almost to touch the other end. He lingered a moment to allow the suspense to build, and then he let go of the rectangular end, only it didn't hit me because he was faking me out. I did not move my arm, so Zach had no more excuse not to really do it. He moved so quickly that for a moment I wasn't sure if he'd faked it again. But I looked at my wrist and the bright red welt was there in the shape of a rectangle. And in an instant I felt as if fire were shooting up my arm.

When I did not cry, Zach gave me one of his rare grins. I was very pleased with myself for having mastered this game, however juvenile it was. Very pleased, until the next morning when everyone else was rubbing painful, rectangular bruises and I hadn't the slightest mark on my arm. Having put the image of the rectangle being drawn way back over my flesh into everyone's head, Zach had barely drawn it back the second time at all.

It wasn't long after that when it occurred to me that I had never been in a fight. Fights did not last long at WSH before the offenders were strapped to beds in separate cells and drugged, but that certainly didn't stop them from happening now and then. One does not lock twenty kids up in a room together for weeks and months and years and expect them all to get along all the time.

Sometimes a patient would damage a staff member, the true enemy, and be sent to juvenile jail. Sometimes a kid would attack an employee of WSH just to be sent to a juvenile jail because those places (except for the two maximum security prisons for youths in the state) were much better than WSH. And in jail they would have a sentence that they would serve and then be free, whereas in a mental institution, you never knew when you might get out, if you ever did at all.

When the other kids were showing their scars and telling their harrowing tales of fights on the outside, I had nothing to add to this conversation. I simply found it amusing that those who had been in the fewest fights told their stories most often.

I wondered if I could ever fight well. Without size or strength, I would need a high tolerance for pain and a lot of experience. Therefore, without much else to do anyway, I started looking to get beat up. There were plenty of over-sized boys around me to provoke, but try as I might, I could not get them to take me seriously. After trying verbally to initiate an incident and failing several times, I steeled myself to the fact that I would have to throw the first punch. I had never punched anyone in my life.

A wiry, sullen boy named Jason happened to be sitting in front of me in the van as it was rattling down the road from school one day. He said something vaguely and teasingly insulting. I don't remember exactly what I said, but I clenched my fists hard and stood up to punch him. I felt a rush of adrenaline as I drove my fists into his face and head as hard as I could, over and over.

It was a few seconds before Jason did anything more than stare dazedly at me, and then he only rather crossly reached over the back of his seat and dug his fingers in around my throat. When he held me this way at arm's length, I could no longer reach his face. I was about to scratch the arm that held me when William, who was sitting next to Jason, turned around and clasped one of my wrists in each of his hands. Jason tightened his grip on my throat slightly until I couldn't breathe, and I had to stop struggling.

Then Jason took his hand away, and I sat there gasping while William and Jason stared at me. Jason was only slightly aggravated and more stunned than anything. At last he said, "Are you joking?"

I bit my lip in frustration and shame. To add to my feeling of stupidity, William asked, "If I let you go will you sit there like a good girl?"

I tried to jerk away from his grip, but I did not even pull his forearms off their resting place on the back of the seat. I sighed and sat obligingly still until he let me go.

As they turned around, Jason said in a low voice to William, "I thought sure she was joking." To which William responded with the air of a parent of a two-year-old, "I dunno what gets into that girl sometimes."

I tried one more time to get in a fight. Derrick only pinned my arms down again, saying, "Calm down, Crazy Girl, I don't wanna hurt you."

I cried out in frustration, "Why not? How else am I gonna learn to fight? I wanna fight, I don't wanna be a wuss!"

Derrick shook his head. "You ain't no wuss, Crazy Girl, you the stubbornest kid I ever saw."

Crazy Girl was what the other kids who were tougher and more jaded than I was always called me. Though mental health workers always called me more politically correct terms like "mentally ill," I found this much more insulting. The adults believed that being different from what is expected was wrong. The other kids thought that being different was wonderful. In a world that had never been anything but oppressive and cruel to any of us, they thought it was crazy for me to still have some innocence, some passion, some caring for other people, and some hope for a better world. They called me crazy with affection. They wanted me to stay that way.

T W E L V E

Josh was about six feet tall at age fourteen and reminded me of a TV star I had a crush on. He
had hit his dad. I wondered how many times his dad had
hit him, and why that wasn't any big deal.

He always wore a long black coat, and I used to pull on
the belt loop in the back when I stood behind him in line.
One day I pulled it right off, and he turned on me to say
angrily, "God damn, what did you go and do that for?"

I told him I could fix it, and he said, "Oh yeah? With
what?"

I said, "Needle and thread," and he pointed out that even
if I could get any, I would not be allowed to keep them
here. I looked at the ground, and when I saw his hand move
out of the corner of my eye, I flinched something awful.
He stared at me, saying, "What, do you think I'm going to
hit you? I wouldn't hit you, just don't pull my God damn
belt loops off!"

Josh and I talked a great deal. He had a little more in
common with me than most of the other kids. We had
both grown up in nice little suburbs where violence goes on
inside freshly painted houses, instead of in the city where it
goes on in the street. Eventually, like Jake's (the boy at
Magna Carta who hit his abusive father with a wrench)
mother, Josh's mother talked his father into letting him
come home, but his situation was not improved, to say the
least.

I sat across from Josh at a card table once and said, "No
kid here will hurt me, even when I'm annoying them.

They're supposed to be so big and bad, but not a one of them ever did anything that any other human being on the face of the earth wouldn't have done in their place. I'm not afraid of them, I'm not afraid of the so-called scum of the earth." I gave a hollow little laugh. "Ha, guess that means I'm not afraid of anyone."

Josh crossed his arms and tilted his chair back. "Well, you're still afraid of *them*," and he nodded toward the staff table, where some fat men and women with upside-down U-mouths sat around a pile of shackles.

I shuddered. I had forgotten about the staff. I never tried to pick a fight with them. I did not want to be touched by any of them. I didn't want to touch them, either, even to kick them in the teeth.

"Josh," I said, "the people that work here, like most people everywhere, I suppose, divide everybody in the world into 'crazy' and 'sane.' They can be real nice to the people on the sane list, like their own kids and their other family and their friends, but if you're on the crazy list then there's nothin' in this world you can do to get them to like you. Even if you were just like somebody they really loved, they wouldn't see that. They will never see you and me. They look at every last kid in this place and see only two words. Mental. Patient."

"So how do us mental patients decide who to like and who to regard as fucked-up, subhuman shit? If we went by the words on our charts like everyone else does, then there's no one around to like, not even ourselves. So we need a new system. It's not so easy as looking at a chart. We have to look at each other. When I mess with one of the kids here, they look at me, they see I'm not much of a threat to them, they like me, too, so they don't hurt me. But the staff wouldn't look at me when a little piece of paper already told them everything they care to know. If I messed with them, they would throw me down and beat the shit out of me and throw me in that God-damn cell.

Just like two-hundred-pound Jonathan. Just like poor defenseless Sam."

Josh's forehead wrinkled a little with sympathy at the horrified expression that came over my face when I talked about Sam. He said, "I sure would be sorry for you if they ever took you down."

I wrapped my arms around myself as a chill came over me. "I don't know what I would do if they ever touched me with their filthy hands. I would die, or kill them, or something, I don't know. I'm so afraid. Funny, isn't it? Not to be afraid of the crazy people in this world, but to be afraid of the normal people because normal people let a little piece of paper tell them how to treat others."

I was never taken down. Even if I had been, I guess I wouldn't have killed anybody, or died. Josh was pretty sure of that. I never gave any of the staff an excuse to touch me; I walked right into the cell when I was told. I turned my head when they were assaulting someone else. I hate myself for doing that. If I had had the courage I would have told them to fuck off, I would have grabbed ahold of them and fought tooth and nail to get them off my friends. I just tried to console myself with the fact that it really wouldn't have done any good.

I was never, ever, put in seclusion—the cell—to prevent "substantial bodily harm to self or others." So every time they did it, it was illegal. The closest I came was to smack the back of one boy's head because he was trying to kiss me when I didn't want him to. I know for a fact that I didn't even hurt him, much less cause "substantial bodily harm." They kept me in the cell for well over the supposed four hours. The boy later told me how sorry he was.

The boy's name was Nick. As a child he had been thrown out of a moving car by his parents and was slightly brain-damaged. He still didn't belong in a mental institution, and I thank God that he was eventually taken in by a foster family. He was only twelve and still very short, but his muscle was beginning to develop and he had beautiful, thick, curly brown hair and brown eyes. He was so handsome already I often wondered what he would look like in a few years.

He was quite infatuated with me at one point and wrote me love letters and poems. He was the only boy there who was neither sickly and puny like Samuel, nor excessively larger and more powerful than me, so I liked to play-wrestle with him sometimes. The outcome would vary. Once I managed to get him into a headlock while we were standing around in front of the school, waiting for the escort. A large, bug-eyed woman stormed out of the building and demanded that I be sent to the cell—not for "assault," but for being "sexually inappropriate." I thought that was really weird.

It was easy enough to get acquainted with the patients on Smith 2 because I was sent to school with them. In time I also got to know the adult patients on Smith 3 and in the other buildings, such as the alcoholic and narcotics building. On any other ward at WSH, "good" patients could sign out for fifteen minutes or so and walk around the grounds. Only the unfortunates on Smith 1 were not allowed this "privilege" because we were the youngest.

The only time a patient on Smith 1 could see the light of day and breathe the outside air without an escort was when they were allowed to sit out on the chain-link-walled porch, which was more accurately called "The Cage." Then, if no one was watching, I could talk to whomever was walking by. The Smith 3 cage was right on top of the Smith 1 cage, and I could talk to the people above me, even though I could not see them. This was how I made friends with a twenty-one-year-old named Kyle. When I saw him in the dining room I thought he was quite handsome and managed to get a note to him saying so.

It was against the rules to pass notes, but it was easy for a patient to do anything they hadn't been caught doing before. (That was why I got Brittany cigarettes. She had been caught bringing some back from pass and was searched more carefully after that. She had to rely on her younger brother to bring her smokes, and he couldn't do that very often. She was very much addicted, and being her friend, I couldn't bear to see her in nicotine fits. I got a smoke for her when I could, and I will never forget standing in line outside the dining room, watched by three staff members, and seeing a perfectly whole cigarette on the ground about three feet away. I casually stooped, reached out and took it, and put it in my pocket. No one knew the difference.)

Anyway, Kyle returned my note. It was very friendly. He told me about himself and said that I was cute and that he wished I was a bit older because then he would ask me out. I was very pleased. That was what gave me away. There should be no such thing as a happy patient at WSH, and the staff was suspicious. The bald farmer told me to bring him what I had in my hand—I hadn't had time to stash the note anywhere. He told me to give it to that woman named Pam, who had cried over me when I first came to WSH, but who didn't seem to like me when I was no longer so helpless.

I did as I was told, even though, as always, I knew they had no right. It was my note, written to me, and no one else's business. Suddenly I remembered that Kyle had signed his name to it, and my hand went instinctively to the note as Pam was reading it. She drew back and snapped, "Don't you snatch things from me! I was going to let this go by with a warning, but now I'm going to report this to the authorities!"

I went over to a dayhall chair next to Jonathan, who had overheard what happened. He said, "Was it from Kyle?"

"Yes."

"Did he sign it?"

"Yes."

"They can send him to jail now, real adult jail, because

he's twenty-one and he was sexually harassing a minor. It'll go on his permanent record too."

"Oh, they can not! It's just a friendly note. He's not interested in me for sex, it says so right on the note!"

Jon shook his head. "That don't matter. They'll send him to jail because he wrote a note to an underage girl. I've seen it happen, just for that."

A bit of nervousness was creeping into me like a cold chill. How could a person be sent to jail for writing a note? But I'd seen stranger things happen—for instance, a person being committed to a mental institution because her parents didn't want her anymore. If only Kyle hadn't signed his name to it, then they would have no proof. Hmm, no proof . . .

Patients were not supposed to go into the little office behind the counter. And we were certainly never supposed to see our charts. I knew that Pam had put the note in my chart. Everyone else was standing in line to go to lunch, so I walked right into the momentarily abandoned office, grabbed my chart, flipped through it until I found the note, and put it in my pocket.

Then I walked out, down the hall, right past the staff and the line of waiting kids, to the bathroom, where I flushed the note down the toilet. I was sad to see it go because I usually kept the notes people gave me, and this would have been a nice one to add to my collection. Then I got back into line with the other patients. In the dining room I saw Kyle and managed to get the message across: "Deny you gave me anything, I flushed it down the toilet." Kyle raised his eyebrows.

When Pam found that the note was gone, she went to interrogate Kyle, and he pretended he had no idea what she was talking about. She then demanded to know what I had done with the note, and I said simply that I had taken it back.

"Take your shoes off, you're going to the cell for stealing!"

Stealing my own stuff. That's what I spent the day in a little white cement cell for, when it was illegal to put me there for any reason other than causing "substantial bodily harm." What was I going to do? Say no? I would have been dragged in and drugged and tied up and my sentence doubled. Call the police and report illegal activity? Ha ha. As if there were any way I could sneak a phone call in the first place, or the police would listen to a mental patient!

There were patients in and out of WSH, although not as often as at Magna Carta. When most patients left, I was usually very upset because they were going to jail, or to a similar institution called a "group home," or back to their abusive families. I even cried when Nick and Derrick, the only kids I knew to be taken in by a foster family, left, because I missed them. But I was glad for them too.

New patients arrived on the ward without warning or explanation. They would just sort of materialize on the dayhall or at school one day. The new patient would sit quietly but apprehensively in one of those farty plastic chairs until one of the other patients took pity on them and attempted to make contact.

My first glimpse of Leo was different from that. He did not quietly accept the shock of discovering that he hadn't just been driven "to the store." When complete strangers were called in to drag him physically onto the ward, Leo struggled. All I really saw was a clump of security guards and other staff members carrying him from the ward entrance on the girls' hall to one of the cells on the boys' hall. Then I saw one of the beds being taken to that cell, and the straps, and a syringe. Two women rolled up a sheet so that everyone on the dayhall could see. We knew it was to be wrapped around the new patient's middle or head because he was "really bad."

Leo's screams echoed and reverberated throughout the entire building. Not even sound escaped those thick cement walls. For a while they were the wordless screams of any tortured animal. Then certain phrases became painfully clear.

"Why don't you kill me? I want to die! I want you to kill me! KILL ME! I WANT TO DIE! I WANT TO DIE!"

Even after all the staff had left him bound hand and foot in the cell, Leo continued his plea. The drugs had little effect; in fact, his words became louder and more desperate with each passing minute.

"I WANT TO KILL MYSELF!! WHY CAN'T I KILL MYSELF?!! I HAVE NO LIFE LEFT! I'M HOLDING ON TO NOTHING! I WANT TO DIE, I WANT IT OVER WITH!! WHO GIVES A FUCK FOR ME OR MY LIFE ANYWAY?!! KILL ME!! I WANT TO DIE!!!"

The patients on the dayhall, only two feet of cement away, were silent. We looked to the staff with anxiety in our eyes. But the staff, seated around the carefully varnished staff table, simply avoided our gaze and attempted to regulate their breathing so that it would not appear as if strapping kids to beds was the only exercise they ever got.

Francis was twelve years old. He was not fat, but very soft and weak. His blue eyes were dilated and staring from whatever drugs he was forced to take. His brown hair stuck out, and his skin was so pale that it was nearly transparent. I don't know what was supposed to be wrong with him; he was certainly not a violent and dangerous criminal sort. I think he was just hyperactive and unwanted, like Tilly had been.

He was never serious, so I never really talked to him. I think that if he had ever tried to be serious, if he had ever thought very hard about what his life consisted of, then he would have gone absolutely mad. So his mind constantly wandered, and his body sought out new movements at every moment to distract himself from the overwhelming horror and hopelessness of his situation. This method of survival kept him from being violent or depressed, but it isolated him from others because he was very annoying.

He jabbered nonstop in a lispy, shrill voice, laughed like a donkey at anything, and gave ear-piercing shrieks when he felt threatened or cheated. I supposed that when he first discovered that his hyperactivity tended to bother the people around him, he used it doubly as a means of revenge on those who were unkind to him. He went around yelling that he was a cat and hissing and clawing in front of people's faces. This power to annoy, since he certainly didn't have the power to do anything else, cheered him up slightly and made him feel more like a person instead of just case number whatever in the corner.

He told me once about his mother. I was sitting on a hill in front of the Smith building with the other kids who were being allowed this privilege under the supervision of a staff member named Barney. (Just as in Magna Carta, where patients could be taken out to the courtyard by any staff member who was nice enough, at WSH patients could be taken out to a patch of grass and mud with a basketball hoop, a swing, and a picnic table.) Francis suddenly ran up to me and began telling me something very breathlessly and excitedly. His loud, squeaky voice hurt my ears, but I listened because I knew I would probably never hear anything else important from him again.

He said, "The social worker found my mother, she found her. She ran away from me when I was a baby. She abandoned me. She came back and took me from the foster homes sometimes and she promised she would never leave me again but she did. She always did. I said don't come back anymore because you will leave me no matter what you say and you're a liar and I hate you. But I didn't mean it. I was glad she came back but then she left again and I haven't seen her in a long time. Nobody knew where she went, the social worker said she would find her and make her pay child support. And she did find her and my mother said that she would not come get me this time. She said she doesn't want me anymore. She won't even talk to me. She doesn't care what happens to me. I hate her. She promised. She is a bitch. And I hate her."

I wanted to ask him where his father was, did he have brothers and sisters, how many foster families had he had, didn't any of them want him now? But Francis ran off as quickly as he had come. He ran over to the other boys who were playing basketball and tried to take the ball. When he was pushed away, he decided he was a cat and he hissed.

I felt sorry for Francis. He was terribly annoying. But I knew that if he had someone to care about him he wouldn't need to be annoying. It wasn't fair.

Then one day Steve was working. I never did like Steve, even though he was one of the staff who would take the kids outside.

Francis was quite hyper that day, and the other patients were complaining about him getting in their faces. Zach drew back his fist, and Francis flinched and screamed. I was playing cards. I paid no attention to Francis's screaming because it was not unusual and because his screams were not real, only attention-getters. I heard Steve call Francis over to the staff table and I could hear him telling Francis to sit down and stop bothering everyone.

I heard Francis hiss, and Steve suddenly began yelling very loudly at him. He told him to stop being such an idiot and said that if he hissed one more time he was going to lock-up. Steve stood up right in front of Francis in a very threatening manner, and Francis backed away, hissing frantically.

I could barely see this happening out of the corner of my eye, and didn't pay much attention to it amid all the other shouting and talking and scuffling. Suddenly Steve threw Francis to the floor, and within seconds there were three people on top of the poor boy. The shackles and chains and straps were hurried into the room. At the sight of them Francis began screaming—real screams. He was squirming on his belly, his face beet red with the effort of breathing with all those people sitting on his back. His arms and legs were flailing until people grabbed them. Then the staff were so crowded around him that I could not really tell what was going on anymore. I heard someone say, "The Side-Rooms are full."

A chair was dragged over next to the pay phone in the corner. Francis was hauled over to it, screaming. His feet were shackled together and his arms were strapped to the chair's arms. A sheet was rolled and wrapped around the back of the chair and his waist. He began shouting that he couldn't breathe, which he obviously could or he wouldn't be able to scream, but the sheet looked very tight indeed. When he was rendered immobile, strapped to that chair like a prisoner awaiting execution by electrocution, the staff stepped away.

When Francis was left in clear view, the other patients grew silent at what was to be seen. Blood drooled thickly over his lip and down his chin to collect in a pool on his shirt. Spots of his blood dotted the floor from beneath the staff table over to the chair in which he was bound like a hostage. As Francis screamed and sobbed, blood mixed with spit sputtered from his mouth. Blood, bright red and pulsing with life. It was doubly shocking splattered violently against the gray, gray room and smeared across Francis's white, white cheek.

Francis's nose was running and tears were flowing down his cheeks. But with his arms strapped tightly to the arms of the chair, there was nothing he could do about it. And no one else cared to remove the evidence of their crime. For what crime had they committed? Making Francis bleed? Even worms bleed.

A woman, I forget who, or if I even knew her, bent down and picked up Francis's glasses, which had fallen to the floor while he was being attacked. They were shattered.

"YOU BROKE MY GLASSES?" Francis shrieked. "HOW WILL I SEE? YOU BROKE MY GLASSES! I'M GOING TO SUE! YOU CAN'T JUST BREAK MY

GLASSES AND GET AWAY WITH IT! SOMEBODY HAS TO PAY FOR THEM! WHO WILL PAY FOR THEM?" He was sobbing and shrieking hysterically. His eyes were enormous with fright and pain and shock. His pale skin was flushed, and the veins in his forehead, neck, and wrists were throbbing.

He writhed and squirmed against his bonds, the leather digging and rubbing against his thin, pale skin. He tried to kick out his feet, but the shackle that bound them together was also attached to the legs of the chair. They had removed his shoes, and the thick leather ankle bands were strapped and locked around his socks. They looked heavy and uncomfortable, clasped by metal locks and attached together with a short chain. He tried to squirm out of his socks and could not. He tried rocking the chair, and discovering that he could do this, gave a hysterical, shrill, joyless laugh.

Steve and the other staff members had settled back down on their cushy chairs around the staff table, just a few feet from the hysterical, bleeding, screaming Francis. They were shuffling their papers as always, and Steve did not even look up as he said, "Francis, if you tip over that chair, no one is going to set you right again."

Francis's screams began again, shrill and real. The ward cleaner appeared on the dayhall with a spray bottle and a cloth. She wiped up Francis's trail of blood as if she were wiping up Kool-Aid. Francis fixed his glazed eyes on her and began to whimper, "Will you wipe this blood off me please? Will you make the bleeding stop? May I have a washrag please? Please?"

The ward cleaner leaned casually over, squirted the blood directly underneath the chair Francis was in, and wiped it up. She did not so much as glance at Francis as she went away.

I wanted to scream. I wanted to cry. I wanted to smash a chair over Steve's face and see how he liked to bleed. Most of all I wanted to wipe Francis's blood and tears away, set him free, and give him a hug. But I did not. I was afraid. So was every other child there. Eventually they went back to playing cards or watching the Nintendo or watching the television with grim expressions. I was nudged, it was my turn, and I turned back to the game in a daze and drew a card.

Francis continued to howl and sob and bleed and writhe over the sounds of rustling papers and shuffling cards and the happy Nintendo song. No one said a word except the staff, who continued to gossip just loud enough to show Francis that he wasn't any big deal.

Francis was still crying and writhing when everyone else went to bed. I came out for a drink of water around midnight, and he was still there. He was perfectly still, like a hunched and subdued statue, staring into space with fatigue and trauma.

The next day Steve called a meeting of every child on the ward and made the following announcement:

"Now, I've been hearing that some people think I hit Francis. I didn't. Francis hit himself. He shouldn't have been struggling against me, and it is all his fault. If I hear anyone accuse me of hitting him again, or if I hear any mention of this incident again, you will go to the Side-Room. I will not stand for this. I do not abuse children."

He glared at each and every one of us in our circle in turn until we looked away.

THIRTEEN

Just a little while after New Year's Day, 1992, another boy arrived on Smith 2. I first saw him as I was walking down the hall at school, past Mr. Hurst's class. I stopped outside the open door—just stopped for no reason whatsoever. What I saw in the next second almost two years ago is more vivid in my mind than any second of yesterday.

Although he was about thirty pounds underweight, he was tall, large-boned, solid. Just as I would have expected, if I had given a thought to what a new boy-patient around here would be built like. And dressed like. He wore a T-shirt, jeans, and a corduroy jacket. He sat with his long legs stretched out easily in front of him, his back and shoulders bent, and his hands wrapped around his elbows—the so-called position of defiance, only I knew it was fear. I couldn't see much of his face, as he kept his head down and let his long blond hair hide him.

There was nothing particularly handsome about him. He was rough. But he gave me the feeling that comes over me in the presence of a puppy or a small child. I wanted to reach out to him, to touch him, but of course that was impossible, and I walked on.

In his first month at WSH, that boy, Joseph, had a girlfriend, but he picked on me constantly. And I teased him right back. What else do a couple of kids that like each other do? Joe was an awfully big kid, though, and a hell of a lot stronger than me. Sometimes he played too rough, and I would get quite desperate.

One evening, when all the good little mental patients on Smith 1 and 2 were taken to the gym to play basketball, Joe discovered he could "palm" my head. I kept pushing him away rather half-heartedly, but he was quite intrigued by how small I was compared with him, so he kept digging his thumb and forefinger into my temples until I blew a fuse. I began to hit him as hard as I could—which wasn't hard at all. I knew I couldn't hurt him, so I had to look as scary and as insanely furious as I could to be taken seriously.

"God damn you, you asshole, you bastard! You leave me the fuck alone, do you hear me?!" I screamed. He drew back, surprised. I took a few steps closer to him to drive him further away, and laid a couple of whole-hearted but completely harmless slaps on his chest and the side of his arm. He flinched, not because it hurt but because he was caught off guard, as I had hoped.

When he stood well enough away from me, and I had spent all my energy trying to look fierce, we stood off and stared at each other. It was then that I noticed two slender scratches up the inside of his forearm. In one of them a bit of blood was welling. My eyes grew wide with horror, and I clapped my hand over my mouth. Never in my life had I bruised or drawn blood on anyone, not even my brother. I hadn't meant to this time either; my nails had just caught him somehow.

Joseph followed my gaze to his arm. He obviously had not even felt such tiny scratches. My eyes traveled back up to his, and then I began to cry. Joseph's forehead wrinkled with confusion that I would cry over such a little thing. He did not know what to do.

I told him I was very sorry to scratch him, and he said he hadn't meant to bother me so much and would I please stop crying. The staff at the gym did not turn me in to be put in the Side-Room, and in fact felt rather sorry for me as I continued to cry. Back on Smith 1, I asked for scissors and a file (you weren't allowed to keep your own, of course) and I cut my nails to the quick. I could not push away the picture of six-foot two-inch Joseph, his large, heavy skeleton strung with sinewy muscle and strength beyond what I could imagine, cowering against the wall as I, eleven inches shorter, fifty pounds lighter, and infinitely less powerful than he, hit him with my relatively harmless hands.

I knew I could never hurt him like that again. Why? Because I loved him more than I had ever loved anything in my life.

By Valentine's Day, Joe's girlfriend had long since been gone from WSH. He put his arms around me and asked me if I would be his girlfriend. I had never felt anything like his fingers against my ribcage. It didn't make me feel afraid, or dirty, or anything like I had felt when Zach and all the other boys had touched me. His hands were so warm, and I could feel that warmth spread through my cold, tense body and soothe it. I grew hotter and hotter until I would have fainted, except I could not take my eyes off his. The answer was yes, yes, yes! But I told him I would think about it. I wanted to see just how serious he was. I never knew for sure what he felt for me, but I felt too strongly for him to keep from saying yes a few days later.

March marked the sixth month of my stay at Wilson State Hospital. I was in pretty bad shape by then.

Without any physical exercise, I was terribly weak, and my muscles twitched often to be moved and stretched. My heart and lungs were so easily strained that sometimes just standing up too quickly gave me palpitations and made me short of breath. I was always tense, so very miserably tense from the noise and confusion all around me and my keepers' eyes on me. It exhausted me; I was always weary.

My mind did not get much strengthening either. School was a joke. The teachers knew it; that's why they turned on dull filmstrips and slept. They were just baby-sitting us loonies for the ward staff. In the beginning I tried to keep my mind sharp on my own, but in the first place there wasn't much material to work with. I was cut off from news of the rest of the world—there were no newspapers or anything. The one magazine subscription someone ever so kindly donated to Smith 1 was *Soybean Journal*. There were no books, paper for drawing and writing was scarce, and anyway, I found no source of inspiration in that place. My ability to concentrate dwindled, and my precious clipboard with my writings on it gathered dust.

Six months hardly seems like a long time anymore. Six months just fly by in a normal or happy life. But six months in a state hospital might as well be six years. Six months of waking at 5:00 A.M., taking a shower in fifteen minutes, sitting on the dayhall, eating, sitting at school, eating, sitting at school some more, sitting on the dayhall, eating, sleeping in my cell, waking at 5:00 A.M., showering, sitting, eating, sitting, sitting, sitting . . .

All the while the staff was yelling, insulting. The kids were fidgeting, arguing, bored out of their fucking skulls, but if they moved around too much or were too loud they were told to go to the cell. And a loud, violent scene would usually follow. It was torture. Pure, cruel torture in a cold, white cement mental institution to top off the years of torture I had suffered from my family.

I learned not even to look at clocks. It can drive a person mad to stare at a second hand, straining to catch every little movement of it, begging it silently to hurry up, and knowing that even if it were spinning around the clock face it wouldn't make anything good, or even just different, happen to you.

The staff always insisted that we watch the clock, that it was our "responsibility" to get where we were going on time. Anyone who remained on the ward when they were supposed to be at breakfast or school or somewhere else would be dragged directly to the Side-Room for the duration of the time of the "activity" that it was their "responsibility" to go to.

I would like to point out once again that this action was entirely illegal. I don't know how it was explained in patient charts that not wanting to go to breakfast or school, or anywhere else for that matter, equals substantial bodily harm to someone. But apparently it was, as the papers were filled out, Dr. Bizaldo signed them, and a child was imprisoned time and time again with no regard for the law or the child's well-being.

Once in lock-up, time becomes slightly important, as I and every other kid wanted to know how long until our release from the sanity-stripping cell. Knowing this is impossible, however, since watches are taken, along with shoes, belts, the contents of pockets, hair fasteners, and anything else "dangerous."

One day Anita, that nasty woman who sent me to Time Out for talking to her, dragged a chair over to one wall and stood on it. All the bored child-patients stared at her as she reached up and removed the wall clock from the wall. She got down with the clock, dragged the chair over to the opposite wall, stood on it again, and fastened the clock in its new position. Having never seen any staff member take any interest in the arrangement of the patients' space, everyone was quite surprised.

Anita shooed away the children who had gathered around her chair. In answer to their question about why she had moved the clock, she responded simply, "Patients in the Side-Room could see it on the other wall." The staff was tired of hearing patients complain and yell from behind steel doors when they knew they were being held much longer than their sentence called for.

My one consolation, for a time, was Joseph. When I saw him, I did not see the stark walls and locks and bars around us. Thoughts of him crowded out the memories of my frightening past, the worry about my bleak future. I felt stronger when I was near him. I felt something that was almost completely foreign to me—joy.

If we had had the chance to get close to each other, would we have been able to trust each other, even though everyone we had ever trusted had stabbed us in the back? If we had had time to spend together, would we have found happiness amid the sea of misery we both drifted aimlessly in? I don't know. I don't know what it would have been like to go to a movie with him and eat out of the same popcorn cup. I don't know what it would have been like to dress up and go to a school dance with him, feel his body close to mine song after song. I don't know what it would have been like to sit under a tree and talk, just talk. These things are forbidden to those deemed "insane."

If Joseph and I were caught touching each other we would be sent to the cell. We had no time to talk; we had to go where we were "supposed" to, or we would be sent to the cell. If any staff member suspected we were getting "too friendly," it could be arranged that the two of us would never lay eyes on each other again. How could we have developed any sort of a relationship in sporadic periods of a few seconds while we stood in terror of being caught together? How were we supposed to get to know each other, learn to trust each other, bond together, feel secure with each other?

If anyone has the answer to that, it certainly isn't me.

My parents' messy divorce was not yet finalized, so both of them still visited me. My father always brought trading cards, and things I wanted to eat so badly that I chewed my pillow at night when I dreamed of them. Then he nodded off to sleep while I babbled in the visitors' room. My mother brought me nothing but her new fantasies of a perfect little household in which she, the poor, abused, ill, single mother "kept us together" ever so bravely and admirably.

In time I was completely caught up in this fantasy myself. It all made sense then: my mother had abused me merely because she was stressed out from being abused by my father. Without him, she would be a new person. Even though she was too sick to work, she would apply for government housing and food stamps. Everything would be different. At last I had a chance at happiness.

I offered to go to court and tell the judge how my father had abused me. I hoped it would speed up the trial so that I could go home with my mother as soon as possible. But my mother told me I didn't need to "stress myself" by going to court. The fact that I had been abused, which I thought was very important, never came up in my parents' divorce proceedings. Of course, neither of my parents wanted it to come out in public that they themselves had abused me, but neither did they want to admit that they had each allowed the other to abuse me, too. They had a silent pact with each other about continuing to cover up what had been done to me. My mother eventually won custody of my brother and me solely because of what she said my father did to her, and because she showed the judge my father's enormous and expensive pornography collection.

My mother went to the state welfare office and "proved," with reports from Heather Williams from Family Matters, Inc., Dr. Kern from Kid Counsel, Dr. Limband from Magna Carta, and Marjory Nelson from the state child protection service (and of course the fact that I was currently residing in a state institution), that I was "mentally disabled." With such a label placed on me, my mother received a special monthly welfare check for my "care."

So after all her months of talk of being stronger without her husband and able to "handle" me, after she had even secured a steady income for herself because of my "mental illness," imagine my indescribable shock when my mother came onto the ward one day and announced that she was going to give me to the state.

Lorri thought my being in state custody was a good idea because then she would have a say in where I would go.

A combination of getting to know me over the past six months, and getting to know my mother, had led Lorri to believe that I would not be much happier with my mother than I was at WSH. She wanted me to go to a "therapeutic" foster home, the home of a child psychologist who was "trained" to work with abused children. I had come to severely mistrust the words "therapeutic," "child psychologist," and "trained." But "foster home" certainly had a better connotation than "loony bin."

Lorri sent all of my records to the local district attorney's office for a summary to be made, and a court date was set. The judge would be presented with a petition that my parents and I had signed, stating the reason I needed to be taken into state custody. The judge would then sign some paper or other making me an official ward of the state.

Lorri made it all sound so easy. In the three weeks that followed my mother's announcement, my spirits were lifted from bitter betrayal and disappointment to new hope. I was going to be saved for sure this time! I pictured the house I would be going to. A nice house perhaps, like Wanda at Magna Carta had described almost a year before, with airy curtains and a comfy bed. I could have my china, my beautiful china, and my guinea pig. Lord, how I missed my sweet little friend Opie. I could go to a new school, and maybe the kids would like me there. Maybe I would be allowed to have friends. Maybe I would get healthy again. Maybe, just maybe, my foster parent would be nice, someone to talk to. I swore to myself that I would do anything the person who took me in and treated me like a human being wanted me to.

At last the court date arrived. I had assured Lorri that I would sign the petition, and of course my mother would, and I had convinced my father to do the same, instead of arguing for custody of me himself.

My mother called Lorri at the very last minute to say that she would not take me to the courthouse because she "refused to be responsible for my behavior there." So I was

driven in a state security transport to the courthouse, where
I found my mother standing by the courtroom door. She
told me that my grandmother and my father were inside,
and that since she had not seen my father since the divorce
hearings she was scared to go in.

I was fourteen, standing for the first time in my life in
court, waiting for my life to be decided for me, and she
wanted me to support *her*. Whatever was she going to do
with herself after she had officially given me away?

As I was standing by her, waiting, I noticed a man in
nice slacks and a tie pacing angrily down the hall. From
his ravings I realized he was furious because the judge had
not sentenced his daughter to jail. She stayed out too late
and did God knows what with God knows whom, and he
just refused to take any responsibility for her actions.

*Oh, she stays out late. What a little criminal. She should be shot,
yes. And that man pacing and screaming and shaking his fist and
demanding that his daughter go to jail is just fine, yes. Poor man. Of
course his children aren't his responsibility.*

I was even more angry when I saw this man's daughter.
She didn't look even as old as me. She was thin and pale
and hunched over in submission. Her bangs half-covered
her sad face. The man began yelling insults and bad things
at her as a woman that I guessed was his wife tried to
calm him. She was dressed nicely, in a ruffly flowered
shirt and business skirt with heels. But her face was wea-
ried and pained. Both the woman and the girl looked so
hurt and subdued and pitiful that I wondered if this man
beat them in addition to this obvious emotional abuse he
inflicted on them.

He was raving now, about what the neighbors would
think, and how he was going to disown the damn girl if
she didn't shape up. I leaned toward my mother and said
loudly, "I wonder what neighbors think of grown men who
throw fits and care more about what the neighbors think
than their family's feelings."

The man whirled around and stared at me furiously. I said, even louder, "I think *he* oughta go to jail, Mom." The man grabbed his jacket off a chair and yanked it over his shoulder and began striding toward me, only he wasn't looking at me anymore.

I said, "I think anybody who doesn't give a shit about their own kids shouldn't have any, and if they do they oughta go to jail."

My mom elbowed me, whispering, "Shut up, Tiffany!"

But I couldn't help it anymore. "Anybody that wants their own flesh and blood to go to jail oughta go themselves, they don't deserve kids, they don't deserve them!"

The man came closer.

"Shut up, Tiffany!"

"What does a kid do wrong? Huh? What does a kid do that's so wrong that their parents didn't teach 'em? That man oughta look at himself, before he goes around cussin' an innocent kid who doesn't know any better than what he taught her!"

The man passed me in a silent rage and went out the door. His wife followed, ignoring her daughter, and the girl slunk out behind. She eyed me in confusion.

When they were all gone my mother said, "Good Lord, Tiffany, I thought that man was going to hit you!"

To which I responded crossly, "He can't hit me, I'm not his own kid."

After half an hour or so, a lady poked her head out of a doorway and asked if I was Tiffany Blake. I said yes, and she told me to come with her.

In a very small room with one glass wall and a table, she told me she was my lawyer. I was rather pleased at the idea of having my very own lawyer, and I smiled at her. She did not smile back. She simply set a piece of paper in front of me, told me it was the petition, and handed me a pen. After a page of my family's addresses and other legal stuff, the thing read as follows:

This petition is based on the following facts:

The County Child Protection Unit first became aware of this situation in April, 1991. On May 6, 1991, Tiffany had been admitted to the Magna Carta Medical Center's Psychiatric Unit, having made a threat to her mother. Upon Tiffany's release from the hospital reports were made of Tiffany's behavior and her parents were afraid of her and for her.

In-home services throught [sic] Family Matters, Inc. were initiated on August 14, 1991, to attempt to assess the situation and keep Tiffany in the home. Tiffany has episodes of such high anxiety that she dissociates, had difficulty remembering, and her ability to concentrate is very poor. Tiffany repeatedly makes accusations of physical and emotional abuse such as drawing bruises on herself with makeup and threatening her brother by putting a belt or rope around his neck. While in-home services were involved numerous crises took place. Recommendations from the assessent [sic] were that Tiffany be placed in a long-term treatment facility to address her severe psychological issues.

On October 15, 1991, Tiffany was placed at Wilson State Hospital wehre [sic] she has received treatment for her diagnosis of Dissociative Disorder. Theri [sic] reports show Tiffany to have benefited from being in the safe, structure [sic], therapeutic environment. At the time of admission, Tiffany was unable to make eye contact and when sitting down or walking her arms would be outstretched. At this time, due to unstable environment [meaning the divorce alone] Wilson is recommending out of home placement.

As I read those words I could see my hands turn as white as the paper they were holding. I was not in the least prepared to look for the first time at even a mere *summary* of the things that had been said and written about me behind my back since before I had even been committed to Magna Carta nearly a year ago. I was horrified, not merely because the petition consisted of lies and misrepresentations, but because of the grammatical errors and typos. It had obviously been whipped out by someone who did hundreds of the things and never really stopped to look at a single one of them.

Not one person involved in my case had ever given me much thought. Was everything said about me a hundred percent true? What was I really like in person? Not one person had ever asked *me* about me. My family had said some things to some "professional." Without stopping to question those things, the "professional" had said I sounded like I had "severe psychological issues." Some other "professional" had read what the first "professional" had said and, without questioning the basis for that first opinion, added his to it, a third one came along, and so on, until—presto! My life was reduced to the meager status of mental patient, and I had never had the slightest idea why until that moment. Oh, why had no one told me sooner? I could have cleared up those awful lies! Or even if no one believed me, they would at least have *heard* a contrary opinion, they would have had to think about my story just a little. They would have had to think about my story *just a little* before deciding whether it was a hundred percent true.

The worst part of that petition was the last part, where someone at WSH claimed that WSH had helped me out of the state of shock I had fallen into when I had first been left there. They forgot to mention that WSH had been the actual cause of that shock. And even if WSH hadn't caused it, the so-called "safe, structure, therapeutic environment" at WSH certainly did nothing to help it. Daniel, the first patient who spoke to me, was the only thing that saved me. I began to tremble when I realized that even if Lorri had not actually written that last paragraph, she had let it slide. She knew it was a lie, an insidious lie geared not only to make me look bad, but to make a place of abject misery seem like a good place to send troubled children.

I sat for a moment without breathing. I felt as though I had been thrown to the ground and kicked in the stomach several times. My lawyer stared at me impatiently.

"What?" I whispered, stunned nearly out of my wits.

"Well, are you going to sign it or aren't you?"

"Sign it!" I gasped. I stared up pleadingly into the eyes of my lawyer, but she gave me a look that said she believed every word of that petition and didn't have time to deal with claims of innocence from the little delinquents she deals with every day.

"Well, what's wrong with it?" she demanded impatiently.

"Everything!" I wailed. "None of it is true! Not a word!"

"So are you refusing to sign it?"

"I can't. It's a lie."

"Look, do you like it at the state hospital?" My lawyer was getting upset now. "All you have to do is sign here, and you can go to a nice foster home. Now isn't that what you want?"

I just stared at her in silence. She was a stranger, a busy stranger, she didn't know me, didn't have time for me. I wondered if she could help me even if she understood. My lips were still trembling, but I wasn't quite crying. I said as clearly as I could, "If I said all this was true, if I agreed that I tried to kill people and stuff like that, then they'd be crazy to send me to a foster home."

"You're just making this harder on yourself."

Then I burst into miserable tears.

"All right," my lawyer said. "What about this don't you like?"

"Everyyy-thiiing!" I sobbed.

"Now calm yourself, and we'll go through this line by line."

"Well, I never threatened my mother, and what on earth does that stupid quote about her being 'afraid of me and for me' have to do with anything? It isn't true anyway, she's never been afraid of me or for me. And I never tried to kill my brother and I never drew any bruises on myself with makeup and I do not have *severe* psychological issues . . ."

My lawyer cut me off with a sharp sigh. She said, "We don't have time to change every word. I'll be right back."

And she was gone. I was alone. I was never so alone in all my life. I was shaking very hard and fighting the overwhelming feeling that I was going to faint. Tears spilled down my cheeks and onto my arms, which were wrapped around my body. This was supposed to be the day I was saved!

My lawyer reappeared in a few minutes with my mother. I choked back my tears so as not to cry in front of that hateful creature who apparently gained some sort of satisfaction from making me suffer. The lawyer said, "Your mom doesn't agree with some of this petition either."

My mother said angrily to the lawyer, "I never said Tiffany threatened me! It's those people at Magna Carta that said that! They're trying to make me look like the bad guy in all this!"

My mother would have thought the petition was fine if she could have been sure I would never get to see it and know she was behind it. Suddenly I knew that was why she had refused to bring me here, hoping I wouldn't be able to come at all.

"All right, all right!" My lawyer sighed again. A man stuck his head into the room and said, "They're ready for you." My lawyer ushered my mother and me into the courtroom. She tried to cross out and rearrange what my mother told her to in the few minutes before the judge showed up, but finally shouted, "You can't cross everything out! You don't have anything left! You don't have a case!"

I have never seen a government official as upset as that

lawyer was. She expected the "criminal" or "crazy" children she "represented" to protest the accusations against them. But how confusing it must have been for her to have my spineless mother suddenly deny those accusations, too.

Then the judge came in. He was a little old man with a hard, pinched face and a gray goatee. He was read the petition and was told that everyone wanted to change everything. He said crossly and simply, "What? Well, then come back when you have a case together and don't waste any more of my time."

And he walked out. And that was all.

FOURTEEN

The lawyer had stated that there was no case. Even the judge had stated that there was no case. There was no case against me if the things in that petition were lies. It was now pretty obvious that those things must be lies, since the woman who had started them was now denying them. But case against me or no case against me, I was driven back to Wilson State Hospital. The ward staff escorted me to the school, where the other children were, as usual.

I saw Joseph in the hall. I ran to him and clutched him with one hand, waving the copy of the petition that had been given to me in the other.

"Oh, Joe!" I burst into tears again. "Look what they said about me! They said I tried to kill my brother, they said I faked my abuse with makeup! It's lies, all lies! I wouldn't sign it, I just couldn't sign it! It was my one ticket out of here, but I couldn't do it, and now what will I do? What will I do?"

He just looked at me rather blankly. I don't think he could understand a word I said through my blubbering. And he didn't know what to do. It was obvious from the look in his eyes that he was sorry for me, but he hadn't the slightest idea what to do.

I was so shaken, I was so low in self-esteem, that I took Joe's silence to mean that he didn't care, that he saw nothing about the petition to disagree with. I ran away, cut to the quick.

Lorri was no help either. She called me into her office

the next day and made it clear she was upset that I had not signed the petition after telling her I would. I told her I wouldn't have even considered signing it if I had known what it said. I told her I had thought that a Child in Need of Care petition would explain that a parent was not capable of caring for a child because the parent was deficient in some way. It had never occurred to me that something could be said to be so wrong with a child that a perfectly normal parent was justified in getting rid of it. I told Lorri I couldn't sign a paper to that effect, especially when the things that were supposed to be so wrong with me weren't even true.

Lorri said it shouldn't make any difference to me what the petition said, what official reason was given for my being taken into state custody, as long as I ended up in state custody somehow so she could put me in a foster home. She said that a petition could not be filed again for another six months, and that then it would be no different.

"Will you refuse again after another six months in this place? Or do you want to wait an entire year from now? Surely you can swallow your pride to save your sanity!"

"Maybe I could, after long enough, confess to lies about myself to save my sanity. But what about this last paragraph? The advertisement for this shithole place? About how the *structure* and the *therapeutic* environment somehow benefited me? If I say that this place did anything but torment me, then other parents will have an excuse to leave their unwanted children here, and I cannot do that. In four years, on my eighteenth birthday, I know I will have to be released as an adult unless someone can prove in court that I'm crazy, and apparently they can't. I would rather wait all that time, I would rather risk my sanity, than walk out of here now and know that I had some part in luring more innocent children here to be tortured for money!"

As spring came again, I began to ache more strongly than I had ever imagined it possible to ache for fresh aii and trees and sun. WSH was always bragging about its acres of grassy grounds with hills and trees and flowers. Indeed, these things are quite wonderful for people, suffering or otherwise, with access to them. As I mentioned before, older patients who were deemed "deserving" could sign out for fifteen minutes, but for me and the others on Smith 1, the great outdoors might just as well have been a photograph pasted behind the thick steel bars.

There was a little person-sized niche in the wall down the hall from my cubicle. There rancid trays were stored sometimes, and there was also, for some obscure reason, a full-length mirror. One day, after what seemed like decades since the ill-fated petition, I passed by that mirror and for some reason noticed my reflection. I stopped short and stared.

It showed. It showed as plain as the nose on my face.

It hadn't come all at once, like a bruise, but it was there now, plain to anyone who wasn't blind. Anyone who looked at me and thought I lived the life of a carefree fourteen-year-old American girl was kidding themselves.

The horribly salty food and lack of exercise had caused poor circulation and swelling. I had gained only a few pounds in the last few months, but I had gone up five clothing sizes, and my jeans pinched my swollen stomach. My cheekbones were invisible, and even my pretty, slender fingers were puffy. My hair was dry, dull, and lifeless. My unsunned skin had a shockingly sallow tone. It sagged in places like an old woman's. Despite the swelling, I was still small and very frail-looking. I stood always with my shoulders rounded in submission, my spine slumped, and my head slightly down. I was out of place, afraid to take up space and never sure where to put my useless hands. The muscles across my face were tense, and the skin under my eyes, stretched. My striking yellow-and-green eyes could not hide what I had seen and how it had affected me. They were hungry. They were pleading.

Signs of suffering are visible in my first-grade school pictures, but it took many years for every feature of my body to be touched. How could I have come to this obviously miserable state without ever being helped? I guessed that my looking like such total shit was blamed, like everything else, on my being "crazy," on that vague little "chemical imbalance" in my head. But I knew that if I were crazy, like Angela at Magna Carta, I would have looked good.

I had wanted to be crazy. I had plumbed the depths of my brain for craziness and tried to let it take over my mind, but it didn't work. I would have come out of my shock sooner or later even if Daniel, that boy who first talked to me, hadn't given me a reason to. I just couldn't totally shut out the things that went on around me, and the way they hurt me. I needed my sanity to fight them. I needed something else besides total immersion in a fantasy world to ease my pain before I became too weak, like my poor Uncle Bob, to walk out into the world alone when I was eighteen.

The front door to the entire Smith building was always unlocked, and sometimes the ward doors were left open for air. Instinctively I began walking down the hall toward the ward door, just walking.

"Hey!" The woman at the staff table called after me. I kept walking. I was going to take a walk. Human beings need walks to be healthy. I hadn't had one damn simple walk since my parents had decided I was too crazy to go out nearly three years before.

Anita was coming in the front door to start her shift. "Where do you think you're going?" was her snotty demand. I did not look at her long, pinched, upside-down-U-lipped face, with those little round snake eyes and those tight little gray rolls on her tiny head. I could not bear the sight of her that day.

"Fuck you, bitch," was all I said.

And she was so stunned, because I had never said anything like that to her, and because I looked so deadly determined, instead of desperate and easily subdued, that she let me pass.

"Do what you like! I'll send security after you for this!"

It had always been so immensely heavy, that door to the world, but it swung away at my touch that day. As I stepped out on the front porch, the sunlight searing my long-imprisoned eyes, all my feelings of rage, defiance, and confinement left me as if someone had pulled a plug out of the bottom of my foot. There was only relief left. Relief and the slightest stirrings of joy. I could not remember the last time that I had stepped out of a building, unescorted and of my own free will.

I held out my arms, as I had dreamed of doing for so long, and felt the warm sun on my goosebump-covered, sickly flesh. I stepped forward as if in a daze, my face drawing into its nearly forgotten smile. I kept walking, faster now.

In the back of my mind there was fear. It was easy enough to walk out like this, but they would come after me, like Anita said. Could I hide? Could I run? Where would I run to? I had nowhere to go, no one to run to. Would they touch me and grab me? They had better not. Would I fight? How much damage could I do before they overpowered me? But I did not want to think of those things; they were trivial compared with enjoying the few precious moments of freedom I had left.

It was a beautiful day. I walked quickly down the hill that we were never allowed to go near. I passed Leo, the boy who had screamed endlessly to be killed, sitting at a picnic table with his visiting mother. We had become close friends, Leo and I. And even his mother, who visited him regularly, seemed to have developed quite a liking for me in the few moments we had spoken.

"Hey, where you goin', Crazy Girl?" Leo wanted to know. There was concern on his face and his mother's. I am sure I must have been a strange sight, stumbling along, frantically absorbing as much of the good in this outdoor world as possible before I was locked away again. I turned my head around to look at them while my feet kept moving forward, and I beamed at them both, responding with near-hysterical joy, "I'm taking a walk!"

How beautiful it was to hear those words roll so casually off my tongue! "I'm going for a walk, a walk!" I said again, more to myself than to Leo and his mother. They shook their heads as I passed them. They knew the price I must pay for a simple walk.

I walked to the stone wall at the end of the hill and climbed up on it. The wall was built against the road that wound slowly through the grounds and led out to the highway. I walked along the top of the wall until I was out of sight of everyone, then sat down on it to rest. The ground on the other side of the wall had sunk farther and farther below the top of the wall as I walked along. I stared down at the rolling land far beneath me. It was beautiful!

I picked up some loose stones and squeezed them, then rubbed them against my bare arms to feel their texture. I thought, sitting there on the wall, that I would rather die than be taken back into that institution.

I could cut my wrists with these stones, or hurl myself off this wall onto the rocky ground below . . .

No. Death would take me away from the enjoyable things in this life, the same as mental institutions do.

I decided to enjoy every minute of my short freedom, right up to the instant when I would be captured and the door of the cell once again slammed behind me. I stood up and breathed deeply again. I listened to the birds chirping and the stillness of the air, and I clutched those two stones in my two fists as I continued on down the rock wall. Soon I could see the gate at the end of the road. It was not guarded, it was just a little gate like a park has.

I walked a little faster. I heard a car grinding slowly up the gravel road behind me. I knew what it wanted. I kept walking and clutching my stones. My heart beat faster.

The gate was close now. I could go by it, but the car couldn't! I could run! But I knew they would get out of the car and chase me, and I could not bear to be touched by those people. I was so weak and flabby and swollen that I knew I would look pretty stupid trying to run, so I stopped still, my heart pounding so hard I wondered if it was possible for it to dislocate itself or something.

The car stopped and a woman stepped out, a woman I didn't know. Thank God it was a woman I did not know instead of someone I had grown to hate! She was wearing a blue security uniform. She was smaller than me, and looked at least thirty but not very old yet, with black hair and browned skin. She walked calmly to me and said quietly, "Tiffany?"

It occurred to me that hardly anyone called me Tiffany anymore. To the other patients I was affectionately know as "Crazy Girl," and to the staff I was just "Cut that out before I lock you up." This woman had been told my name and used it, not as Dr. Limband and all those other people had, but as if maybe those crazy things she was sent after were at least deserving of human names. I wondered what else she had been told about me.

Nothing extravagant, I guessed, because she didn't seem the least bit alarmed. Neither did the man who was leaning casually out the open window of the security car. The woman told me politely to get in the car. I stared at the gate only a few steps away—freedom, only a few steps away. But I knelt ever so slowly, and even more slowly I opened my hands to place my rocks gently on the wall. The woman leaned over. "What are you—oh, you have little rocks."

She opened the back door and I climbed into the back seat, careful not to look at her. I wondered with a little embarrassment what she thought of me, a mental patient, carrying around a bunch of rocks. She went around to the other side of the car and sat next to me. It was obvious she figured I was just a "harmless crazy." It made me angry. If she thought I was so harmless, how could she stand to see me imprisoned among the cruelties she must have witnessed firsthand? How could she take me back to hell so calmly? I wished I could make it hard for her to take me back, but I knew that even the most polite people can get violent when you don't do what they want.

I stared at the gate as we pulled away. I stared at my stones on the wall. I stared at the trees as we began to whiz past them, the sky, the grass, the hills. I had walked a good way. Only a few steps more . . . What if I had found a house and told the people in it my story? Surely they would have helped me. But why? Why would they believe me? Don't all mental hospital escapees say they're not crazy? That they were committed wrongly and mistreated terribly?

Then suddenly I wondered with horror exactly how many of them must be telling the truth, too.

The Smith building loomed before me—the caged side porches, the barred windows, the crumbling brick and cement, the cracking paint and pigeon droppings all over. I could smell it from inside the car. I felt my heart sealing off, silencing the revulsion and hatred I could do nothing about. My body felt numb and weak and shaky. I wondered if I was going to pass out. Then I realized that I never did pass out anymore, because even the deepest realm of my subconscious struggled as best it could to keep anyone at WSH from touching me.

I paused as I was walking up to the cage and stared up at the immense building of doom, trembling. I was pulled forward by the security woman as she got out her keys. Her touch was electric and horrible, but I stifled my desire to scream and run away. Down the hall, Anita was holding open a steel cell door for me with a smug look on her hideous face. I stifled my hatred for her. I took off my shoes and stepped inside the cell. Anita peered through the chicken-wire-embedded window to tell me how very stupid I was to go AWOL.

Coming from the fresh air straight into a small cubicle bulging with the stench of staleness, stuffiness, and age-old human waste was overwhelming. I was glad my stomach was empty, because I would have thrown up if there had been anything in it. I wanted to lie down, but the poisonous odor was concentrated in the plastic mat. It was so dark that my eyes took a long time to adjust. I kept seeing those nice rainbow colors that people see when they go suddenly from brightness to darkness.

I slid down against the wall, conscious of, but too tired to care about, the dried snot on the cement walls that must be smearing against my back. I tried to pretend that the sun was on my arms again, but I was cold and shivering. When the room came into focus, it was so small, so bare, so terrible that again I had to choke back the desire to scream. Those thick, heavy, dirty white walls loomed above my head, unchanging, unmoving, unfeeling, cold.

In the reinforced, wire-embedded, six-by-six-inch window of the scratched, dented blue steel door, I saw Anita's face staring at me with cold satisfaction. I glared at her. She surveyed my small form huddled against the wall of the cement cell behind that door, and she smirked. "Don't go to sleep now," I heard her say before she went on back to her "business."

It was a rule that you were not to sleep at any time except between the time you were supposed to go to bed and five in the morning. This rule especially applied to patients in the Side-Room. If you are sleeping, you are escaping a bit of your punishment, you are not receiving the full subduing effect that being confined in a dirty room for hours upon endless hours can bring. It is more "therapeutic" to fully inhale the aroma of the cell, to stare without relief at your four prison walls, your mind constantly open and awake with nothing to occupy it but the inescapable frenzy induced by confinement and solitude.

Minutes passed. Hours. I did not move. I sat completely motionless and numb. The long, black, fingerlike shadows of the bars and wires on the window crawled slowly across the floor and my body as the sun descended behind a horizon I could not see from the cell. I was given a tray that

I did not touch. In the darkened cell, my senses began to play tricks on me. The walls seemed to waver like a mirage, and my distorted image in the round mirror in the corner seemed to be moving when I wasn't. I was trembling and burning with stress-induced fever.

I was allowed to brush my teeth and go to the bathroom while a woman watched me. I was told to lie down on the mattress and sleep. I asked without tone in my soft, far-away voice if I might have the stuffed bear that I never slept without. One woman said she would ask the doctor. She took her sweet time; I could hear her gossiping with some other staff. An hour or so later she returned to tell me that it was against procedure and not part of my "treatment plan" to have my bear.

Finally the tears that I had struggled to keep inside poured down my cheeks. "Damn it," I sobbed.

The woman's eyes lit up with indignation, and she pinched her mustached mouth angrily. How dare I say a swear word to her! She slammed the steel door, which makes a big enough bang to comfort any cranky two-year-old. She announced loudly to the people around the staff table, "That's just the way she is, she wants everybody to think she's such a nice person, poor, innocent little kid, but when you don't give her what she wants then you see her true nature, mmm-hmm."

I sobbed and sobbed endlessly in the dark cell, the tears and snot rolling down my face and soaking my arms and clothes. I had no Kleenex, of course. I just cried myself dry.

I thought of how that woman would run and grab my chart and scribble in it that I had said a "bad" word because I didn't get my bear. Anyone who read that statement and did not know the circumstances surrounding the incident might be led to believe that I had lost my cool for insignificant reasons. The fact that it was written in a patient chart at a mental institution would lead readers to believe that I not only lost my cool for insignificant reasons, like

most people do now and then, but that it was another indication of my "insanity."

The ball had been rolling too long to stop it now. Account after account of my "insanity" would continue to pile
up, because long ago someone had claimed that I was insane, and everyone after that looked at me through the
lens of that word. Ordinary things that were ignored when
they came from "ordinary" people suddenly held new sig-
nificance when they came from me. I was helpless in the
face of the label "insane." Even when it had been discovered
in court that there was no case against me, the label stuck.

My mother had said all sorts of terrible things about me
long before I was thirteen. She had believed I was insane
since I was about six. But when she spoke words to that
effect, they only floated into the listener's ear. Even I, the
person to whom such words mattered most, cannot remember them specifically. I cannot search my mind and recount
at this moment every negative thing my mother ever said
about me. The specifics have long been forgotten, and this
is as it should be. If the horrible things my mother said
about me had not been written down, then they would
have been forgotten, even by me in time, and the damage
they caused would have healed.

But they were written down. Someone started to write
them down and collect them when I was about thirteen.
The mere fact that my mother's words were written down,
especially by a "professional," somehow made them heav-
ier. The written word—impersonal, unemotional, staring
black letters on white paper—is not easily contradicted,
nor is it ever forgotten. The words stay there, never chang-
ing from the time they are written, ready to be read again
and again, ready to convince another person that I am insane, ready to inflict damage, not just once like spoken
words, but over and over.

The words written about me in my two-thousand-page
"psychiatric record" will haunt me until the end of my days.
Even after I am dead they will lay on shelves in various

places for anyone to pick up, and what difference will it make that years ago in a courtroom it was realized that they weren't necessarily based on fact?

I spent more than thirty hours in a cell for walking out of a mental institution, a mental institution I was placed in and kept in because of words. Whoever said "Sticks and stones will break my bones, but words will never hurt me" never had it written about them that they were insane.

FIFTEEN

My parents' divorce was finalized in April of 1992. My mother cleaned up, winning the house and the car. My father was ordered to pay off all the family's debts and to pay my mother alimony and child support for my brother and even for me, despite the fact that she was already receiving a monthly welfare check for "mentally disabled" me and never spent a penny on me while I was institutionalized anyway. Because she had "proof" that I was insane, the state paid most of the bill for my institutionalization, and what the state didn't cover, my father was ordered to pay by the divorce decree. He eventually went bankrupt, and she made a few thousand dollars off me. She even pretended that she used her alimony check for me so that she wouldn't have to pay so much tax on it.

My mother won sole custody of my brother and me, and even had a restraining order placed on my father so that he couldn't see us anymore without a counselor's permission. I never saw him again. I didn't much care. I hadn't minded him bringing me food and stuff, but as the old saying goes, it was too little, too late. After fourteen years of abuse and total neglect, I didn't suddenly feel attached to him because he had brought me some hamburgers.

I had been home on pass the day his stuff was taken out of the basement where he had stayed, separated by the whole house from my mother, for ten years before they finally got a divorce. The things I saw taken from that basement were utterly bizarre. In my elementary school days, it wouldn't have taken much money to help me feel like I fit in with the other girls. They traded bits of paper with animals stamped on them and sparkly pencils. I begged for little things like this so I could make friends the only way I could see how. I was told by my parents that they were just too poor to buy me a fancy pencil, to buy me a pad of stamped paper, to even buy me new crayons each year. Imagine my surprise when I saw that my father had boxes of fancy pencils in his basement, stacks of colored paper, markers, and countless other things that would have made my artistic heart thump with joy, had he thought to share any of them with his little daughter. The weirdest thing of all was an entire box full of identical dolls. It was buried in the piles of stuff that had packed the basement, and covered with dust. The dolls had sat there for who knows how long, and not one could have been spared for me?

I thought of how fifty-cent toys were not the only thing denied me in my childhood. How hard would it have been to take me to one of the annual father-daughter teas at my church? How much time would it have taken to listen to me talk about my day? How impossible was it, really, to refrain from screaming at and assaulting a little girl? It hurt and angered me to remember how I had been for most of my life—quiet, uncomplaining, striving always to do what others wanted me to do and be, striving to be "good," striving to be "worthy" of love. How ashamed I had been of the times I "lost control" and screamed that I deserved what other children had.

When the rest of the basement was empty, my father's sad parakeet was taken upstairs to the sun, the body of his hamster that had escaped and eaten rat poison was taken out and buried, and I stood alone with the washer and dryer.

For as long as I could remember, I had been forced to do the entire family's washing. I dreaded going into the basement, the monster's lair, for fear he would attack me. The last time it had happened was when I was twelve. I was seeing that counselor I had been taken to after my seventh-grade teacher was so shocked that I would write about a sad, lonely girl who wished she was dead. I told the counselor that my father never said anything nice to me. She suggested that perhaps he did not know that the things he said were unkind, and that I should tell him.

He screamed at me during dinner. I waited until later that night, when I was doing the laundry, and told him that he had hurt my feelings. I was crying. He shouted in an insane rage that he "could hurt me more" and flew at me across the room, slapping me down against the dryer over and over . . .

No, I had no trouble at all ousting him from my life. It was my mother I could not cut myself off from, though she was twice as cruel. My father evoked no pity in any way, but my mother was obviously a terribly ill, weak, piteous woman who hobbled along with a cane. She had been deeply and thoroughly psychologically scarred by her parents and her childhood and her unhappy marriage. She was in such unspeakable physical pain and taking so much medication that it was understandable that she lost control of herself now and then. Also, when she wasn't having a screaming, name-calling fit, she would insist so eloquently that she loved me, that she wanted what was best for me.

If she were anyone but my mother, I could either have refused to see her, or spent time with her and simply ignored her stories about how everyone in the world believed I was a perverted little psychopath with no feelings, while she alone believed that I could be saved. I could have reconciled myself to the fact that her delusions stemmed from her inability to deal with the horrible reality of her own life and had nothing to do with me. But it just hurt and frightened me too much to ignore such things from my very own mother, the only person in the world who had even pretended to care for me. Surely if I just tried hard enough, I could make her stop it, I could make her see reason.

I asked, I demanded, I begged, over and over again, to know exactly who said I was crazy and what proof they had. If she didn't believe them, why was I in a mental institution? Didn't she know that having custody of me meant that she was the only one who could keep me there or take me out? She would repeat her same old lines, claiming that she "didn't have a choice" and that she just couldn't tell me the details because I was "too sick to understand." I always started out completely reasonably, but my frustration would build until I either started screaming at her and cursing her with all my force or merely burst into tears. I begged her to at least stop talking about the subject so our visits would be peaceful, but she brought it up every time I saw her, and we would go round and round the same old bush.

I was often forced to wonder if the problem was really me rather than her. What if what she said was true, that there was this enormous herd of "trained professionals" who unanimously agreed I was a "violent, uncontrollable, manipulative, delusional, irrational psychotic" and believed I required "years of residential care"? If that wasn't true, then why was I in that terrible place? Why hadn't anyone around me ever treated me like a human being with thoughts and feelings deserving of respect? Did I not deserve respect? Could I be crazy and not even know?

During the month of April, in 1992, a new woman secretary appeared in the office at school. Debbie only saw me going back and forth every hour in the halls. I have no idea what on earth possessed her, but she put in a request on the ward to take me out on pass to her house for Easter.

When my mother found out that another woman had requested and received permission to take me to her home, she was quite upset. She drove to WSH immediately and told me not to get my hopes up because no normal person would actually take a mentally disturbed stranger home on a holiday. And even if it did happen, I would be silly to think that this "Debbie woman" and I might ever be close. My mother told me that I could put up a good front, but no one who got to know me or lived with me could stand me, and eventually this "Debbie person" would see what I really was.

Debbie did take me home at Easter as she had said she would. She introduced me to her husband and three children and the extended family that gathered for the holiday meal. I ate and ate, and I liked everyone I met. Apparently they liked me too, because Debbie began taking me home with her regularly.

What my mother had told me was always in the back of my mind. I worried constantly about doing something, anything, wrong or stupid or crazy. I gave myself headaches and tied my stomach in knots worrying. I liked these people so much, I was so grateful to them, that I was sure I would die if they ever saw in me what my mother did.

The way Debbie and her family treated me did much to ease my nervousness, however. They didn't single me out in any way. Just like Debbie's three kids, I went out to dinner with the family and helped around the house. I was in awe of the way that family did things together, and the way people were always stopping by to visit them, or they were visiting someone. It was just the opposite of my closed-up, isolated family. I thought families like Debbie's existed only on television. But here they were for real, and I was part of it. No one cared that Debbie was borrowing me from an insane asylum.

My mother called Lorri one day, as she often did, and said that she was not going to refuse me a "fake" family if that was what I wanted. But she claimed it was her duty to inform Debbie about how "cruel" I was to small animals and children. Lorri called me into her office, and told me that she had talked to my mother, and then Debbie, about my mother's claims that I threw Opie against the wall because he bit me, that I enjoyed torturing him, and that the parents of all the kids I baby-sat for had called my mother and said that I was mean to their kids.

Lorri asked me if this was true and I said no, that I had never even heard these claims before, that none of the parents of any of the kids I baby-sat for had ever complained to me, that Opie had never bit me, and even if he had, I wouldn't have thrown him against the wall or hurt him in any way. Lorri told me she had suspected as much, and that Debbie had said she had absolutely no concerns about her kids or any animals being around me, even alone. Not only that, but she had asked whether as well as going there on day passes, I would like to start spending some nights at her house too.

I was overjoyed to hear what Debbie had said, but my mother's poisonous influence on me could not be completely thrown off. I soon discovered that while Debbie's family distracted me from thoughts of my mother during the day, I was overcome by worry in the dark and loneliness of night. Why was my own mother convinced I could not be trusted with little animals and children? All the children I have ever known have adored me. My little Opie ran toward me squeaking with glee when he saw me. Did my mother and all those people who put me away see something lurking in me that had yet to surface? My mother said Debbie was too nice a person to imagine what I was "really" like. If I spent too much time with her, maybe she would see what my family and everyone else saw in me. And then she would feel horrible that she had brought such a monster into her home, loose around her own innocent children. And she would hate me! Like everyone else!

I began to cry. I was truly terrified that such a thing would happen, as it had happened before. Debbie heard me crying and came to sit with me. I told her that I didn't want to spend the night at her house anymore. I tried to explain that it was just hard for me to understand how strangers could like me when my blood kin despised me with such a passion. She was very kind, and told me she would not make me do anything I wasn't comfortable doing, but she did not understand. She thought she had done something wrong.

Debbie was the one good thing in my existence at WSH that came to me by chance. Everything else I had, I had because I had learned to be sneaky or to throw a tantrum. I sneaked moments alone with Joe, I sat up past bedtime talking to Brittany, I sneaked cigarettes for her, I passed notes, I touched the other patients, and I took a walk that one time—all at great risk because these things were against the rules. I realized rather quickly that the patients at WSH who were quiet and unobtrusive were basically ignored, while the noisy, hyper, tantrum-throwing patients got a lot of attention. I preferred being ignored to being more closely watched and more often harassed by the staff, but when I really needed or wanted something, I learned that throwing a fit was more likely to achieve the desired result than discussing things rationally. The staff, like most people, did what was easiest for them. It is easier to refuse the request of a person who accepts reasonably than to refuse a person who will start screaming and upset the whole ward.

The trick was to have a fit only if it was absolutely necessary. If I had fits all the time, then the shock value would be lost. At first it was rather uncomfortable to be throwing a fit when my nature craved reasonable discussion of problems, but I soon discovered that it was a good release of tension. When the staff tried to take away my acne medication, as they often did because it took some trouble on their part to distribute it to me every day, I lay on my back and screamed until the doctor renewed my prescription.

One day Brittany was considered "well enough" to be given a job. Actually, it was called "Work Therapy," but she received a small paycheck in return for doing odd jobs for an hour after school on weekdays. I made a general nuisance of myself until the ward staff thought it would be nice to get rid of me for an extra hour a day, too.

I didn't mind cleaning toilets and working on an assembly line and loading boxes onto trucks, but I resented the idea that since I was a mental patient, these were the only things I was capable of doing for a living, and then only after extensive "training."

Patients who worked at WSH supposedly received minimum wage for every hour they worked, but they were not allowed to keep more than sixty-four dollars a month. Any amount earned over that went to help pay the bill for WSH's unwanted "treatment." Once a month those in the Work Therapy program were taken to Wal-Mart, or sometimes even to a restaurant, to spend their sixty-four dollars. I was beside myself with the joy of having real soap and shampoo instead of the orange goo that you got a squirt of in the morning at WSH if you didn't have your own things. And food was a good thing too. I stuffed myself silly whenever I got a chance at something with taste.

Joe didn't work at the same time I did, but he was in the work program and went with me on the monthly excursions. Those were the longest periods of time that I could be near him. It was heaven.

There was a little building next to the school where welding and small engine repair and carpentry and other vocational skills were taught. Since vocational skills are (unfairly) considered fields that do not require much intelligence, it was hoped that the best of the mental patients might learn these things and thus serve the society that treats them like shit.

William was taking a welding class. I asked him what welding was, and he explained. I said, "Oh, like in the movie *Flashdance*" (which features a female welder). William said yes, but not to get any ideas because there was no way I, a girl, and a small, weak girl at that, could be good at welding. So I pestered the "principal" at school until he put me in the welding class.

The instructor, Mr. Nichols, was a Vietnam veteran and was very, very calm and rather slow. He had a pleasant face, and I do not believe he ever had a bad thought about anyone. On every "behavior report" he filled out about me he wrote that he had no problem with me, and every day he would fill in that hour's row on my "point sheet" with 5s. He explained everything very slowly and carefully and helped me do whatever there was to do. He seemed to share William's opinion of small girls and welding, and was rather surprised that I never got tired of welding and dropped out of his class. But I loved wearing a welder's helmet and gloves and using a torch. I became pretty good at basic welds, better than William even. He was a little careless.

Once a grinder spark fell on the front of William's shirt, which he had forgotten to tuck in, and a little flame sprang from it. William said, "Um . . . Mr. Nichols . . . Mr. Nichols, I seem to be on fire . . . " and Mr. Nichols just put his gloved hand over the flame. As William examined the charred hole in his shirt, I couldn't help giggling at his amazed expression. He caught another shirt in the working mechanism of the grinder another time. It shredded the bottom of his shirt, and buttons popped off everywhere. Again I was thrown into a giggling fit at the funny look on his face. This time he laughed too.

My mother learned that I was more likely to agree to a visit with her if she brought my brother along. My brother had had a nearly complete change of heart toward me since Thanksgiving Day and the beginning of the divorce. He still didn't know what to think of me and the fact that I was residing in a metal institution, but he had learned he could trust me more than anyone else in the family. He would bring me candy and want to talk with me. He wasn't allowed on the ward, however, because he was only twelve. There was a little sign outside the ward door that prohibited children fourteen and under from entering. If he had been called insane, he could have been admitted to my ward and subjected to any and every torture there. But normal human beings under the age of fourteen were considered too delicate even to *see* the horrors of a mental institution.

I could see my brother in the main visitors' room, outside of all the wards. It was rather fancy compared with the rest of the building, with upholstered furniture and magazines of slightly more interest than *Soybean Journal*. Even though these magazines were mostly for adult women, like *Good Housekeeping* and such, I stole them whenever I was in that room so I would have something to read.

Some of the most disturbing stories of child abuse are found in women's magazines. I read about a little girl who was raped by her father and how he broke her pelvis once and never took her to a doctor. It healed badly and she walked with a limp the rest of her life. Her teachers, her preacher, and others knew that she was being abused, but they never helped her. I read about another girl who was beaten and starved by her parents. When a social worker came to investigate, she was told by the parents that the girl was "accident prone" and "anoretic." So the social worker did nothing. When the girl was twelve she was found abandoned in the back of a truck. She weighed thirty-five pounds, the left side of her face had collapsed from being beaten, and her body temperature was barely over eighty from shock. She spent a year in the hospital, and there was not enough unburned or otherwise undamaged skin left on her body to graft over the worst parts.

These articles distressed me considerably. Compared with what the children in them had suffered, perhaps I had no right to ask for help for what I suffered. But the point of these articles was that even these children, tortured in ways most people think happen only in the dungeons of Third World dictatorships, were not helped either. Millions of women read these magazines. Aren't they at all affected by such stories? If they are, how come child abuse is still one of the top ten killers of children and the number one cause of psychological damage?

I discussed the matter once with a boy named Kevin, an orphan who had lived with various foster families and relatives throughout his life. He was sitting across from me at a card table on the dayhall. I told him how I had been psychologically tormented, constantly verbally abused, expected to be my mother's mother, forbidden a social life, isolated entirely, treated as if I were insane because I walked on my toes when I was seven, and other such silly things. I told him about the physical abuse; I told him the marks of it weren't as obvious as not having enough healthy skin left to graft. I said that emotional abuse isn't obvious at all when parents like mine know how to act like they love their children in front of strangers. I suggested that if the signs of my abuse were visible, maybe someone would have believed me and helped me. I suggested that maybe what happened to me wasn't even abuse, especially compared with what happens to other children.

Kevin responded, "No, that's not it. Maybe your family never abused you in front of anyone, but the effects of abuse are really obvious. The minute I seen the way you were actin' when you first walked in here, and the minute I saw your folks, I knew they had done something really bad to you. And if you ever told anybody that you were abused they should have believed you, especially you, because you can't lie."

"What do you mean I can't lie? I have lied lots in my life!"

Kevin smiled. "Yes, but not very well, not very well at all . . . I can tell right away when you are lying because you are a basically honest person. I can tell that you are not lying when you talk about what your parents did to you. And what they did was bad. Maybe some people have it worse than you, but that don't make what your folks did okay. Nobody would do that to their own kids if they cared about them. Nobody that cares about their kids would leave them here. I don't see how anyone could do such a thing to you. You're a nice little thing and I wouldn't do such a thing to you."

Then he looked down at his fingers, which were picking at each other on the table, and spoke more softly. "It really doesn't matter if no one saw it, because I've been hit in front of so many people and it's just that no one gives a damn, that's all."

I wrinkled my forehead in sympathy. "Really? Who hit you?"

"My uncle. He beat me with a belt, all over. He would come out in the yard or be out in public with me some-where, and unlike your folks he knew that didn't make any difference. He would take off his belt and beat me with it till the blood ran and I would scream. Then he would punch me in the face sometimes. And the neighbors would see, and stand there. And strangers would walk by and turn their heads. It isn't that they don't see, Crazy Girl, it's that they don't want to see. They don't want to get involved, or whatever."

I reached out my hands and Kevin took them in his. I couldn't think of anything to say to comfort the knowledge of such a horrific fact. I just took his hands in mine very discreetly so that the staff would not see and send us to the chair or to the cell for trying to be there for each other.

Kevin was a good friend. He was one of the boys who had discussed me when he thought I could not hear him during my first week at WSH. He would often say to a new patient, "You shoulda seen her when they brought her in, craziest thing I ever saw! Walkin' all around like a zombie and shit, but she's all right. She's real smart. And she's real stubborn, you wouldn't believe her nerve, that's why we call her Crazy Girl."

I was his girlfriend for a while and he gave me a gumball machine ring. The staff promptly took it away from me and punished both of us because patients aren't supposed to give each other things. He was red-haired and blue-eyed and terribly underweight. He was one of the few patients I ever heard was "cured," which meant that after two years at WSH he had learned to do and say and be anything and everything a staff member told him to. He spoke their jargon; he was constantly telling me not to break rules and to be respectful to the staff because then I would be cured too and I could get out of that place.

Once I retorted much too violently, "Oh yeah, well how long have you been in this place since you were fucking cured?" He was obviously aware that this fact contradicted his brainwashing, and it frightened him. If it wasn't true that being "good" was the ticket to being cared about and rescued, then what on earth was? I knew the feeling well, the horror that comes when you have spent years molding yourself into exactly everything someone else says you should be, and you still don't get on the "sane" list. Not only is everyone just as apathetic as they were before, you have lost yourself as well.

Kevin, like all the kids who had known me since the beginning of my imprisonment, watched my physical health deteriorate and my frustration build. He worried about me and put up with a lot from me as more and more anger festered inside of me, with only little cracks that it dared to seep out of.

One of these cracks consisted of becoming increasingly rude and sarcastic as the length of my imprisonment grew. Kevin knew that my anger stemmed from pain and help-lessness and ignored my sharp tongue. So did William and Brittany and Zach, and Leo did for the most part. But even-tually Leo slapped me right across the mouth. I was stunned, not because he had hit me, but because for the first time in my life I had deserved to be hit. I ran my tongue along the inside of my mouth and felt no blood. He had not hit me hard, especially considering his immense strength. Drew, who had seen Leo slap me, could not conceal the

fact that he was laughing. All the kids had been unwilling
to slap me themselves, but had been hoping to see someone
else give me my come-uppance.

I turned red with shame and picked up my hat, which
had fluttered to the ground. Leo watched me uncertainly.
He had meant to do what he did, and he had reason for
it, but he was hoping I would not hate him. I told him I
was sorry I had said what I did and that I was not even
aware of how awful it had been. Leo said, "I didn't think
you did, you've never been like this before. What has gotten into you?"

I looked down at the ground and replied, "I don't know,
just bitter I guess."

Lorri told me in one of our sessions that she noticed I
had picked up a lot of negative behaviors since I had come
to WSH—having fits, becoming more and more deceptive
and rude. I told her I didn't know how else to survive. I
told her I was being squashed from all directions—"can't
do this, can't do that, can't have this, can't have that." It
caused such rage and frustration and despair that it didn't
all fit inside of me. I couldn't just stuff it down somewhere
and live with it quietly; I needed to get rid of it somehow.
I wasn't allowed to get rid of it in good ways, like taking
a walk or spending some time alone or spending time with
friends or having something to do; so it got rid of itself
any way it could.

Lorri said, "I know. This place takes away a person's
choices. I've seen way too many kids come in here like you
and become trapped in the system, and the system changes
them, changes them terribly. That's why I tried so hard to
get you out, you really need to get out. This place is doing
you nothing but harm at this point."

"If you could say that, if you could say that outside of
this office, maybe I could get out." I looked quite hopefully
at her. She sighed and looked away from me. She looked
out through her window, which was barred just like all the
others, and said, more to herself than to me, "Someday I

will. Someday I'm going to write a book about the mental health system and its colossal failures."

"Me too," I said. "I'm going to write a book about this place, about these kids."

Lorri looked back at me sharply. She studied me with a strange expression on her face and said, "Yes. I do believe you'll do just that. And I wish you the best of luck."

SIXTEEN

My mother's birthday was in May. By
that time I had forgiven her again, forgiven everything.
And I had convinced myself that she did not truly hate me
or wish me harm, but was merely weak and easily confused
because of her illness and her stressful life. This view was
encouraged by everyone who worked at WSH. If a patient
refused to visit with his or her parents, no matter how cruel
the parents, then the kid had a problem. The kid was told
that he or she needed to "work things out" before being
considered "cured" and allowed to leave, even if the kid
wasn't going home.

I was expected to get along with my biological parents,
to respect and "honor" them, and to love them, no matter
what they did to me, no matter what they were. The staff
smiled upon me when I made a pot in Mr. Davis's class to
give to my mother for her birthday. It was carefully shaped
and glazed with many colors. I inscribed a loving message
on the bottom and took it back to the ward with me when
it was dry.

I was allowed to call my mother on the pay phone and
speak to her for five minutes. I wanted to tell her I had a
present that I had made especially for her and ask her when
she wanted to come get it. Patients always had to call collect, and my mother had always accepted my calls before.
This time, when the operator told her it was me on the
phone, she sighed like she did when insurance salesmen
called. She said, "Well, I just don't care to speak to her at
the moment," and hung up.

I took the scorned pot back to my room. I was ashamed to think how much work I had put into it. I felt like such a total moron to set myself up like this again and again. Why didn't I believe it when she let it slip time and time again that she just didn't care, that I was only her daughter when she felt like it? Never in my life had I taken my feelings out on inanimate objects. I was raised to believe that only mentally unstable people do that. So, as I stood just inside the door of my room in a mental institution, I knew it wouldn't make my situation any worse to take that damn pot and smash it as hard as I could.

The largest piece left was the one that said, "I love you Mom." I stared at it in horror. It was like an omen. Like a sign that said, "You can get as hurt or as pissed as you like, but you will never get rid of your desire to be loved by that woman."

Drew was my boyfriend for a few weeks, but the rest of the time I knew him, we were just really good friends. He was of average height and extremely skinny because of the drugs he was on. The drugs slowed him down and rendered him rather dopey. He was smart, though, and such a kind, gentle person. His brown, almost black, eyes and hair, his peaceful, unobtrusive way, and his free-form poetry made me think of what my Uncle Bob must have been like at the age of seventeen. They were both diagnosed with bipolar depression.

One day a girl came to Smith 1 who had soft brown eyes and brown hair and looked strangely familiar. Brittany pulled me aside and said, "That's Drew's sister." I was amazed. For some reason, institutions don't like to keep anyone related together.

Her name was Emily, and I was soon good friends with her too. She was only twelve, and seemed even younger than that. She was so innocent. She was soft and slightly pudgy, always wore overalls, and looked quite huggable. After her brother had been taken to WSH, she had been very lonely, and she spent the next few months convincing various people that she had depression too and "needed" to be at WSH. The attachment between Emily and Drew was remarkable. They fought like a regular brother and sister, but Emily could not bear being away from him when he was in a bad place. They looked as much alike as a boy and girl can, and their personalities had a lot in common as well. I have rarely met such a likable pair as those two.

Emily was the last one of the patients I befriended to be left with me as my stay at WSH dragged on and on. Zach's mother showed up out of the blue one day and requested passes with the idea that soon she would take him home for good. When I saw him the day after his first pass, his eerie yellow eyes were bloodshot. He was supposed to be doing "math," but his head kept drooping to his arms on the table. I poked him with my pencil, saying, "Hey, whassa matter with you? Did you stay up all night?"

Without looking up, Zach took my pencil and snapped it in two with one hand. I watched him a minute longer and asked at last, "Are you hungover?"

Zach nodded. I was rather surprised. "But you're only thirteen! How did you get it?"

Zach focused his bleary eyes on me a moment and said, "My mother's boyfriend."

I kept eyeing him as he slumped back onto the table. I noticed an ugly scrape across the back of his ear. "How did you get that?" I wanted to know.

Zach looked up at me again and said, "I was in my mother's chair. She pulled me out by my ear."

I was sure that no one would be stupid enough to send Zach home with a woman who let him get completely wasted and dug her nails into him on purpose, but they did. He went on several passes and came back smashed and upset every time. On the day he left for good, I said sadly, "I bet you will be back in six months."

In less than four months, he was back. He had collected thirteen criminal charges. The police brought him to WSH until he could be tried and sent to jail. I was surprised to see that he was extremely healthy and happy. He had lost any trace of fat and was solid muscle. He had color in his skin and life in his eyes. He had not taken any of the drugs WSH sent home with him, of course, and he was much better off for it. He was not dopey like he had always been before; in fact, he was so rambunctious that I could not go near him or he would accidentally bruise me.

I asked him if it was better here or in jail than it was on the streets, where he had to steal and fight and sleep under bridges to stay alive. I had been under the impression that being a street kid was one of the few fates worse than being a state institution inmate. On the street you didn't know where to find shelter or food, and you were in danger of being assaulted or killed or raped (whether you were a boy or a girl made no difference). Zach said it was better, a thousand times better, on the streets.

He said it is worth anything to be free.

After Loretta left WSH and Smith 1 was hard up for space, I was put back in the double room with Brittany. The view from our window was of two walls lined with barred windows on each side of us and a dumpster in front. Someone from Smith 2 went out to that dumpster each evening to dump the trash of both Smith 1 and 2. William would volunteer, and he would run out to the dumpster and circle back under our window. We could force it open just a tiny crack, and because he was so tall, he could easily slip a note to us. Usually it was addressed to Brittany, but when they had an argument it would be addressed to me. In those notes he would beg me to tell him why Brittany was mad at him and to tell her he was sorry.

Once when Brittany and William had a really bad fight, he sent his fist through a thick pane of glass in his window. (Since WSH was a hundred and twenty-five years old, it still had glass windows instead of Plexiglas. It was the bars that made it impossible for anyone but a tiny contortionist to get out of the windows.)

William's hand was cut all to pieces. He kept a shard of glass and told me he intended to commit suicide since Brittany didn't care for him anymore. I told the staff on my ward that William had spoken to me of suicide and had glass, and I begged them not to let him do it. I felt really stupid to be "narking" on anyone to the staff, and to make things worse, the staff just ignored me. I don't know what would have happened if William and Brittany hadn't made up.

During another fight of theirs, I watched Brittany take a sharp piece of an aluminum can and cut the underside of her forearm. I was horrified as she sliced one tiny streak after another into her soft white flesh. She pressed harder and harder until a bit of blood dribbled down her arm. I tried to wrestle that piece of aluminum away from her, but she was bigger than me. So I just sat with her until she stopped cutting herself.

I did not go to the staff that time. Since Brittany was on the ward they worked on, they might have taken action, but that action would only have been to put her on SP. I thought of how dreadful that experience had been for me, and how it couldn't have prevented me from committing suicide if I had really wanted to. I could have broken my nose on the floor, if I had bashed it hard enough, and shoved the pieces into my brain. Tying a person up and feeding them through a tube so they can't starve themselves is the only way I can think of to keep someone from killing themselves, and what would be the point of living your whole life like that anyway? Most people who think of or attempt suicide don't really want to die. They just need some help living, because that gets really damn hard sometimes.

Brittany was devastated when William's mother came to WSH one day to take him home with her. William had watched his stepfather beat his mother all the time, and one day he took a gun and pointed it at his stepfather's head, saying, "If you ever lay a hand on my mother again, I will kill you." But that did not stop his stepfather, so William's mother had joined the Army to escape him.

Brittany cried and cried, and I guarded the hall as she and William sneaked their last moment alone together. Anybody who thinks "puppy love" doesn't really mean that much should have seen William and Brittany that day, the way they held each other, the look in their eyes. It nearly broke my heart.

William came to me and put his hand out on top of my head, saying with a determined detachment, "Take care of yourself, kid." I looked up, up into his beautiful eyes, and flung my arms around him to sniff, "You should worry about yourself." He was so startled that I would hug him; I had certainly never done such a thing before. He blushed with pleased embarrassment. I could feel every last one of his ribs and the joints of his spine.

When I let him go, he took Brittany's hand and squeezed it, then walked out the door. Brittany watched him disappear down the walk. She knew as well as I did that it wasn't any good place he was walking toward, and that we would never be any good to him again.

All my life my hair and my strange, green-gold eyes were the only physical features I was proud of. I fancied that the rest of me was hideous, but I was complimented on my eyes and my thick, wavy brown hair with its shiny red and gold highlights. When I was young, my grandmother made me wear it in two long braids, but in recent years I had let it cascade freely down to the middle of my back, with only some barrettes or a hairband in front. When it became dull and limp and thin from malnutrition and stress, I decided the only thing I could do was sign up to have it all cut off.

It was a month before the hair-cutter at WSH got around to it. I had really wanted to save what she cut off—

a wigmaker would have paid money for it—but she said she didn't have time to worry about saving it. As that vain piece of me fell in a tangled, worthless mass around my feet, it was all I could do not to cry. No one on the ward failed to point out that I didn't have much left about me that was pretty and that I looked like a boy, although some phrased it more delicately than others.

Society still considers long hair a necessary part of the feminine ideal. I was a good little girl in my pigtails. It was something of a rebellion to get a little bowl cut, with the back so short it might as well have been shaved. I soon realized this, and have kept my hair short ever since.

E ven though Brittany was in the same room with me again, I still didn't see much of her. Her mother had finally started taking her out on passes regularly. Her mother told her that if she "learned to be more responsible" she would put her in a level 4 or 5 group home, and if she was "still responsible" there, she would take Brittany home eventually. (Every place where unwanted children live falls on a "level" of "structure" and "security" from 1 to 6. Level 6 is a mental institution such as WSH, or jail; 1 through 5 are foster homes and group homes. The lower the level, the more humanely the children are treated.) Brittany asked her mother what "more responsible" meant exactly, and she said, "Well, for starters, you could learn to take shorter showers instead of hogging the bathroom."

J onathan attacked me with a tire iron one day in Mr. Nichols's shop class. I was just standing there with my back to him. I don't know if I had a premonition or if some sound he made caught my attention, but I turned around, instinctively ducking when I saw him moving quickly toward me, and the tire iron clanged against the metal-topped table where I had been standing. I still didn't really know what was going on as I ran around to the other side of the table.

"What the hell has gotten into you?" I cried out, as I continued to run around the table to keep it between us as he tried to get within hitting distance. At that very moment Joe walked by outside. Jonathan called to him, "Hey Joe, I'm gonna kill your fucking bitch girlfriend! She called me an asshole!"

Joe was a good distance away. He was startled at the sound of his name. I'm sure he had no idea what Jonathan was talking about, but he understood that Jonathan was being insulting, so he called out "Fuck you!" before walking away.

That Joe would walk away when I was so desperately in need of help shocked me more than turning around to see a tire iron coming at me. I hadn't much time to think about it, though, because I had to deal with Jonathan.

"I never called you an asshole!"

Jonathan, who was also surprised and disappointed that he hadn't been able to draw Joe into the fray, stopped short.

"You didn't? I heard that you did, I heard that you hate me."

It was true that I hadn't thought too highly of him after he had sexually assaulted Diana. But I hadn't even thought of Jonathan or that incident in months. If anyone had told him I was saying things behind his back, it wasn't true.

"I saved you from Zach once, remember?"

"Oh, yeah. Sorry." Jonathan was suddenly sheepish, like the proverbial little kid caught stealing cookies, "I wasn't really going to kill you anyway. I wasn't even going to hit you very hard."

I walked out of the classroom then. Leaving a class was an offense punishable with time in the cell, but I figured Mr. Nichols wasn't going to notice I was gone when he hadn't noticed all that preceded my leaving. I went outside and cried, a little because I had been so frightened, but mostly because of Joe.

Joe was on Thorazine. He was on enough Thorazine to

kill a person smaller than him. Whenever I tried to talk to him now he would look at me blankly, his eyes glazed over. Sometimes I don't think he even knew who I was. He was big, and he knew how to fight, so he had to be completely stoned for the staff to find it easy to take him down. I knew that he had once embarrassed Tyrone by giving him a good punch in the face when he grabbed him. Now Tyrone liked to antagonize Joe, calling him names, calling his mother names, and telling him to try and hit him again. When Joe reacted in his drug-induced stupor, he was easily thrown to the ground and beat up. I would cry then. I would cry again when Joe was released from the cell and I saw his bruises up close, and the cuts on his wrists because the straps had been pulled so tight.

When Joe was a little boy his father broke his arm one time, and his ribs another. His mother eventually ditched his father for a long string of boyfriends who also beat both of them. His mother was an addict who couldn't hold a job and stole for drug money. Joe and his younger brothers and sister were shifted around, homeless sometimes. He had to hide with his mother a lot, from an angry boyfriend, from the cops, from someone she stole from. He never had any stability or security; no one ever took care of him in the least. He grew up uneducated, except for the ways of the streets. He stole, and fought, and lied, and did drugs. When he was fifteen his step-grandfather began sexually molesting him. In frustration, Joe set fire to an abandoned building, and was committed by a juvenile court to WSH.

The most dreadful thing of all was that he was glad to be there. In spite of the way he was treated by the staff, he was glad to have a roof over his head and something (no matter how unhealthy) to eat. He was still assaulted, but not as often and not as seriously as he was on the street. In the first few months of his stay, he gained much-needed weight and made friends with all the other patients.

He was so energetic and playful. He could always make me laugh with his antics and the funny things he said. He made a joke of the staff. When they put him in the cell for swearing, he started saying, "Son of a bean dip, mother frito" instead. I felt lighter and warmer around him. Just to see him walking around with a cigarette outside the barred windows would make me smile. When he held me gently in his arms, nothing in the world seemed painful anymore.

Then they started forcing more and more Thorazine on him. Also, he started going to court to testify against his grandfather. I can't imagine what it would be like to tell a courtroom full of strangers every detail of being sexually abused, especially for a boy. The sexual abuse of young boys is the most hush-hush topic I can think of. The shame of it all somehow falls on the victim. Joe told me he would never feel like a real man again.

His court-appointed lawyer was just like mine had been, hurried, hardened, unsympathetic, interested in getting this case out of the way as soon as possible. These lawyers just didn't have the time or the capacity to think of their cases as real children—real, desperate, trapped children who depended on them to publicly establish the very worth of their souls.

Naturally, the defense wasn't even supposed to be sympathetic toward Joseph. It was their job to make him look like a liar, or just a nut who didn't know what sexual abuse was, or who deserved it. Joe was alone, utterly alone against a system that called what was done to him mere child abuse. Child abuse, different from assault on an adult, a lesser crime, hardly a crime at all, in fact. The case dragged on for months, and I don't think anything ever came of it. It was too painful for Joe to talk about after a while.

As the months passed, Joe was no longer outgoing. The drugs made it impossible for him to be bubbly and entertaining. Those drugs made his mind so fuzzy and his body so weak that he could barely concentrate on and talk about anything, much less the ordeal he was suffering. He shut everyone out, including me.

My response to pain is the opposite. I tell everyone

around me when I am suffering. I reach out for comfort. I knew for a time that I could not get this comfort from Joe because we barely had a chance to be together. But I was horrified to realize that even if that horrid institution was completely torn away and we sat alone on the barren ground where it had stood, there would still be something separating us. I sensed that he was no longer thrilled by the few seconds we had to put our arms around each other. I felt him pushing me away with his frightened heart. He no longer really saw me when he turned his eyes my way. He no longer listened when he sat within hearing distance of my words. He could see and hear and feel nothing but his own misery.

I was frightened by this. I felt betrayed. I felt that if he truly loved me he would try to be closer than ever when he was hurting. Even if he couldn't share his pain with me, I felt that he hadn't any excuse not to try and comfort mine. The clincher came when he started bruising me. He never did it intentionally; he was just so strong and solid and I was so frail and sickly that a careless grasp of my arm left bruises in the shape of his fingers. He bruised my face and my hands and other places, and never even seemed to notice.

I grabbed him by his shirt one day as he walked through the front door of the school, grabbed him hard enough that he would look down at me and follow me into a dark corner. I looked up at him in desperation and said, "Joe I think we should break up."

This was meant merely to get his attention, to make him see how seriously I was concerned about our relationship. I fully expected that he would ask why, and when I told him how he had been making me feel lately, he would promise to think about me more. Then things would be better than before.

But he had been rejected too often to ask why anymore. I could see shock and pain pierce the haze in his eyes. But that was the last thing he wanted me to see, so he turned quickly and walked away. "Fine," was all he said.

The next day he had a new girlfriend, just to show me I wasn't as important to him as I was.

A week later I turned fifteen. I turned fifteen while lying on a prison bed staring at the walls of a cubicle in a state mental hospital.

Naturally my mother had wanted to visit me. What kind of mother would she look like if she didn't visit her poor, crazy daughter on her birthday? But I refused to see her. She left me a cake and a present at the front desk. When the staff member there called me up to give me these things she reproached me for not seeing my mother. She told me that my mother was very nice to bring me things on my birthday when most of the patients' parents never acknowledged their children's existence. I told that woman I wished I had parents like that rather than a mother who abused and ditched me and then confused the issue by bringing me a stupid cake and a little present.

I was comforted for a moment when the woman at the desk also handed me a present and a note from Debbie. I went to my room to open everything (fortunately no one hassled me about not being on the dayhall). The note said that Debbie and her family would take me to a local amusement park that Saturday. I was very flattered and grateful, but nothing could begin to fill the gaping, aching hole inside me that was my heart on my fifteenth birthday.

Brittany was gone on pass. I lay alone on my bed for the rest of the day. Throughout the night I could not sleep. On the first night after Joe and I broke up I had cried so hard for so long that I started vomiting. I woke up the next day with a fever that rattled my teeth. In the days that followed I lost weight and grew very weak. I wanted to stay in bed to recover both physically and emotionally, but if I did not go from class to class, to the dining hall and back, and stay on the dayhall for the rest of the day, then I would be put in the cell. I was afraid that in my condition, being in that dreadful place, watched through the wire window, with nothing to occupy me, would kill me. So at night I slept so hard I did not dream. In the morning I summoned every ounce of strength I had to go about in a daze. I could not cry in front of those people I despised. There was no one to talk to, and no time to think things through until my birthday. By that time I had been holding it in so long it could not come out. My eyes were dry, my body was numb.

That day marked the fifteenth year that I had existed completely disconnected from the rest of the human race. I had always had a general feeling that something was missing from my life, but of course I had no way of knowing exactly what. I had thought I was loved because my mother told me she loved me, because she gave me stuff. Even as I pulled away from this illusion, I replaced it with the idea that friends are the best a person can get, friends like William and Brittany and Debbie. But, while friends are nice, I had discovered on that day five months before, when Joe first touched me, that I desperately needed something more. In that moment I felt something I could never have imagined before. I felt jolted, awakened, alive, and that I had something worth living for.

Joe no longer gave me this feeling. I was left hollower than before. At last, as I lay in that cold, dark, barred, and barren mental institution, I knew I had found exactly what I had been missing. Now it was gone, and I did not know how to go on.

SEVENTEEN

I still loved Joe more than I can describe. I hung around him as much as possible, longing for him. When he wasn't looking at me, I watched him with a pain so deep in my chest that I could hardly breathe. Every move he ever made in front of me—every shift of his muscles, his fingers, his face—was carved into my heart and mind. I can close my eyes nearly two years later and see every feature of him and even everything he ever wore in my presence.

The pain in my heart grew as the pain in his eyes did. His mother wanted to take him out of WSH. He wanted to leave, but he was also afraid of going back to that dreadful life he had led. He was so alone and suffering so terribly. I wanted to comfort him more than I have ever wanted anything in my life.

But he had been nothing but hateful to me since we had broken up. When he caught me looking at him, he would kiss his new girlfriend. I knew that they did not love each other, that their relationship was like all mine had been before him, but he still succeeded in making me insanely jealous. He no longer acknowledged my presence, but behind my back he called me names and spread rumors about me, knowing full well that I would hear about it all.

And so, as much as I loved him, I began to hate him as well. I hated him for hurting me like he did. I especially hated him for hurting me when he was the only person in the world I knew of who could heal me. I thought it was beneath me to spread rumors about him, so I followed him around throwing insults at his back, which he always had turned to me.

All of Smith 1 and 2 was divided between the kids who sympathized with me and thought Joe an asshole, and those who sympathized with him and thought me a bitch. There had been a time when no one at WSH thought me a bitch, a time when I was quiet and unobtrusive and tried to please everyone. Then I learned that either I could sacrifice myself entirely in the hope that everyone else would like me, or I could like myself and to hell with everyone else. So I cut my hair, I started pushing away boys who wanted to feel me up, I started speaking my mind—and all this pissed a lot of people off.

Joe wasn't so popular since he had become so quiet and moody, but he still had his following, including a girl named Stacy. Stacy was fifteen and fancied herself a neo-Nazi. She arrived at WSH with her head shaved and a swastika self-tattooed on her ankle. I liked her anyway, because she was not prejudiced against anyone for their race or religion at all. She lived on the street and needed somewhere to belong, and the neo-Nazis just happened to be around.

Her hair was pretty as it grew back (it is against the rules to have a shaved head at WSH). I liked her sharp, distinguished, yet tiny features and her fair skin. One of her big, pretty eyes was hazel and the other was gray. She was only about my size and even thinner than me. I liked the way she dressed and her homemade jewelry. Of the few things I drew during my imprisonment, some were pictures of her.

We discussed our sorry lives at various intervals. Her father was a junkie who beat her, and she spent most of her time away from "home." I was horrified by her account of street life and pitied her. But, like Zach, Stacy preferred the dangers of the streets to living without freedom or friends. She looked at me with horror and pity when I described my severely isolated and restricted life, and said, "Don't take this the wrong way, but if I were you I would kill myself."

Our friendship, however, paled in comparison to her crush on Joe. A few weeks after my fifteenth birthday, I arrived at school to find that Stacy had drawn a distorted illustration of me and tacked it to the front door. It said in various handwritings, "Tiffany is a fucking bitch, slut, whore." I knew that even if Joe had not written any of it, he knew about it and supported the project wholeheartedly.

Something inside me broke open, and I could not stop the rush of emotion that it had been holding in. I stormed into the building, found Joe, and shouted to his back, "There's the big coward! I believe you have something to say to me, to say to my face, don't you, coward? About how I'm a bitch and a whore?"

Joe tried to walk away. I followed, shrieking, "Don't you walk away this time! Don't you walk away from me and have your little girlfriend do your fightin' for you! If you think I'm a bitch and a whore, you damn well better say it to my face, you God-damn coward!"

He kept walking. I slapped him across his back, hard. Of course it didn't hurt him, but it did get a reaction.

"All right!" Joe turned suddenly. "You're a bitch! Are you satisfied?"

"No, you didn't mean it then! Say it like you mean it!"

He had turned away again as soon as he had called me a bitch and was walking out the door of the school building. It was strictly forbidden to leave that building without a staff escort, and the punishment would be unbearable, but not clearing the air between me and Joe, right there, right then, seemed even more unbearable to me. I could not be convinced that he hated me until he said it to my face.

I followed him up the grassy hill, shaking so hard I could barely stand. Tears began to stream down my face as I shouted between sobs, "Say it like you mean it or tell me what it really is! Tell me why you hurt me so bad when I love you so much!"

I hit him again, to see if it would work this time.

It did.

Joseph turned so sharply that I stepped back. He stared down at me with a strange, stricken expression. There were tears in his own eyes as he cried out, "Stop hitting me! How can I believe you love me when you keep hitting me! How can I believe you love me when you're the one who left me!"

I stared back up at him, with the same expression he had, I'm sure. While he was looking at me, all anger fled from my body, leaving me in a sort of trance. I could do no more than whisper, "I didn't leave you. I just said I thought we should break up. I wanted to talk about it and you wouldn't."

He obviously didn't know what to say to that. We stood there, face to face with the fact that we had cut each other wide open because of a simple misunderstanding. What we were supposed to do now? We were fifteen years old, and confused about everything except the fact that opening yourself up to love means opening yourself up to pain. We were afraid.

What would have happened if we had had a minute more? Would one of us have thought of something to say? If we had started talking, would we have started healing and feeling close again? I'll never know.

The staff of the school building and most of the kids were standing around watching. None of them would make a move to interfere until they saw that Joseph was not going to be violent. If he had started beating the shit out of me for yelling at him, like they expected him to, they would have stayed right where they were. They were all afraid of him without their chains and their drugs and their rent-a-cops handy. But in that moment when he stared at me, showed me the pain in his eyes, he was vulnerable, and they knew it.

Mr. Davis called sharply, "Joseph, you get over here right now." And Joe did. Joe walked away from me again, taking with him the last chance we ever had to make up.

I watched him cross the large patch of grass and disappear inside the door of the school. Mr. Davis and the rest followed. I stood by myself for a minute before I decided I had better go back inside too before security came and grabbed me. I stood in the empty hall, completely drained and confused.

A boy from Smith 2 crept into the hall to taunt me. "Ha, ha, Joe called you a bitch, cause you're a bitch, ha, ha, bitch!"

The spell I had fallen under out on the grass was broken instantly, and rage surged back into me. "Fuck you!" I screamed at him, "I never did anything to you so just FUCK OFF!" I threw my hairband, the only thing I had, at him, and he ran away laughing. It was true that I had never done anything to him; I had never even spoken to him before. I broke into miserable sobs again. I knew Debbie was in the office and had heard me screaming at Joe, and now at this kid. I was so ashamed. I wondered what that boy had been told that made him decide without even talking to me that I was a bitch. It hurt when people did that to me.

In the cell I heard the key in the lock behind me, and the familiar smell of human urine filled my nose. My crying stopped instantly. My long-repressed emotions had rioted, had taken over that day and surged through me with more power than I could bear—love, loneliness, hate, rage, despair, pity, confusion, shame, and now the increasingly familiar yet never any more tolerable horror of that cell. I couldn't take a minute more, and I guess my subconscious knew that in the cell, no one was going to touch me. I took one step toward the window, and in an instant everything was black. When I came to, my knees were bruised and dried blood was smeared across my fingers where I had cut them clutching at the wire on the window as I fell.

The staff kept Joe away from me after that. We were walked to school at different times; we were taken on our monthly excursions to Wal-Mart separately. I only saw him walk by every now and then. I blamed Joe for this, as I blamed him for what I had suffered in the cell. If he had just had the nerve to discuss things with me when our relationship first started to go bad, instead of running away and covering his fear with insults, then the misery of that day and the days that followed would never have happened.

That day I had broken him down. I had proved that he was a coward, that he was too afraid to face me in person. All his insults and dirty tricks were a mere disguise for his hurt and fear and love. I had ripped off that disguise in front of everyone on Smith 1 and 2 and the staff at the school. Never mind that none of them understood a whit of what was going on. Joseph was ashamed at having been exposed. He composed a letter that every patient would know he was giving me. It said that if he had ever loved me, his love was dead as a doornail, and that I had better leave him the fuck alone.

I took this letter seriously. I was numb once more after that day in the cell. I did not cry. I did not show any outward response at all. I simply read those lines over and over in my head for days until I shattered the mirror of my makeup compact. Alone in the bathroom, I took a sharp shard of glass and held it above the white, wasted underside of my arm. I could see the faint blue veins in my wrist, and I knew to slash them vertically so they would be more difficult to sew up. The light glinted off the glass and made a bit of a rainbow.

If the person I loved most in the world did not love me, then how could anyone at all love me, ever? I thought of what my mother had said to me: *If you get close enough to anyone, they will see what you really are. No one can ever love you but me.* And not even she loved me. I could not live without love. I could not live another day in that miserable place without love.

I drove the shard of glass into my arm with a slicing motion. Only a bit of blood welled up, but the pain was so immense that I could not bear to drive the glass into my arm a second time with any more force than the first. I cut into my flesh in frustration again and again, but eventually I was no longer even drawing blood.

I saw in my mind's eye row after row of tiny white cubes with numbers on them, stretched out as far as I could see across the green grass. It was the graveyard of Wilson State Hospital. Mr. Davis had taken his class there one day, and he told us that to protect the "true identity" of mental patients, nothing but a case number was put on their tombstones when they died in the institution. I had said that *was* their true identity, that after being in a mental institution long enough, all you ever are to anybody is a number.

I knew I could not kill myself, because I could not bear the thought of being reduced to nothing but a nameless white cube—of having nothing more to show for my entire existence. I could not bear the thought of the satisfaction, or even indifference, of all those people who knew me and didn't love me when I was laid to rest with a thousand other miserable souls to be as forgotten as they were. I knew that I must live, if only to spite everyone who wanted me to die, or who didn't care if I did.

I picked up all the broken bits of glass and wrapped them in a paper towel before throwing them away. If the staff saw broken glass in the trash, they might start asking questions or searching patients' cubicles. They made periodic searches anyway, looking for collections of too much paper (a "fire hazard") or contraband items such as safety pins, plastic bags, unbent paper clips, makeup, cigarettes . . . If any of these things were found, a patient could be sent to the cell. I didn't want to be responsible for one of those searches. And I certainly didn't want to be responsible for a strip search meant to discover cuts made with bits of found glass. Strip searches are truly one of the most humiliating things a human being can experience. Everyone on Smith 1 was subjected to one once, merely because a woman on the staff couldn't find her ward keys. She had covered them with a paper towel while making her morning coffee.

Smith 4 had been cleared of patients before my arrival for the removal of asbestos. When the removal was done, all of the patients on Smith 3 were moved there, and Smith 3 had its asbestos removed. Smith 2 was next, then Smith 1. I liked being moved up to Smith 4 because its second-story cage allowed me to at least see more of the world that I was not allowed to go out into.

On Smith 4 there was no double room, so I was separated from Brittany again. She had been on pass more often and for more days at a time anyway. She had been taken to see the group home she would be going to. She said she didn't want to go there, but that it would certainly be better than this place.

We stood out in front of the school and waited for the ride that would take her away for good. She stood tall and straight-faced, and I knew she did not want me to cry. I did anyway. She hugged me and said that this was not good-bye; she wanted me to write, and when I was out I could visit her. We did write for a short time, but I never saw her again. It cut a hole in me to see her go, as it had cut a hole in me to see William go, and Zach, and Daniel, and Nick, and Kevin, and Derrick . . .

Drew left months earlier than Emily did. I guess she hadn't given much thought to how she would get out of WSH when she was trying so hard to get in to be near her brother. When at last Drew and his mother came for Emily, Drew sought me out to say hello to me. He found me in a chair by the drinking fountain, holding very still so that the staff would not notice me and force me back onto the dayhall. Even though I smiled to see him again, his face registered shock and horror at the sight of me.

Everyone knew I was sick, and weak, and unhappy. I had been since the day I was brought to that place. It took someone who hadn't seen me for a while to see that I wasn't just sick, I was getting sicker all the time; that I wasn't just weak, I was getting weaker; that I wasn't just unhappy, I was getting more unhappy with every passing day.

"Oh, Crazy Girl." Drew knelt in front of me. "What's happened to you? You look miserable."

"I know," I said, trying not to look directly into his painfully sympathetic gaze.

"Emily told me about Joe. But you want to know somethin', he kept the 'I love you' that you wrote on his history folder. He wouldn't erase it! So don't feel so bad."

"It isn't just Joe." I made a slight gesture toward the dirty white walls, the bars across the windows, the staff around the staff table at the end of the hall, and all the Smith 1 patients crowded into the dayhall in front of them. "It's everything. It's killing me."

Drew pulled me to my feet. It hurt to be moved, but then he put his arms around me. The softness of his flannel shirt soothed me. I placed my ear against his chest and said, "My spirit, I mean. I guess my body will live a long, long time, but my spirit will wither inside of it, and I don't know if it is possible for a spirit to ever be revived after a certain point." I was thinking of my Uncle Bob when I said the last part.

"I know." Drew rubbed my back a little, and I cleared my mind of all thoughts to allow the understanding and comfort he was offering me to reach my heart.

Emily came over in a minute and looked at me as sorrowfully as Drew had. She hugged me too and gave me her address. Then she flung her arms in the air and exclaimed that she was really glad to get the fuck out of that place and that her only sorrow was that she couldn't take me with her. I smiled because I was glad she liked me so much, and also because I had never heard her swear before.

Soon afterward Emily called me and confided that Drew was being given a new drug and going through a bad phase. She told me that she was afraid he was going to kill himself, and she didn't know what to do because nothing she said reached him. I asked her to put him on the phone.

"Drew," I said, "do you know how much Emily loves you?"

Drew answered, "Yes."

"And do you love her at all?"

"Yes."

"Then don't throw that away, do you hear me? I got nobody in this whole world that gives a fuck about me, and I hang on. You've got somebody, so you better hold on too. Emily'd go nuts if anything were to happen to you, so don't you hurt her."

"I know." Drew sighed. "I hope you're doin' all right."

"Not really." And it was the truth.

When I heard that Joseph was leaving WSH I pretended that I didn't care. All through the next week my eyes were dry. All through his last day at WSH, I kept up the appearance of total disconnection. But when the clock showed the exact hour of his departure—one in the afternoon—I burst suddenly into inconsolable tears.

I was ordered by a staff member to get in line to go downstairs for a new "group therapy." I said that I couldn't go, couldn't she see I was crying? I was told that it didn't make any difference, I was to follow my schedule or go to the Side-Room.

I stood and kicked a chair, and as it slid across the floor with a delicious racket, I cried out, "Can't a person cry in this fucking world?"

I was humiliated to be crying like a baby in front of

people who didn't care, but I kept right on crying all the way down the hall and the stairs and into the room where the group was held. I sat there crying and crying and crying. Betty, the group "therapist," suddenly asked her assistant to take over and took me out in the hall.

For a moment I was afraid that I was going to the cell anyway, for disturbing the group. But Betty took pity on me. "Would you like to go for a walk with me?" she asked. I stared up at her in stunned gratitude and nodded.

The July day was unusually cold and dark and drizzly. It had an unreal quality as Betty and I followed the broken walks around the creepy old brick and cement buildings in the heavy mist. A moist chill penetrated my bones, and I shivered with cold and emotion. She asked if it was Joseph.

It was amazing that she, a virtual stranger, would somehow know this when all the stupid people I encountered daily had no clue and didn't care to, either. But I spent no time wondering how she knew. I only sobbed that I truly cared for him and that even though we did nothing but fight anymore, I didn't know how to bear never seeing him again.

"Well, speak of the devil," Betty said. Out of the swirling fog, a familiar form appeared on the path before us. Joe stopped still. It was plain that I was one of the last people he wanted to run into. Betty said, "Hey Joe, I thought you were going at one."

"My mom is late." Joe's face was pale and drawn.

Betty said, "I think someone wants to say good-bye to you. Will you listen to her?"

Joe nodded slowly, and Betty pushed me toward him. I stood right in front of him and stared straight ahead at his shirt pocket for a moment before I gathered the nerve to tilt my head back and look at his face. I was aware that my eyes and nose must be awfully red, my hair was damp, and my face was streaked with tears. My eyes watered and my lips quivered as I studied his expression.

He was as pale as I had ever seen him. He was not

hunched up or fidgety, but he was tense and apprehensive. His eyes were filled with unspeakable terror. Although he was so dreadfully concerned about his future, he managed to look at me, look *at* me instead of past me. His forehead furrowed a little in recognition that I was hurting.

"I will miss you" was all I could whisper.

Joe looked at me a moment and then slowly held out his arms. When I went to them he pulled me close to him tenderly. I nestled my ear over his heart, which was beating more rapidly than usual, and let his familiar and comforting warmth soothe my shivers.

"Do you hate me?" I wanted to know. Joe shook his head.

"Aren't you cold?" I asked, noting that while I trembled in a flannel shirt and jeans, Joe was wearing only a short-sleeved T-shirt and shorts. He shook his head again.

I leaned back to look at his face again. His hands went back to his sides, but I still clutched him. I said, "Are you afraid?"

"Yes."

"Why?"

"I don't want to go home."

I knew exactly how he felt. I knew Joe could come to no good fortune, but I grasped at anything I could to try and comfort him. "Oh, Joe. You'll be okay, I promise you will." I squeezed his arms gently.

Joe looked away. Betty said softly, "Let's get you back where it's warm, Tiffany," and then louder, "Good luck to you, Joe."

I am eternally grateful that someone as compassionate and understanding as Betty was there by my side as I walked slowly away, my head turned to watch Joseph disappear into the fog.

EIGHTEEN

The state governor at the time of my imprisonment made a political tour of all the state institutions and prisons. The day she came to WSH, the cells were emptied, and the children sitting around the dayhall in shackles, cuffs, mitts, or straightjackets were released.

There was a picture of the governor in the local newspaper, which one staff member set out on the ward for her to see. I stared at that paper lying there and wondered how long it had been since I had last had access to a newspaper, to any knowledge whatsoever of the outside world. Before I could get to it, however, another staff member, who apparently did not like the governor, made a face and swept the paper into the trash.

I was very excited about seeing the governor. I prepared a speech in my head, a speech that would pour out my story and the story of all those imprisoned here. I thought that if she only knew what was going on, then she would do something to help us.

I was horrified when the governor arrived on Smith 1 walled in by a crowd of men and women in fancy clothes. She had the biggest, stiffest smile plastered on her face that I had ever seen. She began reaching out and grasping the hands of child victims of abuse and neglect and imprisonment and torment, shaking them, and moving on. Not only that, but she carried a stack of autographed pictures of herself that she passed out among us with glee. I stood rooted to the floor as she whizzed by me, giving me a huge phony smile without looking into my eyes, grabbing my hand,

and giving it a firm shake, while someone with her stuffed one of those autographed pictures into my other hand.

I could think of no way to vent my disgust when the governor, with her big plastic grin, reached for the hand of Samuel, who was standing next to me. Samuel grinned with pleasure, and to my immense satisfaction, he licked every last one of his fingers quickly before grasping the hand of our governor. I snickered as her grin twitched. She got away from us as quickly as possible.

Samuel held his autographed picture gingerly in his shaky fingertips and stuttered, "Who t-this? Her? Her? Euw, she uguly! Uguly! Hee, hee!" and the picture fluttered to the floor. I knew he was not referring to her physical features alone. For all the holes in his mind, no one could pretend to be a caring person to Samuel and get away with it if they weren't.

The last time Sam really talked to me was just before everyone was moved to Smith 4. He was sitting with his green bear, Limey, and rambling on about his brother Skip, whom he had just visited, and giggling like a fiend. I was sitting across from him.

I had learned in time that the brother Sam always bragged about was not big and strong. Skip had Huntington's disease like Sam did, because it is an inherited disease. Skip was put in a separate state institution, where he was probably treated no better than Sam. These dying brothers saw each other twice a year.

I looked at Samuel suddenly and realized that he was looking at me. I also realized that he had been silent for a minute or so. His eyes were so large and so blue. The pupils were so enormous that they nearly swallowed up those blue irises. There was something in Samuel's eyes that I did not understand, something I had never seen before.

I had never really wondered how much Sammy suffered. It was obvious he was dying, but he didn't appear to be in much pain, and he was always babbling so cheerfully and licking his fingers and laughing and hugging his green bear. I assumed he didn't know any better than to be content. Sometimes I wished I was like him in that respect. But now he stared at me and stuttered, "Muh-m-my bruther, m'bruther Skip . . . m'brother Skip is going . . . to die."

I was horrified. Sam kept staring at me through the drug-induced haze in his eyes. Surely he couldn't see very well through pupils that dilated. But there was something back there, something that he was seeing and trying to come to grips with. He rattled off another sentence: "M-Me too. I'm going to die too . . . I'm going to die too . . ." And he licked his fingers.

I stared at him. There was nothing I could do, nothing I could say. I don't think he even wanted an answer; he just wanted to tell someone what he knew. Presently his unstable fingers dropped Limey on the floor. "L'my, L'my, m'green bear . . ."

One day soon after, Sam began walking with a very bad limp, stuttering between finger-licks, "My ankle . . . My ankle hurts . . . It hurts, my ankle . . ."

For three days he hobbled around before someone took a look at his ankle and saw that it was broken. Because of the time it had gone without treatment, and also because of Sam's disease, it never healed as long as he lived—which wasn't very long anyway.

So they gave him a cast, which a few of the nicer staff people signed, and confined him to a wheelchair because there was no way on this earth he could manage crutches. When he kept getting out of his wheelchair and attempting to hobble around, they strapped him into it. It was a sad sight, Sammy constantly swaying and straining against the strap around his waist, abandoned in a corner in a chair he could move no more than he could move a mountain. At least no big fat security men were going to assault him and throw his skinny, sickly body to the ground anymore.

He wasted away quickly after he broke his ankle, losing weight every week, his dilated blue eyes becoming emptier every day. He lost more and more control of his constant motions and could not even keep Limey, his beloved green bear, in his hands for more than a few seconds.

I tried not to think of the ghastly-looking skeleton in the room with me that used to be Sammy, but it would not be still or quiet. He could not hold a conversation, but he rambled and giggled more fervently than ever, until his voice was rasping in his dry throat. I don't think anything he said meant anything to him anymore, even the lines about his brother Skip and his green bear Limey.

I began having a recurring nightmare in which Samuel died and it took the staff three days to notice his body rotting in his bed.

When new patients came to take the place of the old, I would no longer have anything to do with them. I had cared so much for so many friends and had them torn away from me. I knew that whatever situation they were in out there, it was most likely miserable, and there was nothing I could do for them. I refused to care about anyone new. It hurt too much. Each child around me was a separate person with a separate story of violence, loneliness, and desperation. I did not think my brain could contain another such story. The poor kids were so lonely that most of them would try to be friendly with me. I was no longer friendly. I was sharp and angry and weary. I made it plain to all that it was best to leave me alone.

Then came a boy whose name was Darby. He was only twelve, and he arrived at WSH dirty and smelly, with uncombed hair and ratty, worn, ill-fitting, castaway clothing. He was hyperactive, I suppose, and he would throw tantrums and whine. He wore my nerves raw.

It was a month or so before I was seized one day, God knows why, with the impulse to speak to him. He was pacing the dayhall, frustrated and bored. I was sitting at a card table as usual, and I called out, "Hey, Darby, is that your name? Come talk to me."

He walked over slowly and stopped just out of my reach. He was still rather dirty, and although he had been given a few more changes of clothes, they weren't very nice ones, that's for sure. He said, "Why? Why do you want to talk to me?" He seemed terrified. I said softly, "Just come sit still, I won't hurt you."

Darby sat and eyed me. He flinched whenever I moved too quickly, and he could not look me in the eye. I realized that he was brain damaged in some way and had no idea what was happening to him, except that he knew no one cared. There was no doubt that he had been neglected and beaten by whatever miserable excuse for a family he had, probably out of frustration with his simplicity. They might even have caused his brain damage in the first place, either with unspeakable abuse that regressed him emotionally or with a direct blow to the head.

I picked up a crayon from the pile that was lying on the table. I had paper as well. Paper was an unheard-of luxury in that place. When I ran out of my own supply, Lorri had dug up some mental evaluation tests for me to write or draw on the backs of. I held out the crayon and a piece of paper to Darby. "Can you color? Would you like to?" I asked.

He was stunned. "Really? Can I? Would that be okay?"

"Yes," I said.

He took the crayon and paper eagerly, but with reverence, and began in earnest to cover the paper with careful scribbles. He looked up at me with his food-streaked face, beaming, and told me, "You're very nice. You must like me. Do you like me? Will you be my friend?"

Those words struck me to the core. I looked into his hungry, drug-hazed eyes, filled momentarily with happiness because a cross girl in the corner had given him a crayon, and I began to cry.

I had not cried since the day Joe left, a month before.

Throughout my stay at WSH, I had run into a boy named Fernando now and then. Actually, I suppose he was a man, because he was twenty-one years old and lived on Smith 3. One day I was told in hushed tones that he was being moved to the adult ward because he had ripped someone's throat out. I was positively shocked and revolted at the idea (and it took a damn lot to shock and revolt me by then), and I couldn't believe it was true.

I saw Fernando while I was on the porch, and he saw me. I had a vague notion that I should run away in fear and disgust, but I was not the least bit afraid of him. He had always been kind to me. He was wearing, as always, a T-shirt with the sleeves ripped out and some jeans and all his shiny studs in his ear. Fernando wasn't exceptionally big, and he had the sickly skin tone of anyone who is imprisoned away from all that grants human health. It never sunk into my head that he was a killer. I could never quite believe it. He looked a bit like a stereotype of a killer, but he did not have the eyes of a killer.

"Hello, girl," he said to me as always, in his cheerful tones, the way one would address a little niece. I put my hands and forehead on the chain-link and asked very softly, "Fernando, why did they move you to the adult ward?"

Fernando did not avert his eyes, but he was clearly ashamed to answer me that question. "I'm sure you've heard."

I swallowed and wrinkled my forehead. "Aren't they going to press charges—send you to jail?"

"Yeah."

It occurred to me that I should probably not ask personal questions of a person with no qualms about removing someone's throat. But as I said, I was sorry for Fernando; I was never afraid.

"Fernando?" I said. "Why did you do it? Why?"

Fernando raised his cigarette to his mouth, took a drag, exhaled it slowly, and sighed, "Eight years, girl. Eight years I been here."

Then he walked away. And despite all of my shock and revulsion at the time, I wondered how hard it would be for me to try and pull someone's throat out after eight years.

Early in August, in 1992, my mother drove to WSH to announce that she was going to take me home for good.

"What?" It was the only word I could find, I was so stunned.

She explained that her diabetes and neuropathy rendered her unable to work, so now she would be able to monitor me twenty-four hours a day herself. Also, she had discovered that she could arrange "special classes," so "perhaps" I could "manage" my sophomore year in a public school. She told me that WSH was under the impression that I had "improved," and she asked me exactly how I had "changed" and whether I thought I would now be able to "cooperate" with her if she took me home.

Every last fiber of my weakened body exploded with powerless fury. "That is the absolute sickest thing you have ever said to me! My God, you are sick! You are so sick you leave your first-born, your only daughter in hell without a conscience prick for a fucking year and then you ask if that changed her! Well, I'm sick as a dog now, I'm weak now, I'm practically destroyed now, but I suppose that's just what you wanted, isn't it? That's what everybody wants, what everybody calls *improvement* is being so fucking weak that anybody can control me! Well, I'm not so weak I can't still say fuck your *special classes*, fuck your *monitoring*, and *fuck you!* I'm tired of being jerked around by you so just get out of here and don't come back looking for any *improvement* and *changes* 'cause you're never gonna squeeze any out of me!"

My mother pinched her lips together like a pouty baby and glanced over at Lorri in the corner as if to say, "See what that dreadful child did—yelled at her own mother who came to help her, and said the F-word, too!" She waited for Lorri to reprimand me, to tell me that my behavior was inexcusable and that I mustn't act that way if I expected to go home. When Lorri did nothing of the sort, my mother stood dramatically, snatched up her cane, and announced, "I don't have to sit here and take this! Yes, I see you haven't changed at all!"

But as she walked out of the building, I heard Lorri ask her if she still intended to take me home. She said, sniffing as pathetically as she could, "Yes, maybe someday she will come to appreciate all I've done for her."

I told Lorri that if my mother took me home, she'd bring me back within six months. I said I just couldn't take it anymore, I'd rather just stay than be jerked back and forth at the whim of a crazy woman.

Lorri told me I didn't have any choice because that crazy woman was my mother and she had committed me, so she could take me out any time she felt like it.

On August 6, 1992, I packed my things in garbage sacks and hauled them to the car. Samuel squirmed more desperately than ever in his wheelchair as he saw that I was leaving. He licked his fingers madly and called, "Bye, b-b-ye, frnd. Bye frnd, bye, bye . . ." I handed him his green bear from the floor and said good-bye to him, hugging his wasted, fleshless frame. He just kept calling good-bye as I walked off the ward for the last time.

As I climbed into the passenger seat next to my mother, she turned on the radio and handed me her diet cola. She pulled away, humming, as if she were picking me up from a park where she had left me for an afternoon, instead of from a state mental institution where I had suffered unspeakably for nearly a year.

E P I L O G U E

All of this book you have read so far was writ-
ten in between my sixteenth and seventeenth birthdays. Almost four
years later, I added this epilogue.

When I first left Wilson State Hospital, I found myself in a
decent environment for the first time in my life. My mother
moved my brother and me from the town where I grew up
so unhappily to Lawrence, Kansas, the first place that I
affectionately called home. Lawrence has a good housing
program for disabled people and low-income families, so
even though my mother couldn't work anymore, we were
placed in a brand-new house. I loved that cheerful little
place and took very good care of it while I lived there.

I started high school about a week after leaving WSH.
I was afraid that my sickly appearance and crushed spirit
would make me an outcast, but Lawrence High School was
so large and so diverse that hardly anyone was ever singled
out for anything. When I found myself in a place where I
was no longer considered a freak, I actually became very
outgoing, joined the theater, and made several friends. I
met my best friend, Galen Turner, in art class, and he later
became the first person I ever talked to about my experi-
ences as an abused child and mental patient.

Opie, my little guinea pig, was very old by this time,
but he got to spend the last few months of his life reunited
with me. He became frisky and happy again and died
peacefully in his sleep.

I was pretty happy too, except for the fact that I knew

the situation would not last. My mother spent her time wandering through the house like a caged animal. When I was there, she followed me constantly, verbally picking on me about everything she could think of. A few times she tried to harm me physically, but I was old enough, and she was sickly enough, that I simply slipped out of her grasp and took a walk until she had calmed down a little. What frightened me was that she was always talking about how sick I still was, and saying she was going to have me committed again. The thought of it gave me nightmares. Ironically, though, four months after we moved to Lawrence, it was not I but my mother who ended up in a mental institution.

My grandmother came to stay with my brother and me while my mother was gone. She blamed us for my mother's nervous breakdown and did her best to make us miserable. When my mother was released from the hospital, she refused to come home to my brother and me. It was only a few weeks after my brother's thirteenth birthday, and the poor kid, who had been unhappy ever since our parents' divorce, decided to run away. The local police picked him up past curfew at the edge of town and called my grandmother to ask if she wanted him back. She did not, and since running away from home is illegal, my brother was placed in juvenile jail. Since then, he has been kept in high-security group homes, which are run just like the mental institutions I have been in. Because of his "criminal record," he is not eligible for placement in a foster home. After three years of living in high-security group homes, he "spontaneously" developed a chemical imbalance and is now being forced to take antidepressants. The doctor who prescribes these drugs says that it is no surprise that my brother has this problem since it "runs in the family."

My brother has now suffered more than I have at the hands of the child welfare system and the mental health system. He is so miserable and confused at this point that

I am not sure if he will ever recover from the damage done to him.

Soon after my brother ran away, my grandmother told me that she did not plan to stay with me for very long. I knew that when she left I would become a ward of the state, and I was terrified. My friend Galen, who was living with his grandparents, Charles and Mary Michener, invited me over for dinner to meet them and to ask them if I could come to live with them. They said yes.

When the local child welfare department heard that I was going to live with the Micheners, they objected vehemently and took me in a security vehicle to a horrible youth shelter four hours away. I still don't understand why I was forced to grow up with abusive people who didn't even want me simply because they were my blood relatives, but when I had an opportunity to live with an unrelated family who genuinely cared about me, the state would rather pay to imprison me in an overcrowded shelter.

I thought I was doomed to live like my brother until my eighteenth birthday, but to my surprise, the Micheners hired a lawyer and went to court for me. To make a long story short, they were declared my legal guardians, and I went home with them two weeks before my sixteenth birthday.

Three years later, Charles and I were standing in their yard full of June flowers, and he said to me, "I remember that these purple rockets were blooming when you came to us." People look at me funny when I refer to seventy-eight-year-old Charles and Mary as my mom and dad, and to Galen, who is only three months older than I, as my brother, but I don't care. They have been more of a family to me than any of my biological relations ever were. That is why I have changed my last name to Michener.

I have also changed my first name to Anna, to separate myself from my past and to symbolize the fact that I am my own person. I am not the property of the people who bred me. I am not the prisoner of the people with fancy psychiatric lingo in their heads and no love for me in their hearts.

Now that I have passed my eighteenth birthday, I do not have to fear being treated as I was in my childhood. Now that I have sought psychiatric counseling on my own, instead of being brought to it by my parents, my claims of abuse are believed, and the healing process has begun. Now that I am an adult in the eyes of the law, no one can commit me to a mental institution without first proving in court that I am a danger to myself or others. If I am living with someone who mistreats me, I have the legal right to leave. If someone hurts me physically, I can call the police, and they will not refer me to some other agency that calls the assault of innocent children mere "discipline."

I have yet to understand, however, why it is that on my eighteenth birthday, I suddenly had these rights, but on the day before, I did not.

Charles and Mary have given me all that good parents are supposed to. They never told me how I was supposed to be or how I was supposed to live. They showed me. They are hard-working, generous, patient, honest, compassionate, and they treat other people as they would like to be treated themselves. They simply set a good example and trust me to figure out what is best for myself. Sure, they haven't always liked my opinions or the color I dye my hair, but as long as I am not hurting anyone, they have always respected my individuality. This respect has worked miracles for my emotional and mental well-being. And I'm sure that it's a lot easier for them to be themselves and let me be myself than it would be for them to waste their time and energy trying to control every single aspect of my life.

The only thing that bothers me about this fairy-tale ending to my book is the fact that I simply lucked out. I had absolutely no control over my coming to live with Charles and Mary, absolutely no say in my own fate, and this is true of all children in this country. If a child happens to be born to, or come under the guardianship of, people who have the knowledge and the desire to raise them properly, then that child is *lucky*.

It is a sad fact of life that not everyone physically capable of bearing a child is capable of caring for it, or even wants to. What recourse do these unlucky children have? They are pretty much screwed for the next eighteen years, and by then they have been damaged in ways that screw up the rest of their lives, too. Humans learn by example. How can a person be expected to function normally and healthily if they have never seen how that is done?

The problems of abused children are compounded when the mental health community does not acknowledge the source of these problems. Since children do not arrange and pay for their own psychiatric care, it is their parents and other caretakers that clinical psychiatrists must cater to. Imagine what would have happened if any of the people or institutions involved in my case had suggested that the cause of my problems had anything to do with my parents. My parents would simply have taken me elsewhere and paid someone else to see things differently.

It was a lot more convenient for everyone concerned (except me, of course) to blame everything wrong with me, and even some things that weren't wrong with me, on some vague "chemical imbalance" in my brain, then "fix" it by locking me up and drugging me. My family got rid of me without looking bad, and the shrinks and institutions involved made a lot of money.

I don't believe that everyone involved in this system is purposely cheating kids for profit. There are a lot of people out there who buy into the idea that child abuse doesn't happen that much anymore, that genetics and biological disorders are the only other explanation for deviant behavior, and that drugs and mental institutions actually help.

I hope that my story helps to dispel these myths. If the things that I describe are the things that I have experienced and witnessed in one little part of the Midwest, imagine what is going on throughout the country. The sexual abuse, physical and emotional abuse, and neglect of children is still going strong. The only thing that has changed recently is a sudden resurgence of denial. And this denial is most prevalent in the shockingly impotent child protection services and mental health community.

Drugs are being used increasingly to subdue and control children with mental or emotional problems rather than to help them. Sometimes psychiatric drugs are useful when dealing with extremely dangerous behavior or mood swings, but they should never be relied upon as the single answer to anyone's problems. And drugs should not be forced on anyone, regardless of age, without a court order.

As long as children have no rights or power of their own, then, intentionally or not, there will always be those who will exploit them.